TELL ME A STORY

TELL ME A STORY

◻

A New Look at Real and Artificial Memory

◻

ROGER C. SCHANK

Charles Scribner's Sons   New York

Collier Macmillan Canada   Toronto

Maxwell Macmillan International
New York   Oxford   Singapore   Sydney

Acknowledgments for reprint permissions appear on page 255.

Charles Scribner's Sons
Macmillan Publishing Company
866 Third Avenue, New York, NY 10022

Collier Macmillan Canada, Inc.
1200 Eglinton Avenue East, Suite 200
Don Mills, Ontario M3C 3N1

Library of Congress Cataloging-in-Publication Data
Schank, Roger C., 1946-
   Tell me a story: a new look at real and artificial memory /
by Roger C. Schank.
      p.   cm.
   Includes index.
   ISBN 0-684-19049-4
   1. Intellect. 2. Memory. 3. Storytelling—Psychological aspects.
4. Artificial intelligence.   I. Title.
BF431.S277   1990
153—dc20   90-35836   CIP
Macmillan books are available at special discounts for bulk purchases
for sales promotions, premiums, fund-raising, or educational use.
For details, contact:

Special Sales Director
Macmillan Publishing Company
866 Third Avenue
New York, NY 10022

1   3   5   7   9   10   8   6   4   2

Printed in the United States of America

To Diane, who likes my stories

Contents

❑

Preface

❑

People know a lot. They know Aunt Martha's birthday and they know what flavor ice cream little Johnny likes. They know how to drive a car, how to cook dinner, how to operate the heating system in their houses, and how to type. They know how to follow the directions that someone gives them, and they know how to tell their needs and desires to their friends. Human intelligence is bound up with each and every one of these activities, and we recognize in our fellow human beings differences in intelligence by noticing who understands us more easily, who can fill in the blanks and figure things out without instruction, and who needs to be led by the nose every step of the way.

When it comes to thinking about the intelligence of people we use two standard methods. Either we try to assess people's intelligence by making them take a multiple-choice test involving a lot of mathematics as well as verbal and spatial reasoning skills, or else we simply make a guess by talking with them and observing them over a period of time in a variety of activities. The first method is the one that schools use, and the second method is the one that individuals who do not have a professional interest in the assessment of intelligence use. Most people are happy to assess the intelligence of others by talking to them and listening to what they say back.

When it comes to computers, however, all bets are off. Both computer professionals and people who have no interest in computers at all change their positions on assessing intelligence if the intelligence of computers is up for discussion. Computer professionals believe that making computers intelligent means endowing them with logical reasoning abilities and detailed expertise in various domains. They have been fascinated from the beginning of the age of computers with making computers play chess, prove theorems, do formal mathematical reasoning, and lately with the idea of making computers expert in such enterprises as finding oil and doing retirement planning. The concept of intelligent computers, to most computer professionals, has meant the creation of programs that do tasks that only very intelligent people can do.

To the layperson, computer intelligence is a different thing. Most people who have little familiarity with computers fall into one of two categories when the idea of intelligent machines comes up. Either they are willing to ascribe intelligence to a machine that does something that they themselves cannot do—for example, beating them in chess or doing some complex calculation—or else they are unwilling to allow a machine any intelligence, no matter what feat it may perform, intelligence being a quality ascribable only to creatures made of flesh and blood.

This book is not about computers but about intelligence. For more than twenty years, I have been concerned with the attempt to create intelligent machines. I have watched as people extolled the intelligence capabilities of computer programs that I knew only too well had very little real knowledge, much less intelligence, in them. At the same time, more and more computer capabilities have been available to the general public, capabilities that have, by and large, both impressed their users with the fantastic things these machines can do and served to further the impression that computers are, nevertheless, inherently quite stupid.

The interesting subject underlying any discussion about the potential for artificial intelligence should be the nature of intelligence in general. Even if machines can do interesting things, perhaps ascribing intelligence to them does not make much sense. Similarly, just because machines act stupidly on some occasions, refusing to ascribe intelligence to them may not make any more sense. But to decide that intelligence is a property only of animate objects certainly doesn't make sense either. Intelligence can only mean intelligent behavior. Any entity capable of behavior could, at least in principle, be capable of intelligent behavior. The issue for anyone interested in intelligence, then, is what behaviors signify intelligence.

For years I have been fascinated by the seemingly intrinsic human desire to tell a good story. Children love to hear stories. Adults love to read or watch reproductions of long stories and love to tell and listen to shorter stories. People need to talk, to tell about what has happened to them, and they need to hear about what has happened to others, especially when the others are people they care about or who have had experiences relevant to the hearer's own life.

We assess the intelligence of others on the basis of the stories that they tell and on the basis of their receptivity to our own stories. At first glance, this seems like an awkward way to judge intelligence. Why does a good listener seem intelligent? What could the ability to tell an interesting story at just the right moment have to do with intelligence? We view intelligence as being intimately bound up with the notion of understanding. When people seem to truly understand something we have said, we give them high marks. We like them and appreciate them. But how can we determine that they have, in fact, understood us? We cannot really believe that intermittent head nodding and sage um-hums indicate real understanding. What else is there to go by? Our only real recourse, outside of administering some kind of intelligence test, is to listen to what our listeners say in response to what we have told them. The more that they say back that seems to relate in a significant way to what we have said, the more they seem to have understood. In order to respond effectively, a listener must therefore have something to say. But we have lots to say, potentially. We have a memory full of experiences that we can tell to others. Finding the right ones, having the right ones come to mind at the right times, having created accounts of the right ones in anticipation of their eventual use in this way, are all significant aspects of intelligent behavior. Finding and listening to stories might seem like peripheral aspects of intelligence. But if you think about what intelligent computers should be like, an ability to tell us what we want to know, combined with an ability to understand what we really need to know about, are critical aspects of the problem.

Clearly, then, at least two aspects of intelligence are critical for either humans or computers. One is to have something to say, to know something worth telling, and the other is to be able to determine others' needs and abilities well enough to know what is worth telling them.

To put this another way, our interest in telling and hearing stories is strongly related to the nature of intelligence. In our laboratory today, we are attempting to build machines that have interesting stories to tell and procedures that enable them to tell these stories at the right time. Our machines do not solve puzzles, nor do they do mathematics. Rather, our aim is to make them interesting to talk to, an aspect of intelligence often ignored by computer professionals and intelligence assessors.

This book, then, is about how we think—not how we think about mathematics, but how we think about life. It is not about machines but about people. It represents an attempt to look at the problem of mind in a different way than usual. The intention is to understand how human memory works, why it works the way it does, and what the implications are for those of us who are attempting to understand what thinking is about. Its main assertion is that, while thinking is certainly a complex activity, it may not be quite as complex as many believe. There are some essentially quite simple mechanisms that underlie an important part of the process of thinking. Thinking depends very much on storytelling and story understanding, and this is the subject of this book.

Members of my laboratory have contributed to this work in a variety of ways. Some of my students have been working on storytelling computer programs which are in various stages of completion. Talking to them about this work has been quite important to me as I was writing this book. In particular, I want to thank Eric Domeshek, Bill Ferguson, Eric Jones, Alex Kass, Robin Burke, and Chris Owens. Colleagues who have helpfully discussed aspects of this work with me were Larry Birnbaum, Chris Riesbeck, and especially Bob Abelson, who listened to my stories about stories every Tuesday at lunch. I sincerely want to thank Liza Cobbett, who worked very carefully with me on the manuscript of this book during its latter stages in an attempt to make it really work. I want to thank the Defense Advanced Research Projects Agency, the Office of Naval Research, and the Air Force Office of Scientific Research, whose support for my laboratory at Yale University made this work possible. Recently, I have moved to Northwestern University to start The Institute for the Learning Sciences. I want to thank the many people whose lives were uprooted by the move to Northwestern for bearing with me, and the Arthur Andersen Worldwide Organization for supporting this new institute, whose goal it is to learn more about minds so that we can build machines that can help educate minds.

February, 1990
The Institute for the Learning Sciences
Northwestern University
Evanston, Illinois

TELL ME A STORY

□ 1 □

Knowledge Is Stories

□

"No generalization is worth a damn, including this one."
Oliver Wendell Holmes

PEOPLE remember what happens to them, and they tell other people what they remember. People learn from what happens to them, and they guide their future actions accordingly. Intelligence, in the popular mind, refers to the capacity to solve complex problems, but another way of looking at the issue might be to say that intelligence is really about understanding what has happened well enough to be able to predict when it might happen again. To be a successful predictor of future events, one has to have explained confusing prior events successfully. Explaining the world (at least to yourself) is a critical aspect of intelligence. Comprehending events around you depends upon having a memory of prior events available for helping in the interpretation of new events.

We get reminded of what has happened to us previously for a very good reason. Reminding is the mind's method of coordinating past events with current events to enable generalization and prediction. Intelligence depends upon the ability to translate descriptions of new events into labels that help in the retrieval of prior events. One can't be said to know something if one can't find it in memory when it is needed. Finding a relevant past experience that will help make sense of a new experience is at the core of intelligent behavior.

Research into the mechanisms of intelligence tends to dwell on the techniques of puzzle solving, planning, and the understanding of complex, even bizarre situations, such as the "Missionary and the Cannibals" problem or the "Tower of Hanoi" problem. Traditionally, intelligence tests are problem-solving tests, and the most difficult questions on College Board exams and other standardized tests involve solving a problem one has never encountered before or attempting one that appears commonplace but may have an unusual twist. But why do we imagine that intelligence is best gauged by problem-solving ability? Why not by an analytical ability about problems for which there is no clear solution, such as the kind of people-oriented problems that we encounter every day?

Seeing the mysterious workings of people's minds as discrete processes that can be told to a computer means analyzing each and every mental action that people can perform in terms that are clear and precise. Work in Artificial Intelligence (AI), which is the enterprise of systematically looking at what it means to think, must make explicit what is implicit about how minds work. We need to know how people do the ordinary things, not the extraordinary. Expertise is nice to model on a computer, but it won't tell us as much about thinking as modeling on a child or an adult engaged in his or her daily activities, doing simple things like talking or reading or watching television.

Does Thinking Really Involve Thinking?

Upon an initial examination of human mental processes, the task of building a machine that is an effective simulation of these processes seems formidable. And, as years of only small progress in AI can attest, that task *is* formidable. Not only can people talk and chew gum at the same time, but also we can reason, extrapolate, induce, deduce, contradict, and complain. We can retrieve long-lost items from memory and create new ideas and thoughts at the drop of a hat. We can understand situations and ideas that we have never seen before as well as criticize the ideas of others. In fact, human mental ability is nothing short of phenomenal. Any human, even the dullest of us, is unbelievably intelligent.

The story may have another side, however. Consider, for example, the answers to the following question, obtained by a Connecticut radio station (WHCN in Hartford) in a man-in-the-street interview spot called "60 Seconds":

Does the thought of catching AIDS scare you?
1. Oh, yeah, I think it would scare anybody.
2. No, it doesn't. This country is qualified to deal with the problem.
3. Yeah, it could be deadly.
4. It's like having cancer; you don't know when you can get that.
5. Everything scares you. If it happens, it happens.
6. It does, I'd be cautious. Like when I visit Provincetown, or something, I wait till I leave the city before I have anything to drink.
7. Can girls get it?
8. Yes, it does.
9. It's spreading throughout the country at a very fast pace.
10. There are so many other things around that you can catch without indulging in sexual intercourse, I'm not as worried about AIDS as I am about any other things that I can catch by breathing.
11. Yes, it would frighten me.
12. Yes, definitely. Especially going in for operations with blood transfusions.
13. You probably all have it anyway.

How intelligent do you have to be in order to think up answers like the thirteen that appear above? The computer scientist says, "Very intelligent; do you realize how many complex processes are hidden in the production of those simple answers?" But to the general public these answers are at best naive, at worst stupid. Both sides are right.

The process of thinking up answers to unexpected questions is at once extremely creative and very simple. When you read the next set of questions and answers, ask yourself the following two questions: Was the person who thought up this answer someone whom I would consider to be very smart? Would a computer program that thought up these answers, without any preparation or anticipation that these questions were to be asked, be considered to be reasonably smart?

What do you think about the situation right now in South Africa?
1. There's definitely some investigation into the civil rights problems going on down there.
2. The police arrested people. Yeah, if it happens here, how would we feel here? Just empathize with those people and hope that our government steps in and does something?
3. It is ultimately ridiculous. Everybody should be what they want to be.
4. Why should there be violence?
5. That's bad, that's bad up there. I be thinking why we don't take no kind of action—America takes no kind of action.
6. Really not that up with it.
7. It's just gonna antagonize the people. I think they really have to end apartheid really more quickly than they are doing.
8. You know I prayed the United States to send a little more help out there.
9. Kind of terrible.
10. I don't see any change. Isn't that what the government was doing in the first place, was just taking whatever liberties they want?

So, which is it? Are the ten people we have heard from above rather dull, or was the computer that generated these responses rather bright? This is not an issue of whether machines are unjustly glorified or people unjustly denigrated. Rather, the real question is how people figure out what to say. The problem here revolves around a rather limited but interesting form of creativity. Namely, is the process of generating novel answers to questions one of tremendous brilliance and complexity, or is it straightforward and routine? What differentiates people who give wise answers to such questions from those who give dull ones? Could we get a computer to generate such answers? If we did and if the method we used to do it were the obvious dull one, namely printing out previously prepared statements, how wrong a method would this be?

Certain aspects of human thought may be simpler than many scientists have imagined. Certainly the overwhelming complexity of the thinking process seems startling when so many humans actually seem to do so little inventive thinking. The creative aspects of the answers above seem limited indeed. Scientists who seek general principles upon which the mind is based might do better by observing the behavior of people and attempting to postulate the simplest possible mechanisms that might replicate that behavior.

With this in mind consider another set of interview responses.

Should the U.S. impose economic sanctions on South Africa?
1. Yes, because I think no matter what color you are—black or white—you should have equal opportunity.
2. I don't think so. I think Ronald Reagan is just keeping his face out of everything.
3. Well, it all depends whether or not Africa wants to be like America or not.
4. They should retain the government of South Africa to help those people who need it.
5. I think definitely, definitely so somebody having their rights taken away from them—I think definitely without question.
6. I sure would like to go over there and find out what's going on first.
7. I don't think they want me over there anyway.

Did any of these answers demand serious thinking on the part of the speaker? Clearly the answer is no. Generating these responses did not require the full force of our reasoning ability, complete with inferencing, reasoning from general principles, application of specific background knowledge, and so on. It could have, of course. One of the respondents could have given a carefully reasoned and original answer. But none of them did, nor is that sort of behavior very common.

My claim is that these answers were *already* available in memory, or to put this another way, the responder already knew *an* answer. People have opinions about a large range of topics. They know what they think, and more importantly, they have already thought up what they are likely to say long before they say it. The respondents' actual task here was to determine which of the many answers they already knew was relevant to the question at hand. The view of intelligence that I am espousing here is that most answers, indeed a great deal of what people say at any time, do not require—nor do they receive—much thought. Consider the two responses below, for example:

1. Yes, because I think no matter what color you are—black or white—you should have equal opportunity.
2. I don't think so. I think Ronald Reagan is just keeping his face out of everything.

When speakers come up with answers such as these, they are actually just digging them out of their memory. They are not really "thinking them up." The person who gave answer number two above doesn't necessarily have the construction "just keeping his face out of everything" stored as part of a set of feelings about Reagan, but already has an idea about Reagan that can be applied to nearly any situation in which an opinion about Reagan is called for.

The construction of answers by such interviewees is novel and, I have asserted, in a sense creative. Certainly, a computer able to answer such a topical question without prior knowledge of the kind of question to be asked and without previously prepared print statements would be impressive. We would be impressed because the machine would appear to be, in a rather dull way, creative; that is, it would seem to have had to make up these answers on its own. And such limited creativity is, in fact, quite difficult. But it is a much simpler process than is ordinarily thought of when we think about what people do when they engage in conversation.

The process of creativity of the sort we are talking about depends upon explanation. An understander of the world is an explainer of the world. In order to understand a story, a sentence, a question, or a scene, you have to explain to yourself exactly why the people you are hearing about or observing are doing what they're doing. You need to know or figure out the intentions of the people you interact with and to anticipate what might happen next. Since people don't make a habit of telling you these things all the time, understanding entails, at least in part, figuring this out for yourself. In other words, everyday understanding is a creative process that requires you to construct explanations for behaviors and events that have occurred. Commenting upon the behavior of others adds one more level of complexity to the process. But not everyone is brilliant. These wildly complex processes would seem at first glance to be too much for the average person to bear. Nevertheless, some very unintelligent people manage to understand the world they live in fairly well. Can it really be all that difficult?

Scripts

The answer is no, and one reason is *scripts*. In the mid-seventies at Yale in our work on designing programs that understand English, or natural language processing, we invented the concept of a script. A script is a set of expectations about what will happen next in a well-understood situation. In a sense, many situations in life have the people who participate in them seemingly reading their roles in a kind of play. The waitress reads from the waitress part in the restaurant script, and the customer reads the lines of the customer. Life experience means quite often knowing how to act and how others will act in given stereotypical situations. That knowledge is called a script.

Scripts are useful for a variety of reasons. They make clear what is supposed to happen and what various acts on the part of others are supposed to indicate. They make mental processing easier by allowing us to think less, in essence. You don't have to figure out every time you enter a restaurant how to convince someone to feed you. All you really have to know is the restaurant script and your part in that script.

Scripts are useful for understanding the actions of others as long as we know the script they are following. Scripts also enable computers to understand stories about stereotypical situations. When a paragraph is about a restaurant, we can realize with very little effort that we need not wonder why the waitress agreed to bring what was asked for, and we can assume that what was ordered was what was eaten. To put this another way, not everything in the world is worthy of equal amounts of thought, and restaurant stories are readily understandable by a computer armed with a good enough restaurant script. In fact, not too much thinking has to be done by a computer or a person if the right script is available. One just has to play one's part, and events usually transpire the way they are supposed to. You don't have to infer the intentions of the waitress if her intentions are already well known. Why concentrate one's mental time on the obvious?

Taken as a strong hypothesis about the nature of human thought, scripts obviate the need to think; no matter what the situation, people may do no more in thinking than to apply a script. This hypothesis holds that everything is a script and very little thought is spontaneous. Given a situation, there are rules to follow, the way things are supposed to be. We can follow those rules and not think at all. This works for all of us some of the time. People have thousands of highly personal scripts used on a daily basis that others do not share. Every mundane aspect of life that requires little or no thought, such as sitting in your chair or pouring your daily orange juice, can be assumed to be a script. In fact, much of our early education revolves around learning the scripts that others expect us to follow. But this can all be carried a bit too far. Situations that one person sees as following a script may seem quite open-ended to another person. The more scripts you know, the more situations will exist in which you feel comfortable and capable of playing your role effectively. But the more scripts you know, the more situations you will fail to wonder about, be confused by, and have to figure out on your own. Script-based understanding is a double-edged sword.

Scripts are also a kind of memory structure. They serve to tell us how to act without our being aware that we are using them. They serve to store knowledge that we have about certain situations. They serve as a kind of storehouse of old experiences of a certain type in terms of which new experiences of the same type are encoded. When something new happens to us in a restaurant which tells us more about restaurants, we must have someplace to put that new information so that we will be wiser next time. Scripts change over time, therefore, and embody what we have learned. For this reason, my restaurant script won't be exactly like yours, but they will both include information such as: *One can expect forks to be available without asking unless the restaurant is Japanese.* Thinking in most contexts means finding the right script to use, rather than generating new ideas and questions; so, essentially, we find it easier to apply scripts than to reason out every new situation from scratch. But scripts aren't the complete answer. Obviously, we can understand some novel experiences even if no script seems to apply. We do this by seeing new experiences in terms of old experiences.

When a prior experience is indexed cleverly, we can call it to mind to help us understand a current situation. This process can lead to brand-new insights. All people reason from experience. The differences among reasoners depend upon how they have coded their prior experiences in the first place. We are not all reminded of the same things at the same time. Let me give you an example.

Recently, I attended an informal talk by a leader of the sixties counterculture. These days he describes himself as a performer, a kind of comedian. In the sixties, he was also a performer. His humor was part of what made the counterculture so appealing. I was rather surprised, however, that he now saw himself as a performer. True, he got paid for performing, but he still cared deeply about the same issues he had always cared about. I told him that he reminded me of Jimmy Swaggart, the television evangelist. Naturally, he was curious as to why I thought this. I said that Jimmy Swaggart was only masquerading as a righteous man, getting paid well for performing when he was trying to hide the sinner that he really was. The sixties leader was also getting paid for performing as a clown when he was actually hiding the political reformer that he really was. In both cases, the masquerade was easy to see through; what was odd was that the performers seemed unable to see through it themselves.

For me, Jimmy Swaggart, like any other experience, is a case. It is not a particular case but a generalization over a set of experiences which one could label as: *Convincing speaker makes living at pretend-*

ing he is something he is not. I labeled the case of Jimmy Swaggart in such a way as to have it come to mind when hearing the counterculture hero speak. I reasoned about him by using the case of Jimmy Swaggart, and thus was able to come to some conclusions and insights about both. Mulling over the behavior of both men in turn reminded me of Ronald Reagan. His case was also labeled in my mind as a performer who got mixed up about his perceived role and his actual role.

The mind depends upon data in order to give it something to reflect upon. Where is this data to come from? Of course, movies, books, newspapers, and television provide much of this data. But in many ways the most important data we have comes from within. We learn from reconsidering experiences we have already had in light of new information. We form insights by comparing what we are currently examining with what we have already examined. To do this effectively, we had to have been very clever in how we labeled the data we originally perceived so we can find it again in circumstances that we could not have anticipated initially.

If a prior experience is understood only in terms of the generalization or principle behind the case, we don't have as many places to put the new case in memory. We can tell people abstract rules of thumb which we have derived from prior experiences, but it is very difficult for other people to learn from these. We have difficulty remembering such abstractions, but we *can* more easily remember a good story. Stories give life to past experience. Stories make the events in memory memorable to others and to ourselves. This is one of the reasons why people like to tell stories.

We are more persuasive when we tell stories. For example, we can simply state our beliefs, or we can tell stories that illustrate them. If John explains to Bill that he is in a quandary about whether to court Mary or Jane, and if after listening to John's description, Bill responds "Mary," his reply would usually be seen as useless advice. We need justifications for the beliefs of others in order to begin to believe them ourselves. If Bill responds, "Mary, because Mary is Irish, and Irish women make good wives," he is being more helpful but not necessarily more believable. But if Bill responds with a story about a similar situation that he was in or that he heard about and how the choice was made in that case and how it worked out, John is likely to be quite interested and to take the advice offered by the story more to heart. Why?

As we have seen, thinking involves indexing. In order to assimilate a case, we must attach it someplace in memory. Information without access to that information is not information at all. Memory, in order to be effective, must contain both specific experiences (memories) and labels (memory traces). The more information we are provided with about a situation, the more places we can attach it to in memory and the more ways it can be compared with other cases in memory. Thus, a story is useful because it comes with many indices. These indices may be locations, attitudes, quandaries, decisions, conclusions, or whatever. The more indices we have for a story that is being told, the more places it can reside in memory. Consequently, we are more likely to remember a story and to relate it to experiences already in memory. In other words, the more indices, the greater the number of comparisons with prior experiences and hence the greater the learning.

Let me tell a story to illustrate my point. A friend and I were discussing stories and then moved on to a discussion about Jewish attitudes toward intermarriage. He said that two Jewish friends of his mother had gone out when they were young women, and when they'd returned home, their mother had asked them what they had done that day. They'd responded that they had played tennis. Their mother had asked whom they had played with, and they had said, "Two guys." The mother had then asked what kind of guys, and they had responded, "Italian," to which the mother had said: "Another day wasted."

In hearing this story, I asked my friend what he thought would have happened in our discussion of Jewish attitudes if instead of telling this story he had said, "I knew someone who thought that playing tennis with Italians was a waste of time," or "Some mothers don't want their daughters to spend time with non-Jews." Stories illustrate points better than simply stating the points themselves because, if the story is good enough, you usually don't have to state your point at all; the hearer thinks about what you have said and figures out the point independently. The more work the hearer does, the more he or she will get out of your story.

Intelligence and Stories

This book is about stories. Human memory is story-based. Not all memories are stories. Rather, stories are especially interesting prior experiences, ones that we learn from. Cooking up egg foo yung is not a story. We would want to find that experience when we wanted to cook it again or when we wanted to cook up some new adaptation of egg foo yung. But the time we lost our cat while cooking egg foo yung would be a story (if there were, in fact, something interesting about the relationship between the two). Not every experience makes a good story, but, if it does, the experience will be easier to remember.

Why do we tell stories? How do we find them? Do we have any knowledge that is not encoded as stories? Does having stories available enable us to think less? When people listen to each other's stories are they really listening or only listening well enough to find an index to one of their own stories so that they will have something to say in response? How do stories become memories in the first place? These are some of the questions that naturally arise when one asserts that memory is story-based.

Our knowledge of the world is more or less equivalent to the set of experiences that we have had, but our communication is limited by the number of stories we know to tell. In other words, all we have are experiences, but all we can effectively tell others are stories. Oddly enough, we come to rely upon our own stories so much that it seems that all we can tell ourselves are stories as well. Communication consists of selecting the stories that we know and telling them to others at the right time. Learning from one's own experiences depends upon being able to communicate our experiences as stories to others.

For expository purposes I will use three models to illustrate the way intelligence and stories are related: the first is the librarian; the second is the grandfather; and the third is the logician. In AI, we tend to talk about modeling people, but part of the problem is deciding exactly what kind of people we are talking about.

Let's start with the librarian model. No one would doubt that a librarian, at least a human librarian, is intelligent. If we describe our interests well enough to a librarian, he may do one of three things. He might tell us where in the library to look for what we want, he might be able to find a book that fits what we have described perfectly although he has no idea of the actual contents, or he might be reminded of something he has read that suits us exactly. The process by which he does any of these things is intelligent, and in all three cases involves exactly the same issue, namely effective labeling. Now we naturally assume that the librarian is intelligent no matter which of the three courses of action he performs. However, if we attempted to develop a computer librarian, it would certainly seem intelligent enough if it could tell us where to look for a book, even more intelligent if it could select a book for us, and maximally intelligent if it were reminded of a book it had read and could converse with us about it.

Why does it matter which of these answers seems most intelligent? Has the computer librarian understood us? What is the difference between intelligence and understanding? Imagine a program that has thousands of screens of information that it can call up, each quite different. If it calls up the screen we want when we want it, it would certainly be doing its job, but would it be intelligent? Most people probably would say that a computer was not intelligent if it was only responding to our request for information by some simple label, such as a number. So, if we typed "2786" and got the screen that had that number, no one would assume that any intelligence was involved. Computers exist that can do such retrieval, and no one considers them to be intelligent.

Now imagine that the correct screen appears when we type something more complicated, such as "Who were the major league stolen-base leaders in the last ten years?" Such a program would seem intelligent if it provided the right answer, but the difference between the two programs would be no more than the complexity of the labeling of the screens and the ability of the program to translate the input typed by the user of the program into labels that call up the screens.

Returning to our librarian, we may find him very intelligent if he called up exactly the book we wanted, but his intelligence would be in translating what we said into the system of labels by which all the books he knows about have been encoded. Now imagine a computer version of this librarian that responded to our requests with just the book we had in mind and then, say, printed that book on our screen. Such a program would seem quite intelligent, but obviously the program wouldn't know what it was talking about. It could retrieve the book, but it wouldn't understand the book. In fact, it wouldn't necessarily even know what was in the book, apart from knowing a set of labels that described the book sufficiently to enable retrieval.

With this in mind, let's consider the grandfather model. The grandfather I have in mind is one who seems to tell the same story over and over again. Everyone has heard his favorite stories many times, but they indulge him by listening to them once again. Every now and then a new story appears, or at least one that no one remembers hearing before. When this happens, even the grandfather is surprised, and he enjoys telling the story more than usual. In some sense, the grandfather model is really just a crystallization of something we all do.

Is our grandfather wise? We need to know the difference between intelligence and wisdom. Here again we confront another subjective distinction that is very difficult to articulate. Nevertheless, we are willing to ascribe wisdom to those who are not so quick to draw conclusions but rather who see many sides of a problem and attempt to draw reasonable analogies. Or to put this another way, wisdom is often ascribed to those who can tell just the right story at the right moment and who often have a large number of stories to tell. Furthermore, these stories rarely draw every conclusion for their hearer. Rather, they present information, often leaving out the final conclusions.

The difference between our grandfather model and a model with wisdom is really just the difference between a system that can recall only a small number of stories, thus being reminded of and repeating each of them quite often, and one that does not repeat its stories but

tells just the right story at the right time. In other words, a computer
that had thousands or hundreds of thousands of stories and carefully
selected which ones to tell might well be considered to be not only
intelligent but also wise, even though it might not have understood
the very stories it was telling. The appearance of intelligence depends
very strongly upon what one says, ignoring, ironically, an assessment
of what one truly understands about what one has said.

Now let's consider the logician model. This model has been paro-
died in the popular mind by the Mr. Spock character in "Star Trek"
and, in general, is an image associated with scientists. The idea
behind the logician model of intelligence is that every problem can
be reduced to first principles and decided on the basis of some logic.
In popular fiction, such logical characters often fail to have some
emotional quality that makes them human in the audience's eyes. In
fact, any live logician model would have two more serious problems
in real life. The first is an understanding problem, and the second a
discovery problem.

The understanding problem is simply that humans are not really
set up to understand logic. People tell stories because they know that
others like to hear stories. The reason that people like to hear stories,
however, is not transparent to them. People need a context to help
them relate what they have heard to what they already know. We
understand events in terms of events we have already understood.
When a decision-making heuristic, or rule of thumb, is presented to
us without a context, we cannot decide the validity of the rule we
have heard, nor do we know where to store this rule in our memories. Thus, what we are presented is both difficult to evaluate and
difficult to remember, making it virtually useless. People who fail to
couch what they have to say in memorable stories will have their
rules fall on deaf ears despite their best intentions and despite the
best intentions of their listeners. A good teacher is not one who
explains things correctly but one who couches explanations in a
memorable (i.e., an interesting) format.

What makes us intelligent is our ability to find out what we know
when we need to know it. What we actually know is all the stories,
experiences, "facts," little epithets, points of view, and so on that we
have gathered over the years. Each of these is like a screen full of

information in a computer. Each screen has a label, and to find that screen, we must produce that label. Part of our intelligence is devoted to decoding inputs from the outside world sufficiently well so that these inputs produce labels that bring our own experiences to mind. When our own experiences come to mind, we can adapt them to a new situation if we are problem-solving, reduce them to a one-liner if we are in a short conversation, or tell them whole if we have an interested listener. We can compare two stories and attempt to find the similarities and differences, or we can alter a story to invent a new one for some purpose.

One consequence of this model of intelligence, especially of any computer implementation of this model, is that such a system runs the risk of being described as only appearing to be intelligent without actually being intelligent. In some sense, intelligence is in the eye of the beholder, and most beholders are very prejudiced by skin. If the skin of the teller of the story is fleshy and humanlike, we are likely to consider the algorithm that produced the story to be an intelligent one, except perhaps in the case of the grandfather who we would agree was intelligent but is now telling the same story too often. But if the skin is plastic and we suspect that a computer is inside we are likely to claim that the algorithms being used to produce the same story were somehow just unintelligent retrieval methods.

In the end all we have, machine or human, are stories and methods of finding and using those stories.

Knowledge, then, is experiences and stories, and intelligence is the apt use of experience and the creation and telling of stories. Memory is memory for stories, and the major processes of memory are the creation, storage, and retrieval of stories. To build models of intelligence or simply to understand the nature of intelligence we must understand the role that stories play in memory. We must know how events become stories and how these stories are stored and later retrieved. We must know the indices we construct that label stories, and we must determine how and why such indices are created. A good theory of mind must include theories about how the stories of others are decoded to find indices to enable their retrieval and storage, as well as theories of how and why our own stories appear in our minds in response. It must also contain a model of how and why we create new stories and of what happens to experiences that do not get encoded as stories. What we know is embodied in what we tell, and, as we shall see, what we tell strongly determines what we know. We know what we tell, and we tell what we know.

Conversation Is Reminding

If intelligence isn't embodied in problem-solving, where is it best expressed? Most of us are called upon to make judgments of the intelligence of others every day. We do so naturally in the course of our everyday conversations. How do we judge intelligence? What do we base our judgments on? Are our judgments reasonable?

Since we tend to confound the issues of intelligence and intellectual difficulty, problem-solving ability seems a more reasonable measure of intelligence than does the ability to participate in a conversation. After all, anyone can talk, but people nevertheless judge the intelligence of their conversational partners all the time without giving them puzzles to solve or reviewing their IQ scores. In some way that most people understand implicitly but not explicitly, performance in a conversation is an excellent measure of intelligence. This natural province of the layperson is also the natural province of the AI researcher. Moreover, the lack of computer programs that display conversational ability gives observers good reason to doubt the successes of AI. Not surprisingly, a program called ELIZA that employed very little in the way of AI technology was for years one of the best known "successes" of AI precisely because it could engage in a seemingly natural conversation.

Below is an often-cited conversation from that program:

PATIENT: Men are all alike.
COMPUTER: In what way?
PATIENT: They're always bugging us about something or other.
COMPUTER: Can you think of a specific example?
PATIENT: Well, my boyfriend made me come here.
COMPUTER: Your boyfriend made you come here?
PATIENT: He says I'm depressed much of the time.

COMPUTER: I am sorry to hear you are depressed.
PATIENT: It's true. I am unhappy.
COMPUTER: Do you think coming here will help you not to be
           unhappy?
PATIENT: I need some help. That much seems certain.
COMPUTER: What would it mean to you if you got some help?
PATIENT: Perhaps I could learn to get along with my mother.
COMPUTER: Tell me more about your family.
PATIENT: My mother takes care of me.
COMPUTER: Who else in your family takes care of you?
PATIENT: My father.
COMPUTER: Your father?
PATIENT: You are like my father in some ways.
COMPUTER: What resemblance do you see?
PATIENT: You are not very aggressive, but I think you don't want
           me to notice that.
COMPUTER: What makes you think I am not very aggressive?
PATIENT: You don't argue with me.
COMPUTER: Why do you think I don't argue with you?
PATIENT: You are afraid of me.
COMPUTER: Does it please you to believe I am afraid of you?
PATIENT: My father is afraid of everybody.
COMPUTER: What else comes to mind when you think of your father?
PATIENT: Bullies.
COMPUTER: Does that have anything to do with the fact that your
           boyfriend made you come here?

Why does this conversation make one feel that ELIZA is intelligent? ELIZA seems intelligent, not because it understood what the "patient" said, but because its responses relate to the patient's statements. As long as a listener responds to what we have said with a relevant comment, we can be quite forgiving. We readily assume understanding and intelligence on the part of the people or programs with whom we interact until we are given reason not to. Had ELIZA given a few irrelevant answers, had it had nothing to say that seemed to relate to what the patient said, we would have considered it dull indeed. But it kept up its end of the conversation, and that is an important aspect of how we judge intelligence.

What is it about conversation that strikes at the heart of intelligence? The answer to this question is both easy and far from obvious—real conversations involve, at virtually every stage, *reminding*. Now, it is not at all obvious that conversation is based upon reminding. The question to think about is how, after someone says something to you in a conversation, something comes to mind to say back. Even the simplest of responses have to be found somewhere in memory. One has to be reminded of what one thinks about a given subject in order to express that thought. Such remindings don't give one the same feeling as remindings of the "I haven't thought of that experience in thirty years" variety, but they are functionally much the same thing. So although Joseph Weizenbaum, the author of ELIZA, wasn't thinking about reminding when he wrote ELIZA, and even though his "theory of reminding" was trivial indeed, he still had to concern himself with how and where to find whatever ELIZA was to say next.

Reminding is the basis of much of our conversation and our thought. Even in casual conversations, we tell each other entertaining stories that come to mind without realizing how they came to mind or why they came to mind. But these seemingly random remindings are not random at all. In order to learn or understand something, our minds attempt to process everything we see and hear by comparison to what we have already experienced. From these remindings we gain new insights about the world around us.

What follows describes a real conversation that shows how we connect seemingly random or unimportant remindings with a view to explaining a situation we have never really understood that well.

John and Sam went to a university cafeteria for lunch. Sam got into the sandwich line, where the server, a young woman, was slicing roast beef, ham, corned beef, etc. Sam saw a nice looking piece of meat on the side of the cut roast beef, and ordered a roast beef sandwich. However, the server had previously cut some beef off, and she put this previously sliced beef into the sandwich. It wasn't nearly as nice as the meat that was still unsliced. When they got seated at their table in the dining room, Sam turned to John and said, "Boy, have I ever been suckered!" and he explained what had happened.

John said, "No, you haven't been suckered, because my impression of the word 'suckered' is that it implies serious attempt to defraud. You want a real suckering experience? On our trip to Spain, we were driving across the country, and we came to this tiny village. We went into a little store run by someone who looked just like a Gypsy lady. We bought some cheese and great bread and really nice looking sausage and some wine. Then we had it all wrapped up, and we drove out of the town. We parked in a secluded location, found a hill with some trees, climbed up to the top, and sat down, looking out over the beautiful countryside. Then we opened the wine and unwrapped the food. Garbage. All there was was garbage, carefully wrapped garbage. Now that was a suckering experience. The Gypsy lady suckered us."

Sam thought the story was pretty good and was reminded of an experience of his. "I went to Mexico with a friend," Sam said. "My friend tried to bargain for a hat. He started at one hundred pesos and tried to get the price down to fifty. But the guy wouldn't go below seventy-five. So he quit. Just then, someone else walked up and bought a hat without bargaining. He paid the full one hundred pesos. So my friend went back up to the guy and said, 'Look, if you give it to me for fifty, you will have gotten your price from both of us if you average it out.' And he did. So someone else was suckered, and my friend took advantage of it."

"Well," said John, "that reminds me of a similar incident that happened in Mexico, except that the result was just the reverse. This was a long time ago, way back in 1957, just after I graduated from MIT. I had driven down to the Yucatan with some friends. There we saw some really lovely hammocks. One friend, who was raised in Mexico and spoke fluent Spanish, bargained the price way down, and then bought one. So I walked up and said, 'I want one too.' But now the price went back to the original price, and try as I might, I couldn't get the price down to anything close to what my friend had just paid. I haven't thought about that incident in years—and it's been twenty-three years since it happened."

This is a rather typical reminding-driven conversation. People tend to trade stories as they are reminded of them. Sam tells about something that happened to him, and it reminds John of something like it that he experienced. This in turn reminds Sam of a good story, and so on. People trade jokes, stories about illnesses, yarns about the opposite sex, and so on. People exchange stories all the time, even though the significance of their remindings doesn't usually occur to them. People tell each other stories based on what sticks out as funny or odd. When something is unusual, we keep it around so that we can match it with other things that are unusual in the same way. In being reminded, we use our previous experiences to understand our current ones. When someone tells an irrelevant or pointless story, you feel that you have been misunderstood. When someone tells you a story in response to one you have told that captures an important generalization between the two, you believe that you have been "really understood," and you ascribe qualities of high intelligence and perception to your listener.

The mechanisms of reminding that we use in making connections are the very same mechanisms that we use in a conversation. We must think of something to say in response to what we have heard. This is fundamentally the same process that we use in understanding anything and hence in responding internally to anything. In other words, it doesn't matter whether we are called upon to respond to what we have just heard or whether we are not expected to, such as when reading, hearing a lecture, or watching a movie. The mental processes are the same in each case. We understand by getting reminded. Whether we choose to tell that reminding to others is a matter of assessing correctly the social situation in which we find ourselves. Expressing our opinion in the middle of a movie theater would be considered odd. Stating it when asked by our date after the movie would be reasonable. In either case, the process is the same. We must be reminded of our opinion, and often that opinion is a story that existed in our heads prior to the input that evoked it.

Intelligence and Storytelling

To the extent that intelligence is bound up with our ability to tell the right story at the right time, understanding a story means being able to correlate the story we are hearing with one that we already know. Below is a real example of this process in a story and a reminding that a student of mine told me.

INITIAL STORY

After several years of waiting for the bus at night without having any threatening encounters, a student had a scare. She was in a dangerous neighborhood and was nervous about being mugged. Instead, she was hit in the face by a snowball which broke her glasses. The next day, she went to an optician in another bad neighborhood to have her glasses fixed, but while waiting she began to feel uneasy. She was the only customer, and the young man and woman who worked there were acting strangely. She was still jittery from the night before and wanted to leave. In order to leave, however, she had to ask the very people she was afraid of to give back her glasses. Nevertheless she asked for them and of course got them back.

REMINDING

In Wouk's *Winds of War,* Natalie, trying to get out of Nazi-threatened Europe, goes to the Lufthansa office to pick up tickets. She has to give the ticket agents her passport—her major protection as a Jew and an American—but feels reasonably safe until the Lufthansa employees request she fill out a form that asks for her religion. This shakes her, and she decides that flying Lufthansa is even more dangerous than its alternatives. She wants to get out of the ticket office and abort the whole transaction, but the Germans still have her passport! She asks for it back, and they refuse to return it at first, but she finally manages to get safely out of the Lufthansa office with her passport.

The similarity between these two stories is striking, down to the details of the feelings and attitudes on the parts of the participants. We must have very complex and detailed memories, indeed, to be reminded of one of these stories by the other, a reminding that requires the ability to store and retrieve these stories on the basis of a set of rather subtle details. The value of the reminding in this case is fairly clear. By storing information about the problems of others, even if they are fictional characters, we can learn from their actions. When our own circumstances match those of people we have heard about, we can conclude that we need to modify our behavior so as to learn from the commonality of experience. Here, the student presumably learned a new lesson: Hold on to your valuable possessions when you are frightened. Without them, you may not be able to get away.

In the following reminding story, we again have a situation where someone is reminded of a movie by his own life. Instead of saying something original or in some way adapting the original for a new purpose, the actor here just used the old story verbatim.

INITIAL STORY

A man met a woman, and they talked about life for a few hours and began to feel very close to each other. But she was married and was afraid to go further. The man went back to his hotel and the woman to her home. Later, the man received a call from the woman saying that she had to see him before he caught his plane the next morning but that she wasn't sure she knew how to get away from home without causing trouble.

REMINDING

The man found himself thinking about the movie *Casablanca* and Woody Allen's related movie *Play It Again Sam*. In both of these movies, a woman must decide whether to leave with her husband on a plane or to remain behind with another man. The man says, "If you don't go now, you will regret it, maybe not now, and maybe not tomorrow, but soon and for the rest of your life." Woody Allen says the line and then says that he has always wanted to say it. The man in our story found himself reminded of the line and used it as Woody Allen did.

What can we make of remindings such as the one given above? The circumstances are very similar—planes, extramarital affairs, life decisions, and so on, enter in all three cases. Human memory is a cluster of experiences, each labeled in complex ways. These labels allow for the retrieval of relevant experiences at the right time so that we have a story to tell. The process of labeling these stories is not transparent to us as understanders of these stories. We do not realize that we are creating such labels, nor do we realize that we know the labels we have previously created well enough to be able to use them as aids in retrieval. It is only through a comparison of actual remindings, by looking at the similarities between two stories, one of which was retrieved in response to an attempt to understand the other, that we can begin to see the mental labels that the mind relies upon. Understanding means constructing such labels and using them to retrieve similar situations in which those labels have been previously used. Figuring out how to behave in a new situation is most certainly helped by being reminded of an old situation that is like the new situation. The old situation then becomes a guide to follow or even a guide to what not to do. But all this depends upon finding something relevant to use as a guide in the first place.

Storytelling as Understanding

Storytelling and understanding are functionally the same thing. Conversation is no more than responsive storytelling. The process of reminding is what controls understanding and, therefore, conversation. Thus, seen this way, conversations are really a series of remindings of already-processed stories. The mind can be seen as a collection of stories, collections of experiences one has already had. Conversationalists are looking to tell one of their stories. They are looking to tell a good one, a right one, but to do this they must be reminded of one of the ones that they know.

Viewed this way, it is almost as if we never say anything new; we just find what we have already said and say it again. But we don't do this freely or randomly. There is a method to this system. We are always looking for the closest possible matches. We seek to retrieve stories that seem to us to be identical. We are looking to say, in effect, *Well, something like that happened to me too* or *I had an idea about something like that myself.* In order to do this, we must adopt a point of view that allows us to see a situation or experience as an instance of "something like that." In other words, we must evaluate experiences with an intention of matching them to what we already have experienced.

Generation by Storytelling

The story-based conception of generation presupposes that everything you might ever want to say has already been thought up. This is not as strange an idea as it seems. I am not suggesting that every sentence one will ever say is sitting in memory word for word. Rather, adults have views of the world that are expressed by ideas they already have thought up and have probably expressed many times. When asked for your view of Reagan, for example, you don't usually consider the problem for the first time. What you say, however, may not be something you have ever said before. Certainly, you are not likely to say word for word what you have said before. Nevertheless, what you say will have a certain familiarity to it and will be something that you have thought before and possibly expressed in other words. Your views evolve, so what you say one time will not be identical to what you say the next time. But the relation between the two will be strong and will occur to you as you begin to construct your new thoughts. New ideas depend upon old ones.

So the main issue in generation is really the accessing of whatever you already think about something and the expression of those thoughts. When we tell a story, we are doing the same thing. We are accessing the gist of that story and then reexpressing that gist in language. Our own personal stories are not identical each time we tell them with respect to the words that we say, but the ideas behind them are more or less the same. In other words, we take the gist of a story as it exists in memory and then transform that gist into a verbal expression of the story that perhaps leaves out one point or embellishes another. The words we choose may depend upon the audience. The ideas expressed may depend upon our reinterpretation of past events in light of events that have occurred since the story being told took place.

This transformation of the gist of a story into a realization of that story in language has its parallel in everyday conversation. Once conversation is redefined as basically mutual reminding, the generation of responses becomes no more than accessing the gist of whatever one was reminded of and the transformation of that gist into language. Surely this is not, however, the only kind of generation that occurs. People can think on their feet occasionally, usually by remembering a situation in one domain and applying their reasoning to another. For example, when a politically naive individual was asked how he would derail Dukakis's presidential campaign if he were George Bush, he replied as follows:

The first thing that popped into my mind was *All the King's Men*, which is a novel about Huey Long, and Huey Long's favorite tactic for derailing an opposing politician was to get the dirt on him. Another tactic that comes to mind is that I would do whatever I could to suggest that I was not, in fact, connected to Reagan. Just as George Steinbrenner, let's say, does damage to the image of the New York Yankees today. There are thousands of people who would root for the Yankees if George Steinbrenner were not the boss.

In this example, the speaker was reminded of Huey Long and George Steinbrenner. By applying analogies to the political scene, he was able to think on his feet and to answer the question. But even here the respondent is looking for relevant stories. He may never have made this particular analogy before, but he had abstracted features from situations before and he had stored certain information in his memory in terms of those features. Even innovative thinking relies upon the mechanisms of reminding and the transformation of existing stories to new situations. However, most of what people say on a day-to-day basis has already been said before in a very similar form.

Therefore, to put this in the simplest possible terms, the problem of generating language can be reduced to the problem of selecting the gist or gists of thousands or millions of not necessarily conscious ideas to be transformed into a particular linguistic expression of those ideas. In other words, taking one's part in a conversation means no more than searching for what one has already thought up and saying it. Even thinking on your feet and creating something new to say still relies upon using something that you have thought about before. Participating in a conversation means reminding oneself of a good story to tell, either by telling one you have already told or by the far more difficult process of creating a new one. Because the creation process is so difficult, when we choose to say something, we usually have said it before. Not all conversations are one story after another, but in a group situation especially that tends to be the case.

Stories are everywhere, but not all stories look like stories. If you consider a story to be a previously prepared gist of something to say, something that you have said before or heard another say, then a great deal of conversation is simply mutual storytelling. Moreover, if the majority of what we say is in our memories in the form of previously prepared stories, the way we look at the nature of understanding and what it means to be intelligent must change. Is being very intelligent just having a great many stories to tell? Does it mean being better at finding relevant stories to tell? Is it adapting superficially irrelevant stories into relevant ones, i.e., finding a story in one domain and applying it by analogy to another? Maybe it means combining stories and making generalizations from them—or, perhaps intelligence is embodied in the initial process of collecting stories to tell in the first place.

□ 2 □
Where Stories Come From and Why We Tell Them

□

I WAS SITTING in my office one day when three people came in, one at a time, to talk to me. The first was a foreign student who was about to become a graduate student. He told me the following story.

In order to go to graduate school, I had to postpone going into the army. Ordinarily, three years of service are required, but my country decided that if I wanted to study for a Ph.D. now, I would owe them five years after I finish my studies. I agreed to this, but after I agreed, my country called and said I would owe six years of service. Again I agreed, and again I received a call saying that now they had decided seven years would be required. What should I do?

The second person who entered my office was someone who worked for me. This was his story:

My ex-wife just called. She's moving back to town, and she's planning to put our child in public school here. She's had him in private school, but now she wants me to pay the tuition money to her instead. She isn't planning on working and is trying to get me to support her. I just called my lawyer to ask him what to do.

The third person was a friend. He had been looking to change jobs and had negotiated a fine deal for himself in another town. This was his story:

I've been busy selling my house and otherwise preparing for the move. All of a sudden, my appointment has been stopped at the highest levels of the company. No one will tell me why, but I think someone who was my enemy in the past has a friend at the company. And I think she wrote a letter that prejudiced them against me. I'm very upset.

Everyday human communication revolves around stories such as these. Where do we get stories to tell? Obviously, stories digest one's experiences. We tell what happened to us. But we also create stories. I, for example, had a story to tell at the end of that day about how people mistreat one another, and I needed to tell it.

When people talk to you, they can only tell you what they know. And the knowledge that people have about the world around them is really no more than the set of experiences that they have had. Now, of course, not every experience that someone has had is worth remembering, let alone telling to someone else. The experiences we do remember form the set of stories that constitute our view of the world and characterize our beliefs. In some sense, we may not even know what our own view of the world is until we are reminded of and tell stories that illustrate our opinion on some aspect of the world.

Types of Stories

With the exception of certain questions and some straightforward and factual answers, such as "What room is Jones in?" followed by "1244," everything people say regarding their opinions or experiences is a story of some sort. Some stories are too dull to worry about, but the process of search, retrieval, and adaptation of stories is the same whether the story is long or short. One question is where stories come from. We start life without stories, and we go through life acquiring them. Some are handed to us directly by others and some we invent for ourselves.

With respect to the issue of where stories come from, there are five basic types of stories:

1. official
2. invented (adapted)
3. firsthand experiential
4. secondhand
5. culturally common

Official Stories

Official stories are those we learn from an official place, such as school or church or a business or from the government. They are stories that have been told many times, and no one knows or cares who thought them up first. Governments and other official bodies have a kind of script for inventing them, and people in general know how much credence to give them. We know official stories about the creation of the universe, for example. Science has its versions, and religions have theirs. From time to time, we tell an official story because our job requires us to or because the official story is the only one we know.

Official stories are those that our boss, our government, our parents, or anyone in authority instructs us to tell. They are repeated as originally related. People can tell their own official stories. For example, Gary Hart in the 1987–1988 political campaign told an official story about his alleged lover Donna Rice that it seemed no one, not even he, could have believed. But it was the official story. One of my favorite official stories is about Sydney Biddle Barrows, the so-called Mayflower Madam. The following was taken from the *New York Post:*

MAYFLOWER MADAM SAILS
INTO A NEW BUSINESS

The Mayflower Madam, a thirty-three-year-old blonde blueblood awaiting trial on charges of running a $1000-a-night prostitution ring, is back in business as the Makeover Madam. She has founded a house-call service for women who want to eat better, dress better, and look better, called We Can Work It Out. Sydney Biddle Barrows, the beautiful descendant of Mayflower pilgrims, will send training counselors to enforce tough diet and exercise regimens on middle-class women.

Her attorney and friend, Risa Dickstein, yesterday told of the project, still in its infancy. In a three-hundred-page motion filed in Manhattan Supreme Court, Mrs. Dickstein asked for a dismissal of the charges against Miss Barrows on grounds ranging from insufficient evidence to prosecutorial misconduct.

She painted a heartwarming picture of the woman accused of running a prostitution ring for high-class clients. She said Miss Barrows:

voluntarily reads to a blind college student and helps him with term
papers in a program to aid the handicapped;
instructed her employees to patronize an Upper West Side food
store because it supplied free meals to the needy on
Thanksgiving;
doesn't drink, smoke, or take drugs—not even aspirin;
has the support of her mother, stepfather, and siblings in her ordeal;
lost the love of her natural father because of her arrest.

Mrs. Dickstein said in her motion that Miss Barrows has a totally unblemished record. It is undisputed that she comes from a family which is well recognized not only as law-abiding but also for its commitment to public service. She is accurately viewed by those who know her well as a well-bred, well-educated, responsible citizen for her community.

The defense argues that the escort agencies run by Miss Barrows were legitimate businesses in which clients paid for companionship. Sex, when it took place, was indulged in freely by the escorts—and at no extra charge.

Official stories are ones that have been carefully constructed by one or more people to tell a version of events that is sanitized and presumed to be less likely to get anyone in trouble. Alternatively, official stories are often the position of a group that has a message to sell and treats that message independently of the facts. A rather grisly example of this was recently placed on a billboard overlooking I-95 in Bridgeport, Connecticut. The sign showed an iridescent skeleton crawling into a body bag. The legend over the picture said: "AIDS—It's a Hop in the Sack." Such epithets are quite typical of official stories. The facts are made simple, often to the point of being wrong, so that a message can be made public. Official stories often leave out details that would make things clearer in order to portray situations as being less complicated than they are.

The overall intention of an official story is to make complex issues seem clearer than they otherwise might appear. When we don't have answers, official stories give us those answers. We learn these stories when we have no stories of our own for those particular situations. As soon as we do have a story of our own that we believe more than the official version, we tend to ignore the official story.

Invented Stories

Obviously, people can make up stories, but the process of story creation and invention is one of adaptation rather than creation out of nothing. Official stories are made up by adapting real stories into appropriately sterilized stories. Invented stories can also, of course, be official stories. In any case, the processes behind the creation of these two story types are remarkably similar. Both of these story types tend to use a real story, that is, a firsthand experiential story, something that really happened to somebody, and then expand upon that story in some way.

The invented story expands upon an experience for the purpose of entertainment, sometimes leaving the original experience unrecognizable in the process. The official story is created in the same way, albeit for a different purpose. An official story tends to obscure the facts of the original experience for the purposes of eliminating culpability on the part of the actors in the story.

Invented stories are also created brand-new by authors, by parents, and often by people who pose a hypothetical case in order to make a point in an argument; however, even brand-new invented stories are usually adaptations of previous stories and frequently, but by no means always, have a point. They tend to be much less rich in detail at first, but their continued elaboration can make them very rich over time.

A good way to understand the story invention process is to observe it firsthand. Unfortunately, when people create a new story, we have difficulty knowing exactly how they found the various pieces of the story they are telling. We cannot easily know what has been invented out of thin air and what has been adapted from prior experiences or other stories. We can reasonably assume, however, that true creation can hardly exist with respect to stories. Every story we tell has to have its basis in something that we have already experienced. Of course, the better we are at telling stories, the better we are at giving them the appearance of being complete fiction. This can mean that even we as tellers see the story as fictional, not realizing the adaptation process that we ourselves have used. Even stories that are pure fantasy are adaptations of more realistic stories where certain constraints of the real world are relaxed. People can take past experiences, consciously or unconsciously, and modify them into stories where the original experience is completely hidden.

One way to see this is to observe a child who is learning to tell stories. When my daughter, Hana, was very little, I recorded some stories that she told at various ages. Here are some of them, taken from *Scripts, Plans, Goals and Understanding* (Roger Schank and Robert Abelson; Hillsdale, NJ: Lawrence Erlbaum Associates, 1977). Hana, age two years, eleven months:

PAPA: I met you in the plant store and then what happened?
HANA: I don't know.
PAPA: Oh, come on, I thought you were going to tell me a story.
HANA: I went on a bike and you drived, and you buckled me in and
       we went riding the park, and droved and went on one swing
       and then the other swing and two swings and then we, I went
       on two slides and then went in the sandbox and then I met
       somebody, and then I met, and then I went right on our
       bicycle, and took the thing off and and and we went on and

you drived on and then you taked the one street and then you
ride on the other side and then we were home and then we
were opened, I opened, you opened, I opened the door and
then I went right in and I take my jacket off and said hang up
your coat and I hanged up my coat and said and went right in
the kitchen and and was almost time to dinner.

PAPA: And then what happened?

HANA: I don't know.

PAPA: What happened after you took your coat off?

HANA: Then we went take a nap and you were and then we, you, we
went to the plant store and then Nadine was at home and
then at our home, and then she was clean, changed, cleared
all the rugs, and then I wake woke up and then I I was . . .
went into living room and there's something I didn't ask her
and and then she I didn't want and watched and watched
cartoons. I watched this, I watched, I did, when we got home
I watched I watched TV um "Sesame Street." That's the end.

This is a story in the sense that it is what my daughter told when
she was asked to tell a story. But obviously she has just recapped the
day's experiences. By age four, Hana could really invent a new story.
The story itself is invented in the sense that it didn't happen as such,
but each individual event in the story did happen. Hana had experienced it all before; she just adapted the events for her use here. We
lose coherence here because Hana hasn't yet learned standard coherent story forms that an adult might know. Other than that, though,
the process of story creation is remarkably similar to the adult process.

PAPA: Tell me a story.

HANA: Once upon a time there was a little girl and she lived with her
mother and father in a big house, not an apartment house, and
she was born in California. She has her own passport, her
brother has a passport, too. Everyone has a passport, you
know that, 'cause they have to have passports for special
reasons. They went out to London and they had a good time
there. They went riding on horses and they had real good
times. They played. They brang lots of toys to play with, even

books. Well, books are not such things to play with, you read them. And so then they went out, and then they saw a rabbit and they said hi to the rabbit, and then they said would the rabbit be their pet. But the rabbit said it couldn't be their pet and then they came up to a kitten. They said to the kitten, "Could we have a kitten?" And then, after they had the kitten for their own, then they named it, Joan, Joe, and then they walked on. The kitten was almost in danger. It got struck by a big wolf came and almost tried to bite it and then eat it, but it finally chased the wolf out and Mama and Papa got danger, Hana helped, Joshua was too little, he just said "ah da" to the wolf. And then they came up to a great forest, they had lots of pine trees. And then they came up something shiny with bright eyes, another kitten, instead it was a mother. And so, they took good care of the two kittens and then rode back to where they were, and got, and then went to sleep, and often got dressed the next morning and went out to have their breakfast. They had Chinese breakfast, but Hana in case didn't bring the cat and left it outside by mistake, and Mama and Daddy, locked it in a cage. It was barking the next day, and meowing the next day, and then, away from danger, they saw balloons and then one bursted the balloon and then they got all the rest of the balloons. They had all the money that they needed for to buy a balloon. It was free. They didn't know that, so they paid some money. And then they got all the money that they paid. And then they went home to their own real house and wrote down that they had a good time and sended it to someone and everyone got a chance to read that. And then they had such good time, they had a jolly time here and from all you, this is telling the story. That's the end.

Story invention, for children or adults, is a process of the massaging of reality. How reality is massaged, how old stories are transformed into new ones, depends upon the goals of the teller. If the teller has something to hide, a fantasy to express, a political point to make, whatever, the original story can be changed in a variety of ways. Invention is not a process that comes from nowhere.

Firsthand Stories

People tell about their own experiences all the time, but they do not necessarily tell about the same experience in the same way every time. The telling process, even in the relating of a firsthand experience, can be a highly inventive process. That is, the art of storytelling involves finding good ways to express one's experiences in a way appropriate to the listener. A fine line exists, therefore, between invented stories and the relation of firsthand experiences. The entertainment factor exists in relating firsthand experiences just as it does in inventing stories. Nobody wants to listen to what happened to you today unless you can make what happened appear interesting. The process of livening up an experience can involve simply telling that experience in such a way as to eliminate the dullest parts, or it also can involve "jacking up" the dull parts by playing with the facts.

Firsthand experiential stories are the type of stories we talk about most. They represent our own personal experiences. Some of these experiences have been digested and analyzed so that we know their point or points and are reminded of them when those points come up. But many firsthand stories come up because of random associations, and many have no intended point; they are just stories about ourselves which have not necessarily been fully understood and from which no conclusions may have yet been drawn. Or more often firsthand stories are told because they relate information that is nonstandard in some way. We don't tell about experiences that we believe everyone else has also had. We tell about what we believe to be unusual. The more usual such an experience is, the less we want to tell about it. Good stories are about things that are unusual and could not have easily been predicted.

Secondhand Stories

Secondhand stories are acquired secondhand. We often tell the stories of others. Telling secondhand experiences tends to be a much more straightforward process than telling firsthand stories, because the task is mostly an attempt at proper recall of the facts as they were heard. The problem, of course, is that we can't recall all the facts, even when the event being related is firsthand, much less when it is secondhand. Here again, "facts" are made up as needed to preserve coherence, although tellers may not actually be aware that they are making up part of the story. The parlor game of telephone relies upon the inability of people to recall and to relate properly what they have just heard.

Secondhand experiential stories are simply the firsthand stories of others that we have heard and remembered. Usually the indices to them are much less rich, much more specific. These stories often have clear points and are frequently remembered in terms of the points that they are intended to illustrate.

Culturally Common Stories

The culturally common story is not as obvious a category as the other four. We get culturally common stories from our environment. No one person tells them, and no one person makes them up. They are pervasive nevertheless. Below are two examples of culturally common stories, again taken from a movie, this time *Casablanca:*

YVONNE: Will I see you tonight?
RICK: I never make plans that far ahead.

CAPTAIN RENAULT: And what in heaven's name brought you to Casablanca?
RICK: My health. I came to Casablanca for the waters.
RENAULT: Waters? What waters? We're in the desert.
RICK: I was misinformed.

Both of the above statements by Rick are stories. Obviously, they are not your usual kind of story and to all outward appearances seem to be merely tag lines that are meant to be funny. But the reason one can speak in such a shorthand and humorous way and be understood not only by one's listener but also by a movie audience is that both statements are simply cryptic ways of referring to well-known stories, stories that the movie writers, in this instance, are assuming their audience knows.

Culturally common stories are usually referred to rather than told. For example, the following one-liner from the Woody Allen movie *Love and Death* is a reference to stories that we all know about insurance salesmen:

There are worse things in life than death—If you have ever spent an evening with an insurance salesman, you know what I mean.

The commonality of our culture's views of insurance salesmen allows us to communicate in this way about insurance salesmen. The culturally common story here is simply that insurance salesmen are boring and painful to listen to.

To a large extent, a story's usefulness depends upon how much of the original detail has remained over time. An ossified story is useful as a rule applicable to many specific situations but not to all the situations which in its original form it might have been. A story still present in its full form in memory can be applied to a variety of situations but not necessarily as widely as a distilled story. Memory richness versus memory succinctness is a trade-off between multiple labels, or ways of referring to a story, with general applicability and few labels with specific applicability.

On the other hand, distilling a story sufficiently gives back its general applicability. A proverb is an ossified distilled story, but it has lost so much of its original detail that it needs the hearer to supply some detail. Thus a proverb can be seen to carry with it great wisdom because the hearer has supplied the specific referents to the general frame which is the proverb. This is the case with the *I Ching,* a collection of ossified distilled stories that seem to contain great wisdom when one adds one's own details. The following, a comment on the Hsu hexagram, is a passage from the *I Ching:*

2.   The second line, undivided, shows its subject waiting on the sand (of the mountain stream). He will (suffer) the small (injury of) being spoken (against), but in the end there will be good fortune.

3. The third line, undivided, shows its subject in mud (close by the stream). He thereby invites the approach of injury.
4. The fourth line, divided, shows its subject waiting in (the place of) blood. But he will get out of the cavern.

In some sense, much of what we consider to be creativity is no more than the adaptation of a story from one domain for use in another. Taking a neutral story and adding detail can also be considered to be creative; indeed, many new stories for television are written in precisely this way. We are also creative when we understand the stories of others by adding details of our own lives that allow us to read more into a story than may have been put there by the author. In each case, the story adapted from the original is now a story in its own right and can be stored in memory with new indices.

The opposite side of the coin is that some stories get told in their least detailed form, making them understandable only to those who already know them. Such stories can become so short that they do not in any way appear to be stories, and in some obvious sense, they are not stories. Maybe the best way to illustrate what I mean here is by a well-known joke.

The prisoners in a maximum-security prison had little to entertain themselves with so they told jokes to each other. But they had long since run out of new jokes to tell, so they simply numbered the jokes and yelled out the numbers. A new prisoner hearing "forty-two," "sixty-four," "one hundred eight" being yelled down the hall with raucous laughter following each number asked about what was happening, and it was explained to him. He asked if he could try it, and his cellmate said sure. He hollered "thirty-six," and nothing happened. Next he tried "twenty-seven" and still nothing. The new prisoner finally asked his cellmate what was wrong, and he replied, "You didn't tell them so well."

Is "forty-two" a story? Of course it is, and it isn't. It doesn't sound like a story; it's more the name of a story, so to speak. In some sense, every story is simply the name of a longer story. No one tells all the details of any story, so each story is shortened. How much shortening has to take place until there is no story left? A story shortened so that it ceases to be understood is no longer a story, but what is understandable to one person may not be understandable to another, so it is clear that "story" is a relative term. In any case, as long as it *is* understood, it remains a story. For this reason, there are some very short stories.

One of my favorite short stories comes from the movie *Manhattan:*

YALE: She's gorgeous.
ISAAC: She's seventeen. I'm forty-two, and she's seventeen.

More needn't be said here because the point has been made without saying more. We all know stories or can imagine stories involving the complexity of a relationship between a forty-two-year-old man and a seventeen-year-old girl. Of course, the movie goes on to tell exactly that story. The referent here is to a story we all know which then serves as the basis for the new story we are about to hear.

Why We Tell Stories

People can be viewed in some sense as repositories of stories. Old people most obviously tell the same story again and again, but many people have a number of stories to tell and take the occasion to tell them whenever that opportunity arises. When we look at particular stories, we can think about the points that they express and attempt to understand why a given story may have come to mind at any specific point in a conversation, but particular stories don't really matter. The issue here is why do we tell stories at all? What is interesting about stories? What is the point of telling a story instead of just saying what we want to say directly? In order to understand why we tell stories, we must identify the goals that people have in a conversation. Because stories are usually told to someone and not to an empty room, no story commonly satisfies only one goal. Rather, tellers may have one goal for themselves and another goal for their listeners.

In broad terms, then, we usually have one of three basic reasons for telling stories. First, we may derive some satisfaction from telling a story. Second, we may derive satisfaction from the effect we believe, or convince ourselves to believe, that a story will have on our listener. Or third, we sometimes tell a story because of the effect we believe that the story will have on the conversation itself. We can categorize our intentions in storytelling as follows:

> **Category 1:** Me-goals (the intentions that storytellers have with respect to themselves)
>
> **Category 2:** You-goals (the intentions that storytellers have with respect to others)
>
> **Category 3:** Conversational goals (the intentions that storytellers have with respect to the conversation itself)

Me-goals

The first category, me-goals, includes our intentions in telling stories to satisfy our own personal goals. When we tell stories to others, we often do so entirely because of our own goals for ourselves that are satisfied by the listener paying attention in the desired way. Tellers can have five intentions with respect to themselves: to achieve catharsis, to get attention, to win approval, to seek advice, or to describe themselves. Several intentions are frequently present at once. For example, imagine a man at a party where he sees a woman he wants to meet. He begins to tell a story that is designed immediately to get the attention of the group he is talking to and ultimately to get the woman's approval for his being sensitive. The story he chooses is self-descriptive and tells about a horrible situation that allows him to become emotional in the telling. As a result of telling the story, he feels better, but, more important, the woman in the group notices him, likes his emotional qualities, and feels that she can tell him something that will help him in his predicament. We can see that the teller's intentions fall into all categories.

In the following scene from the movie *The Apartment,* a character tells a story to prevent herself from committing suicide on Christmas. Her intention, in other words, is cathartic:

I think I'm going to give it all up. Why do people have to love people, anyway? I don't want it. What do you call it when somebody keeps getting smashed up in automobile accidents? That's me with men. I've been jinxed from the word go—first time I was ever kissed was in a cemetery. I was fifteen—we used to go there to smoke. His name was George—he threw me over for a drum majorette. I just have this talent for falling in love with the wrong guy in the wrong place at the wrong time. The last one was manager of a finance company, back home in Pittsburgh—they found a little shortage in his accounts, but he asked me to wait for him—he'll be out in 1965. So I came to New York and moved in with my sister and her husband—he drives a cab. They sent me to secretarial school, and I applied for a job with Consolidated—but I flunked the typing test—oh, I can type up a storm, but I can't spell. So they gave me a pair of white gloves and stuck me in an elevator—that's how I met Jeff—Oh, God, I'm so fouled up. What am I going to do now? Maybe he does love me—only he doesn't have the nerve to tell his wife.

The teller of this story needs to explain why she has reached an emotional crisis and doesn't seem especially interested in how the listener feels about what she says. Of course, we can't know for sure what her attitude toward the listener is. She may intend to elicit an emotional response from him, and his reaction to her, if sympathetic, may affect how successfully cathartic the telling of her story is. But either way, telling her story attempts to accomplish the hoped-for catharsis.

In response to her story, the listener offers a story of his own which falls not into the me-goals but into the you-goals category, a story told to have an effect on someone else. He tells the story seemingly to display some kind of feeling—"We are in this together"—for the teller of the original story:

I know how you feel, Miss Kubelik. You think it's the end of the world—but it's not, really. I went through exactly the same thing myself. Well, maybe not exactly—I tried to do it with a gun. She was the wife of my best friend, and I was mad for her. But I knew it was hopeless—so I decided to end it all. I went to a pawnshop and bought a .45 automatic and drove up to Eden Park—do you know Cincinnati? Anyway, I parked the car and loaded the gun—well, you read in the papers all the time that people shoot themselves, but believe me, it's not that easy—I mean, how do you do it? Here or here or here [with cocked finger, he points to his temple, mouth, and chest]. You know where I finally shot myself? [Indicates knee.] Here. While I was sitting there, trying to make my mind up, a cop stuck his head in the car, because I was illegally parked—so I started to hide the gun under the seat, and it went off—pow! Took me a year before I could bend my knee—but I got over the girl in three weeks. She still lives in Cincinnati, has four kids, gained twenty pounds—she—Here's the fruitcake. [Shows it to her under Christmas tree.] And you want to see my knee?

Within the me-goal category, we also tell stories expressly to get attention. One way to grab attention is to tell stories that will interest the group one is involved with at the moment. The teller of attention-getting stories often wants to impress listeners as being very funny or sympathetic or honest or powerful, etc. The teller may have the allied intention of entertaining the listener so that the teller can continue telling stories and thus remain the center of attention. In the following story from Tennessee Williams's *The Glass Menagerie*, a woman tries to win the approval of a gentleman caller and in the process draw attention to the virtues of her exceedingly shy daughter:

It's rare for a girl as sweet an' pretty as Laura to be domestic! But Laura is, thank heavens, not only pretty but also very domestic. I'm not at all. I never was a bit. I never could make a thing but angel food cake. Well, in the South we had so many servants. Gone, gone, gone. All vestige of gracious living! Gone completely! I wasn't prepared for what the future brought me. All of my gentlemen callers were sons of planters and so of course I assumed that I would be married to one and raise my family on a large piece of land with plenty of servants. But man proposes—and woman accepts the proposal! To vary that old saying a little bit—I married no planter! I married a man who worked for the telephone company! That gallantly smiling gentleman over there! . . . A telephone man who fell in love with long-distance! Now he travels and I don't even know where!

We tell stories to describe ourselves not only so others can understand who we are but also so we can understand ourselves. Telling our stories allows us to compile our personal mythology, and the collection of stories we have compiled is to some extent who we are, what we have to say about the world, and tells the world the state of our mental health.

To some extent, our stories, because they are shaped by memory processes that do not always have their basis in hard fact, are all fictions. But these fictions are based on real experiences and are our only avenue to those experiences. We interpret reality through our stories and open our realities up to others when we tell our stories. We can also tell stories to escape reality, to paint a picture that is more like what we would like to have happened than what actually happened. But, it should be understood, this is to some extent what we do all the time with stories. The extent to which we can stretch reality and still be considered mentally healthy is not all that clear.

Our intentions in telling self-descriptive stories are often complex. Our goals with respect to ourselves and to others are sometimes complementary and sometimes contradictory. One might, for example, tell a story hoping to rekindle a friendship in the eyes of another but in reality attempting to manipulate the other for personal gain.

Because telling a self-descriptive story often satisfies at least two goals, me-goals and you-goals, and often the conversational-goal as well, the self-descriptive prototype is both common and important. People have a great many things to say about themselves for a great many reasons and thus have many stories to illustrate various aspects of their personalities, their points of view, and their hopes and their problems. As we saw in the story sequence from *The Apartment,* the description of the woman's problem reminded her listener of a similar problem in his own life. His quickness in telling the story suggests that he has told the story before. People love to match stories, communicating by having similar experiences to relate. For this reason, we tend to tell the same stories over and over until we fashion a stock story which illustrates a point about ourselves effectively. The man, however, also intended to make a further point to the woman about the resilience of human beings and thus to prevent her suicide.

In the following story from *Long Day's Journey into Night,* a man tries to justify choosing a low-cost state sanitarium for his ill son by recounting events from his own childhood that shaped his character. Again, his story seems to be well rehearsed to illustrate a basic point about himself:

We never had clothes enough to wear, nor food enough to eat. Well, I remember one Thanksgiving, or maybe it was Christmas, when some Yank in whose house Mother had been scrubbing gave her a dollar extra for a present, and on the way home she spent it all on food. . . . It was in those days I learned to be a miser. A dollar was worth so much then. And once you've learned a lesson, it's hard to unlearn it. You have to look for bargains. If I took this state farm sanitarium for a good bargain, you'll have to forgive me. The doctors did tell me it's a good place.

Another example, but much shorter, of telling a stock story to describe oneself occurs in the movie *A Thousand Clowns:*

MURRAY: You're going to have to stop crying.
SANDRA: I cry all the time, and I laugh at the wrong places in the
            movies.

The story—crying all the time, laughing at the wrong places in the movies—is an example of a personal myth derived from our experiences and confirmed again in the telling. Here, the story has been reduced again and again until only its essential message remains.

The next story from *All the President's Men* is another example of a self-descriptive narrative. Woodward and Bernstein are in their car, parked outside the house of yet another CREEP employee on their list. The frustrations of working for a newspaper are getting to Bernstein. He attempts to make sense of his present work by remembering an incident early on in his career:

My first day as a copyboy I was sixteen and wearing my only grown-up suit—it was cream colored. At two-thirty, the head copyboy comes running up to me and says, "My God, haven't you washed the carbon paper yet? If it's not washed by three, it'll never be dry for tomorrow." And I said, "Am I supposed to do that?" and he said, "Absolutely, it's crucial." So I run around and grab all the carbon paper from all the desks and take it to the men's room. I'm standing there washing it, and it's splashing all over me, and the editor comes in to take a leak, and he says, "What the fuck do you think you're doing?" And I said, "It's two-thirty. I'm washing the carbon paper."

I'm beginning to feel like I never stopped.

We also acquire personal myths from our parents, teachers, friends, enemies—in short, from anyone who tells us stories about ourselves. Listening to and telling these stories has an effect on memory which makes it almost impossible not to believe the stories that describe who we are. The following stories are examples of self-descriptive myths initiated by other family members; thus, the process of telling begins with a you-goal intention, and the retelling involves the me-goal intention. In the first example from Elizabeth Stone's *Black Sheep and Kissing Cousins,* Peter Mott, a nuclear physicist, attempts to explain why he and his sister defined themselves according to their mother's story.

My mother's father, whom she always saw as a comforter, had died. . . . Then her two sisters died—one of scarlet fever and the other of spilling boiling water on herself. Then my grandmother, my mother's mother, died of a heart attack. My mother was pregnant with my sister at this time, and so they named my sister Blanche, which had been my grandmother's name. In fact my grandmother's maiden name was Kane, and they named my sister Blanche Kane Mott. . . . My mother was in terrible shape. . . . She was hospitalized—she had a nervous breakdown—and there was a nursemaid to take care of my sister. . . . My mother could never bring herself to use the name Blanche with my sister, so she called her Missy. It was just too much, the death was too much and the daughter was too much. Perhaps my sister was just too much of a reminder. But anyhow, my sister was the one in the family who could do nothing right. As a consequence, she was raised as if she were dirt, or incompetent, or terrible. Growing up, I didn't consciously recognize how my sister was being devalued, but one of the most extraordinary aspects of all this family stuff is that for most of my adult life, I dealt with my sister as my mother had dealt with her. As for me . . . I was "the Golden Boy." The doctor told my mother to have another child to make her well. I was that child, and I could do no wrong.

In the following passage from *The Pawnbroker,* the narrator tells a story about himself, but he also has a conversational goal in telling the story—to respond to a question. Sol Nazerman has been a survivor of the death camps for twenty years. His wife and children died at Auschwitz. Before the war, he was a professor at the University of Cracow, but now he runs a pawnshop in Spanish Harlem. One evening, his apprentice asks Sol, "How come you people come to business so naturally?" Sol responds:

You begin . . . you begin with several thousand years during which you have nothing except a great bearded legend. Nothing else. You have not land to grow food on. No land on which to hunt. Not enough time in one place to have a geography, or an army, or a land-myth. You have only a little brain in your head and this bearded legend to sustain you . . . convince you there is something special about you, even in your poverty. But this little brain . . . that is the real key. With it you obtain a small piece of cloth, wool, silk, cotton—it doesn't matter. You take this cloth, and you cut it in two and sell the two pieces for a penny or two more than you paid for the one. With this money, then, you buy a slightly larger piece of cloth. Which perhaps may be cut into three pieces. And sold for three pennies profit. You must never succumb to buying an extra piece of bread at this point. Or a toy for your child. Immediately you must repeat the process. And so you continue until there is no longer any temptation to dig in the earth and grow food. No longer any desire to gaze at limitless land which is in your name. You repeat this process over and over for centuries. And then, all of a sudden, you discover you have a mercantile heritage. You are known as a merchant. You're also known as a man with secret resources, usurer, pawnbroker, a witch, or what have you.

But by then it is instinct. Do you understand?

We tell stories like this in order to express our feelings, to get out our anger, or to explain ourselves in some fundamental way. These stories become who we are and telling them allows us to feel these feelings that define us yet again. We avoid telling stories that evoke feelings that we do not care to relive.

You-goals

Obviously, the above story contains many unspoken stories, but unspoken stories, as other survivors of Auschwitz have testified, change substantively in memory or disappear altogether. The survivors of the Holocaust tell stories to preserve their memories for themselves and for their listeners. Their intentions in recounting what happened to them at the hands of the Nazis fall within both the me-goal and the you-goal categories.

As we have already seen, when we tell stories about ourselves our goals are often internal and difficult to determine, but when we tell stories intended for other people our goals tend to fall within five categories:

to illustrate a point
to make the listener feel some way or another
to tell a story that transports the listener
to transfer some piece of information in our head into the
    head of the listener
to summarize significant events

Most stories have a point, or at least are supposed to have one. What exactly a point is, is difficult to define, but we know when one is missing. In such cases, we ask *What's your point?* We tell stories, then, to illustrate points we wish to make or to help listeners achieve their goals. In an essay in which he reflects on the costs of personal success, Tennessee Williams illustrates his point with a story.

I lived on room service. But in this, too, there was disenchantment. Sometime between the moment when I ordered dinner over the phone and when it was rolled into my living room like a corpse on a rubber-wheeled table, I lost all interest in it. Once I ordered a sirloin steak and a chocolate sundae, but everything was so cunningly disguised on the table that I mistook the chocolate sauce for gravy and poured it over the sirloin steak. . . .

I got so sick of hearing people say, "I loved your play!" that I could not say thank you anymore. I choked on the words and turned rudely away from the usually sincere person. I no longer felt any pride in the play itself but began to dislike it, probably because I felt too lifeless inside ever to create another. . . .

This curious condition persisted about three months, till late spring, when I decided to have another eye operation mainly because of the excuse it gave me to withdraw from the world behind a gauze mask. . . .

Well, the gauze mask served a purpose. While I was resting in the hospital the friends whom I had neglected or affronted in one way or another began to call on me and now that I was in pain and darkness, their voices seemed to have changed. . . .

When the gauze mask was removed, I found myself in a readjusted world. I checked out of the handsome suite at the first-class hotel, packed my papers and a few incidental belongings, and left for Mexico, an elemental country where you can quickly forget the false dignities and conceits imposed by success, a country where vagrants innocent as children curl up to sleep on the pavements and human voices, especially when their language is not familiar to the ear, are soft as birds'. My public self, that artifice of mirrors, did not exist here and so my natural being was resumed.

A second reason for telling stories with you-goals is to make the listener feel some way or other, in other words, to tell an affective story. Trying to get someone to fall in love with you or to make a special exception in your pathetic case or simply to feel better is typical of the affective intention. We can, of course, have goals for both ourselves and others in a story we tell; sometimes the distinction can be confusing. However, stories that are intended to make somebody feel something are very common and very important. They may also make the teller feel something as well, often unintentionally.

In a passage from *Below the Line*, the narrator recalls telling an affective story that failed to achieve the effect he wanted:

One day—this is how I got in the worst trouble—my baby was crying. We didn't have no money, no food, so I went to the grocery store. I told the owner—he knew that I had boughten there before—I told the owner, I was crying, I told him, "Please can you do me a favor, give me a dozen eggs, a loaf of bread, a gallon of milk, and I'll pay you back in the morning." He told me no. So I went back home and I took out my gun and I went back. I said, "Now give it to me." Then I went back home. Within fifteen minutes they locked me up, but I didn't care. I did it for my kids.

For reasons similar to telling affective stories, we tell transportive stories to make others experience certain sensations, feelings, or attitudes vicariously. One way to achieve this effect is to be clever enough in our descriptive capabilities in order to make listeners come to view the scene the way we want them to. Usually, we have some additional purpose in mind when we tell a transportive story; nevertheless, stories are so often heavily laden with description of a transportive nature, we should recognize the transportive intention independently of other motivations. In the play *That Championship Season,* a high school basketball team gets together for a reunion with their old coach. The coach reminisces:

You were a rare and a beautiful thing, boys . . . a miracle to see people play beautifully together . . . like when I was a boy . . . long time past . . . the whole town would come together. We'd have these huge picnics, great feasts of picnics. My father ran the only bank in town. An elegant man. Bach was played in his house. He quoted Shakespeare, "To be or not to be, that's the question." Shoulders like a king . . . he carried me on his back into the freezing, God, yes, waters of the lake. So clear you could see the white pebbles on the bottom. Gone now, all gone, vanished. Lake, picnic grounds, gone now. All concrete and wires and glass now. Used car lots now. Phil's trucks came and took it away. . . . Jesus, I can still see buckets of ice cream . . . great red slabs of beef . . . kites, yes, the sky full of blue and red kites, men playing horseshoes, big silver pails of beer, in the late afternoon the men would dive from the high rocks, so high they made you dizzy to look down. I watched my father dive and turn and glisten in the sun, falling like a bird falls, and knife the water so clean as to leave only ripples.

We have similar intentions in telling stories that summarize significant events, i.e., historical synopses, and in telling stories that transfer information. Tellers want their listeners to know whatever it is they are telling them. Teachers want their students to know certain information; parents want children to know how to behave, how to play safely, etc.; and people who are talking to one another want their friends and associates to know about their lives or about various events in the world. All of them want to transfer some piece of knowledge in their heads into the heads of their listeners. Historical synopsis is a special case of transfer where the teller must reduce a tremendous amount of information into a form small enough to be absorbed.

Conversational Goals

The above stories have been relayed without the context of a surrounding conversation. When we tell stories within a conversation, the goals that need to be satisfied are more complex. The following set of intentions, unlike the others we have discussed, has nothing to do with the content of the conversation. People do not always speak to communicate some specific piece of information or remark. Sometimes we speak solely to keep on being able to speak or simply to get the general topic of the story on the floor for discussion. For example, we might tell a story about a problem in a particular relationship if we wanted to discuss relationships in general. Our intention, then, would be *topic opening*. On the other hand, we might open a new topic in order to close off or avoid another; in this case, our intention would be *topic changing*. We also tell stories to revive conversation. For example, in airplanes two people seated next to each other often tell stories for the sole purpose of having something to do during the flight. When the conversation bogs down, one of the speakers will tell a story to *continue* the conversation. So that the conversational partner won't go away or talk to someone else, often the speaker tells a story just to keep the conversation going.

A more significant but still in essence structural part of the storytelling process in a conversation involves the relationship that exists between the partners in a conversation. When someone tells a story, he or she expects conversational politeness, a response of some sort. Therefore, when you tell a story in turn, you may have no point in mind other than to be *responsive*.

One of the goals of history synopsis is often conversational as well. Above, we saw an example of history synopsis told to satisfy the you-goals, but often these stories are responses to direct requests for stories, rather than spontaneous remindings. When we ask certain questions, we expect stories as answers. We associate stories with life events such as the story of our choosing a college, the story of our first job, the story of the birth of our child, the story of our first love, and the story of our marriage. Since these stories have usually been told many times, they often have rehearsed and well-planned versions. Sometimes we get the whole story, and sometimes we get partial or cryptic stories. Below is an example from *Manhattan* of a cryptic yet revealing shorthand depiction of an obviously much larger history.

MARY: Why did you get divorced?
ISAAC: My wife left me for another woman.

Another category of responsive story is the argument. When you tell a story that implies something is wrong with yourself, you may hope for a story that disputes your point. Sometimes, you make an assertion, however, without intending to stir an *argumentative* response but do so anyway. Of course, not all arguments are unfriendly; mutual storytelling, even in the form of an argument, can make the storytellers feel closer to each other.

Stories can also be used as a defense. Sometimes we tell a story to *distract* our listeners from what they want to discuss. Many times we tell stories to avoid whatever it is we should be talking about, as a defense against what other people are liable to say. We distract our conversational partners by giving them a range of other things to think about. Such stories are often made up on the fly, but sometimes they have been previously constructed and are retrieved because they relate superficially to the question at hand. The goal of such a story is to avoid telling a different story. The reasons for distraction/obfuscation may be as simple as maintaining conversational sociability to avoid an argument or a painful or perhaps embarrassing subject. Obversely, the reason may be psychologically complex. Someone with a checkered past might obfuscate when relating certain experiences if fearful of losing a friendship. Similarly, we may obfuscate to protect a family member or ourselves if we perceive a question as a threat. An example of this kind of story from *A Thousand Clowns* follows. In this story, Murray tells a joke to avoid being sad about something else, to avoid telling the story he should be telling:

SANDRA: Which job did you get?

MURRAY: I shall now leave you breathless with this strange and wondrous tale of this sturdy lad's adventures today in downtown Oz. Picture if you will, me. I am walking on East Fifty-first Street about an hour ago practicing how to say "I am sorry" with a little style.

SANDRA: Sorry about what?

MURRAY: Oh, not for anything—just rehearsing, you know how you are walking down the street talking to yourself, and suddenly you say something to yourself out loud? So I said: "I'm sorry"—and this fellow walking by, a complete stranger, said: "That's all right, Mac," and goes right on. He immediately forgave me. Now five o'clock rush hour in midtown, you could say "Sir, your hair is on fire," and they wouldn't even hear you. So I decided to test the whole thing out scientifically. I just stood there saying "I'm sorry" to everyone who came by. . . . Of course I got a few funny looks—but seventy-five percent of them forgave me. . . . I could run up on the roof right now, and I would say I'm sorry and a half a million people would say, "That's OK, just see that you don't do it again."

SANDRA: You didn't take any of the jobs.

MURRAY: I'm sorry. I'm very sorry. Damn it, lady, that was a beautiful apology. You got to love a guy who apologizes so well. I rehearsed it. Oh, Sandy, that's the most you should expect from life—a really good apology for all the things you won't get.

Conclusion

The various combinations of our intentions affect the processes that transform the gists of the stories that we have in our memories into the actual stories that we tell. We don't remember the stories that we tell or hear, in the sense that we cannot recall all the words. We extract gists when we listen to stories, and we recast gists when we transform them into actual stories. These memory processes—extraction of gists from stories for storage in memory and transformation of gists into stories that express an intention—are fundamental to the thinking process. How these processes work is the subject of later chapters.

I might add that the most you can expect from an intelligent being is a really good story. To get human beings to be intelligent means getting them to have stories to tell and having them hear and perhaps use the stories of others. Now, by stories here, recall that I mean having a set of interesting things that one has already thought up and stored, ready to say when necessary. There are other aspects to intelligence that come into play to finish the process to make something that is intelligent seem very intelligent. The first is storytelling ability. How a story is told greatly affects the receptivity of the listener. Good storytellers will make their stories seem interesting and that interestingness makes the stories more memorable and hence more useful to an understander. Good storytellers cause positive responses in their listeners. Thus, good storytellers seem very intelligent.

But intelligence is also manifest in the content of what one has to say. And new content, innovative ideas are seen by listeners as marking intelligence as well. We like inventive stories, even when told badly, because their new content excites us, and we deem the tellers of those stories to be intelligent as well.

Whatever the reason for telling a story, and whatever the origin of the content of the story, the concept here is a rather simple one. Intelligence means having stories to tell. If those stories are told well or are innovative in some way, so much the better, but a being must have a set of stories and tell them for the right reasons at the right time in order to be intelligent.

It would seem, then, that the cliché "Experience is the best teacher" is quite true. We learn from experience, or to put this more strongly, what we learn *are* experiences. The educational point that follows from this is that we must teach cases and the adaptation of cases by telling stories, not teach rules and the use of rules by citing rules. We may never find ourselves in a situation where the rules we were taught apply exactly. Ordinarily, we find answers for ourselves. Lots of stories and cases help, but methods of applying these stories and cases, especially in places where they weren't originally supposed to apply, help more.

□ 3 □

Understanding Other People's Stories

□

LET ME tell a story: I went to visit a cousin of mine who is curious about why family members turned out the way they did. She asked me whether I knew anything of interest about our mutual grandfather. I told her my father always says his father (our grandfather) never really talked to or had much time for him. My father explains this reticence in a variety of ways having to do with how much work my grandfather had to do. Recently, however, I heard that whenever he didn't have much work, my grandfather would go to the movies by himself. My cousin was very excited by this information and ran to tell her grown-up daughter. It seems that both my cousin and her daughter have the habit of going to the movies alone and thought that they were quite odd to do this. They found something fascinating about the fact that their ancestor did the same thing. I found it all quite confusing myself. My cousin and her daughter are very gregarious people. My grandfather never spoke to anybody. My point was that growing up with this man as a father was probably difficult. My cousin's point was something else entirely. When I noted the differences in our perspective, she was too excited about discovering our grandfather's predisposition for going to the movies alone to consider another point of view.

People are only able to hear part of what is being said to them. Some of the reasons for this are obvious. Most of what we hear is complex and has so many possible avenues of interpretation and provides so many possible inference paths that people must make their choices as they listen. We cannot think about all the possible ramifications of something we are being told. So we pay attention to what interests us.

Interest can be expressed in a variety of ways, but one way is to focus on the things you were looking for, ignoring the things you were not prepared to deal with. Another way to look at this is to take the view that, since we can only understand things that relate to our own experiences, it is actually very difficult to hear things that people say to us that are not interpretable through those experiences. In other words, we hear what we are capable of hearing. When what we hear relates to what we know, what we care about, or what we were prepared to hear, we can understand quite easily what someone is saying to us. If we have heard the same story or a similar story before we can also understand more easily what we are being told.

Understanding, for a listener, means mapping the speaker's stories onto the listener's stories. One of the most interesting aspects of the way stories are used in memory is the effect they have on understanding. Different people understand the same story differently precisely because the stories they already know are different. Understanders attempt to construe new stories that they hear as old stories they have heard before. It follows then that one of the major problems in understanding is identifying which of all the stories you already know is being told to you yet again.

In the shallowest form of understanding, a hearer has only one story that he wants to tell. No matter what you say to him, he tells you his story. He understands what you say as something that reminds him of the story that he wanted to tell in the first place. Thus, his understanding algorithm needn't have more in it than a detector for when you have stopped talking, and perhaps he doesn't even need that. One typical case of this kind of understanding involves people who we might label as crazy, people who just rattle on without regard to the world around them.

In the world of computers, we have an analog in machines that do their thing irrespective of the wishes of the user because the user either doesn't know how to communicate instructions to the machine or else doesn't know how to stop the machine once it has begun to do its thing. The crazy person or the user-hostile computer has a story to tell, and it may not really care about whether you want to hear that story. For them, understanding means no more than unrestrained storytelling.

A less shallow form of understanding takes place when listeners with many stories to tell pay enough attention to what you have said in order to relate the story in their repertoire that is most closely connected to what they have heard. But, in a sense, this still seemingly shallow understanding may be all we can really expect most of the time. Now, this view may seem rather radical. After all, we do see and hear new things every day. To say that we never have to understand any story that is brand-new may be overstating the case. And, of course, we do get presented with new stories. My point is that we don't really understand them.

Well, more accurately, we don't understand them as new stories. They may be new enough, but we nevertheless persist in seeing them as old stories. To understand what I mean here, consider the possibility of this hypothesis in its strongest form. Let us assume an understander who knows three stories. No matter what story you tell him, he will tell one of his three stories back. If understanding means matching the story we are hearing to the stories we have already heard, the strong form of my hypothesis states that an understander must decide which of the three stories he knows is most applicable. When he has found some way to relate the new story to an old one that he knows, we can claim that he has understood the new story as well as could be hoped for.

Looked at this way, the strong hypothesis appears somewhat silly. Why should we label as "understanding" a process that merely differentiates among three stories? In some sense, we shouldn't. But let's consider the same situation where the understander knows ten thousand stories. When he selects one to tell as a response to the new one that he has heard, he will most likely seem more profound than the understander who has only three stories. If he has used sound principles for selecting a story to tell from his data base of ten thousand, we are unlikely to dispute his having understood the original story. But naturally the process of understanding in both cases is identical; only our subjective judgment allows us to decide that one understander seems to have "really" understood. We cannot look inside people's heads to see what the difference in their understanding of a new story is; therefore, from an objective evaluation of the output alone, we still can measure understanding only by how effectively and reasonably we think the responsive story relates to the input story.

Now, my argument here is that all that people are doing when they understand is figuring out what story to tell. Thus, the understanding process involves extracting elements from the input story that are precisely those elements used to label old stories in memory. In other words, understanding is really the process of index extraction. Further, index extraction is an idiosyncratic process that depends upon what stories you have stored away and what indices you have used to label those stories. In some sense, then, no two people can really understand a story in the same way. You can't understand a story that you haven't previously understood because understanding means finding (and telling) a story that you have previously understood. Finding some familiar element causes us to activate the story that is labeled by that familiar element, and we understand the new story as if it were an exemplar of that old element. In this way, we find things to say to those who talk to us. These things differ considerably from person to person, thus accounting for the very different ways in which two people can understand the same story.

Find an Anomaly, Ask a Question, Get a Story

People have powerful models of the world. Through these models, which are based on the accumulated set of experiences that a person has had, new experiences are interpreted. When the new experiences that we perceive fit nicely into the framework of expectations that we have derived from experience, we believe ourselves to have understood the experience or the person who has related the experience. Understanding something or someone is, after all, a relative issue. We only understand part of what could have gone on in a situation that is being described to us, for example. But we can act as if we have understood when we can derive information from the description that we know how to place properly in our memory store. In other words, understanding, rightly or wrongly, usually means being able to add information to memory.

But we dislike failing to understand. When what we have been asked to understand is anomalous in some way, failing to correspond to what we expect, we must reevaluate what is going on. We must attempt to explain why we were wrong in our expectations. A failure to have things turn out as expected indicates a failure in understanding. People desire very much to remedy such failures. We ask ourselves questions about what was going on. The answer to these questions often results in a story.

People are constantly questioning themselves and one another in a quest to find out why someone has performed an action and what the consequences of that action are likely to be. Thus, in order to find out how we learn, we must find out how we know that we need to learn. In other words, we need to know how we discover anomalies. How do we know that something did not fit?

The premise here is that whenever an action takes place, in order to discover what might be anomalous about it, we have to have been asking ourselves a set of questions about the nature of that action. Anomalies occur when the answers to one or more of those questions is unknown. Then we seek to explain what was going on, and then we learn.

To get a handle on this process, we must attempt to sort out the kinds of anomalies that there are. Knowing the kinds of anomalies gives us two advantages. In order for us to see something as anomalous, we must have been unable to answer a question about some circumstance. So first we must discover the questions that are routinely asked as a part of the understanding process.

Every time that someone does something, we as observers, in our attempt to interpret the action we are observing, check to see whether that action *makes sense*. But actions do not make sense absolutely. That is, we cannot determine whether actions make sense except by comparing them with other actions. In a world where everyone walks around with his thumb in his mouth, we don't need to explain why a given individual has his thumb in his mouth. In a world where no one does this, we must explain why a given individual does have his thumb in his mouth. Clearly, making sense, and thus the idea of an anomaly in general, is a relative thing.

Relative to what? Naturally, the answer is relative to the stories one already knows. We are satisfied, as observers of actions, when the stories we hear match our own stories. When the match is very similar, we tell our version of the story. When the match is hardly a match at all, when we have a contradictory story, we tell it. Actually, the middle cases are the most interesting—when we have no story to tell. What do we do then? We look for one. We do this by asking ourselves questions.

People are not processing information with the intent of finding out whether something is anomalous and needs explaining, at least not consciously. In fact, quite the opposite is the case. We are trying to determine the place for an action that we observe. To do this, we must find a place in memory that was expecting this new action. Of course, we may not find one, since not everything in life can be anticipated. So, as understanders, we ask ourselves, unconsciously of course, *What story do I know that relates to the incoming story?*

Nonanomalous Curiosity

We might be tempted to imagine that we create questions for ourselves only when our curiosity is aroused by confusion about something in the world that we have observed, but we are often forced by the social circumstances that we find ourselves in to create questions for ourselves to answer. When somebody says something to us, we are supposed to say something back. But what? Is there always something worth saying? Whether or not we have something important to say, given that we have to have something to say and given that this happens to us all the time, we have developed various methods of coping with this situation. We ask ourselves questions.

Clearly the questions that we ask ourselves about what others have told us cannot be solely dependent upon what we have heard. In a sense, since we are both asking and answering these questions, we need to know that we can answer a question before we ask it. That is, the questions that we ask serve as memory calls, requests to get information from memory that will be of use in the formulation of a response to what we have heard.

We are concerned here with input stories that are responded to by stories. In other words, we want to know what questions one might ask oneself in response to a story that would allow a story of one's own to come to mind. We can start simply by considering the paradigmatic case where the response to a story is a story where one says, "The same thing happened to me." The call to memory that might retrieve a story where the same thing happened is obviously not likely to be *Look for the same thing*. First, the same thing that happened is rarely the same thing literally at all. Second, the characterization of the initial story would have to be stored in memory within certain parameters. In other words, in order to find a possible response story in memory, one must be looking for any story that meets a set of criteria that might be described as "The same thing happened to me."

Well, obviously, the same thing never actually happens to anybody. What actually occurs are episodes in memory that bear some superficial similarity to the input story. Probably more differences exist in an "identical story" than similarities. Certainly places and people, time and context, are usually quite different. What is the same then?

Sameness, at the level we are discussing, exists with respect to plans, the goals that drive those plans, and the themes that drive those goals. Thus, when someone tells you a story, you ask yourself: *Are there any events in my memory where I had a similar goal for a similar reason?* In other words, when we hear a story, we ask whether at the broadest possible level of interpretation we already know a story like the one we are hearing. But possibly the similarity would not exist at the level of plans. That is, one could easily recognize a similar situation and suggest an alternative plan that might have been followed, based upon one's own experience. So we can match new stories to old ones on the basis of identical goals. Therefore, one question that we can expect people to ask themselves is: *Do I have a story in memory where the main goal is the same as that being pursued in the story I am hearing?*

Indexing Stories

If our knowledge is really a collection of hundreds of thousands of stories, then finding the one we need leaves us with a massive indexing problem. Of course, finding stories is a problem that people seem to manage with some ease, if not with perfection. So we probably have some method that works. To see what I mean here, let's consider an actual situation of story understanding.

A group of people heard two monologues from the movies *Diner* and *The Breakfast Club*. In each monologue, the speaker tells some listeners about a problem of his. The subjects in this informal experiment were asked to imagine that they were the friend whose advice was being solicited or to expect that, as conversational partners, they would have to say something back. The subjects were asked, therefore, to tell a story or to give some advice or to comment in any way that came to mind. What are the indices available from Shrevie's story? In light of the responses to Shrevie's story, indexing is a highly subjective process—clearly, there is no right answer to this question. Our interest lies in how the same story can be understood differently by different people. With that in mind, let's look at the responses to find the indices that the subjects actually must have constructed in order to have made the matches that they did in telling their stories.

Here is the first story, from *Diner,* exactly as it was read to the students, from *The Actor's Book of Movie Monologues* (Marisa Smith and Amy Schewel, eds.; New York: Penguin, 1986).

TIME: 1959
PLACE: Baltimore, Maryland

A group of six high-school friends get together around the Christmas–New Year holidays. Most of them have stayed in town after graduation. Shrevie, the first of the group to get married, works in an appliance store and nurtures his obsession for his record collection. He can tell you what's on the flip side of practically every record he owns. His collection is kept in frighteningly fastidious condition—with a detailed system of categories that would put the Library of Congress to shame.

Eddie, his pal, a ferociously loyal Baltimore Colts fan, is planning on marrying Elise on New Year's Eve on the condition that she pass an outrageously difficult football quiz he has prepared for her. One night, in front of the local diner where the guys hang out, two days before the test, three days before the wedding, Eddie asks Shrevie if he's happy with his marriage to his wife, Beth. Shrevie answers.

SHREVIE: You know the big part of the problem? When we were dating we spent most of our time talking about sex. *Why* couldn't I do it? *Where* could we do it? Were her parents going to be out *so* we could do it. Talking about being alone for a weekend. A whole night. You know. Everything was talking about gettin' sex or planning our wedding. Then when you're married . . . It's crazy. You can have it whenever you want. You wake up. She's there. You come home from work. She's there. So all the sex-planning talk is over. And the wedding-planning talk. We can sit up here and bullshit the night away, but I can't have a five-minute conversation with Beth. But I'm not putting the blame on her. We've just got nothing to talk about.

The first subject chose to tell a story about a friend of his:

SUBJECT 1:   In high school, I had a friend named Larry who was a couple of years older than me. We were the two computer jocks in school. His dad had died, and his mother was sort of on hard times. But Larry was doing OK, and we used to go to the beach together. We had this great arrangement with the computer teacher. The teacher would teach one day, and we would teach one day. This was summer school. The day that we taught the teacher would take off, and the day the teacher taught, we would take off and go to the beach. It was a great way to get summer school credit. I think about where I am now, and where Larry is. Larry didn't go to college. He didn't really take his hacking talents anywhere. He got married as soon as he got out of high school. He was a manager of a Shakey's in Hollywood. Now he's a group manager at Shakey's in Mar Vista, and he's married to this stupid woman. It's really a sad story. The guy just exploded—and he had all that potential. He just didn't know what to do once he got out of high school. He didn't know what to do with himself, so he got married and got a job like he was supposed to.

One thing that we do when we understand a story is to relate that story to something in our own lives. But to what? One thing seems clear. Potentially, we can see Shrevie's story in many ways. Subject 1 understood Shrevie's story by relating it to one about a friend of his whose life never amounted to much. In other words, according to his value system, he saw Shrevie's statement as a story about how one can get trapped into a dull life by marrying right out of high school. To put this another way, Subject 1 seems to believe that marrying too young leads to a dull and pointless life. Subject 1 also probably believed this prior to hearing Shrevie's story. Thus, we know two things. First, Subject 1 drew a conclusion from Shrevie's story that confirmed a view he already had about the perils of marrying too early. Second, he already had labeled a story in his own memory with such an index.

So the first index we shall identify is:

INDEX 1: Marrying too early can lead to a dull and pointless life.

Actually, we cannot say for sure that this is the index that Subject 1 used. What other matches are there between Subject 1's story and Shrevie's story? Both stories are also about the following:

INDEX 2: Blindly following scripts that are chosen for you in life can cause you to raise questions when it is too late.

This index, also, might not be the one that Subject 1 actually used, although clearly Subject 1 believes this generally and believes this about Shrevie specifically. However, and here is the important point, the story that Subject 1 heard, namely a story about the futility of early marriage, was not the same story that the other subjects heard at all.

Now let's consider how Subject 2's understanding of Shrevie's story differed from Subject 1's understanding:

SUBJECT 2:   I had the same experience. Basically you desire things that you can't have, and often once you can have them, you don't desire them as much. I remember that with a woman I was always interested in sexually over the course of many years. Either she had boyfriends or I had girl-friends, and we never consummated our relationship. For four or five years, I always kept in contact with her, wrote letters, and so forth, but independently of anything else, I considered her a friend. A year or two ago, we did end up having sex. What's interesting to me is that, afterwards, I wasn't all that interested in her friendship. Now we sort of occasionally make efforts to see each other, but I find that I don't have much motiva-tion. It's very disillusioning. I realize that most of my interest in her must have been sexual, particularly in trying to get something I couldn't have, and not in her, herself. That reminds me of this situation. You seem to be saying a similar thing which is that you thought you really loved your wife when she was your fiancée, but now that you have her, you realize that what you really wanted was the conquest. Part of it is political. I guess the opposite story that I could tell is about a woman I knew a year ago. I saw her for about two months, very heavily, but it was a platonic relationship pretty much because she had a boyfriend, and we were still trying to decide what would happen if we didn't want to meet behind his back. In the end, she decided to stay with him. She has remained in my mind very, very strongly. I think the reason for this is that I didn't succeed in the conquest. So she occupies my imagination disproportionately. Well, is there any solution to this? One relationship that I had was very successful for three years. Why did it survive once we had sex very regularly? I think the answer is that there has to be a lot of intrinsic interest in the person outside of sex and the relationship. So if it is just the conquest, then you lose interest. It's not that having sex makes it less interesting—it's more that what really is often at issue is the power relationship. If that's all there is to the relationship, making the conquest, then it won't last.

Subject 2 sees Shrevie's story as a story about sex, not early marriage. He understands Shrevie to be saying that he got married as a way of getting sex on a regular basis. Here are some of the indices that Subject 2 explicitly mentions:

INDEX 3: You desire things you can't have, and then when you can have them you don't desire them so much.

INDEX 4: Desiring sex clouds your judgment about whether you really like and want to spend time with the person you desire.

INDEX 5: Good relationships depend upon intrinsic interest in a person, not sex.

INDEX 6: The exercise of power in the form of sexual conquests can be a strong motivating force.

Notice that while this interpretation is a perfectly reasonable way to understand Shrevie's story, it simply isn't the way Subject 1 understood it. Subject 1 sees the story as one about the promise of life unfulfilled. Subject 2 sees this story as one about the hazards of thinking with your sex organ. Clearly, this story is about both of these things. Surely Subjects 1 and 2 would agree that the other's interpretation is valid, but what each learned from the story is different.

One question to ask here is what kind of animals these indices are. They look a great deal like beliefs. In a sense, I am arguing that each subject learned very little precisely because they both saw the stories as simply verifying already-held beliefs. The four indices above are certainly things that Subject 2 believes, but they are also labels that the mind uses to find what it knows. It almost couldn't be any other way.

Consider for a moment what it might mean to believe something and not be able to justify why one believes what one believes. Certainly inarticulate people have difficulty with that sort of thing. And, in fact, we do use that ability, namely the ability to justify one's beliefs with evidence, as a measure of intelligence and reasonableness. In other words, we expect intelligent people to have a story to tell that explains why they believe what they believe. But how can they do this? The mental mechanisms that are available must be ones that connect beliefs to stories. The fact that we can do this is obvious.

It follows, therefore, that beliefs are one possible index in memory. Construct a belief and you should be able to find a story that exemplifies that belief.

Thus, for Subject 2 at least, beliefs and indices are one and the same. Understanding, then, in this model depends upon being able to see one's own beliefs in whatever one is trying to understand. Understanding Shrevie's story for Subject 2 meant identifying what he believed about what was happening to Shrevie, but the beliefs expressed in the story that Shrevie told are Shrevie's beliefs. So what we are seeing in the understanding process is the attempt to understand the beliefs of another in terms of one's own beliefs.

An index is a juxtaposition of another person's beliefs, made evident by statements or actions, with one's own beliefs. Indices are not beliefs, but are actually beliefs about beliefs. In other words, our reactions to the implicit beliefs of others cause us to consider what we believe about the same subject. We can either directly access what we believe by finding our own belief and telling a story that exemplifies it, or we can use the belief expressed in the story as if it were one of our own and see what story we might have stored away in memory under that label. Alternatively, we can create a new belief that is a juxtaposition of what we heard and what we might think about what we heard. This new belief might already exist and thus we would find another story to tell, but possibly the new belief will be entirely new. If this is the case, we need to create a story that exemplifies the belief or it will be lost.

Indices are phenomenally complicated and phenomenally important. We find what we want to say effortlessly and unconsciously. But to do so, we must construct complex labels of events that describe their content, their import, their relation to what we know and what we believe, and much more. It is effective indexing that allows us to have stories to tell and enables us to learn from the juxtaposition of others' stories and the stories that we are reminded of.

Let's now consider another subject:

SUBJECT 3:   There seems to be a real pattern of joking between guys that are married and guys that are not married or are about to be married. I've been having some conversations like this because I'm getting married in the fall. I think there is a standard pattern that's involved in these stories. Unmarried guys and married guys joke to each other a lot about sex. I remember hearing the comment, jokingly said because I am getting married soon, "Oh, you'll be married, and you'll understand it someday, my boy." It seems to be a comment that sometimes is said seriously, but a whole bunch of jokes are based around it.

Subject 3 is a very clear example of an idiosyncratic understander. Obviously, he had been talking with many people about getting married and had been subjected to various jokes about sex and marriage. He sees Shrevie's story as yet another person bothering him with worries about why one should not get married. Obviously, that was not the intent of Shrevie's story. Shrevie did not say what he did with Subject 3 in mind. Equally obviously, Subject 3 knew this. Nevertheless, Subject 3 took Shrevie's story personally as yet another married person trying to scare him about getting married. He, too, had heard this story before, but the story he had heard was about why marriage will make you unhappy. Note that neither of the previous two subjects sees the story in this way.

With that in mind, let's look at another response. Subject 4 understood Shrevie's story in terms of the belief that Shrevie had expressed:

SUBJECT 4: Something like that happened to me with my girlfriend. It must have been right after things had gotten past the initial stage, that we really knew we were together, and we started sleeping together. I remember I was sitting on the floor one morning, and she was doing something in the kitchen. So I said to her, "What do lovers do when they're not eating or screwing?" She threw a spoon at me. She didn't think much of the question. But I think it was a question that bothered me for a long time. We had to kind of learn what to do and what we were going to talk about and what we were going to do when we weren't eating and screwing and doing the things that we knew we had to do anyway.

Subject 4 understood this story exactly as it appeared on the surface. While the other subjects tried to relate the story to some deeper theme about marriage or life or sex, Subject 4 asked himself the question: *Well, what else is there to do with a mate other than screw and eat?* This question strikes at the heart of Shrevie's story in some sense. Rather than read a deeper meaning into the story, why did Subject 4 only see the superficial question? Because he had already asked himself that question. In other words, Subject 4 had seen this story before in his own life exactly as Shrevie presented it. The index here is:

INDEX 7:   What do lovers do when they are not screwing or eating?

While indices clearly can be beliefs, indices can obviously be questions also. This assertion is obvious because people can answer questions. In order to answer them, they must be able to use something in them to find a story in memory. But what?

People can ask and answer their own question rather easily. They can query themselves about real world facts (What was the name of George Washington's wife?), about internal facts (What is my favorite flavor of ice cream?), about recent history (Where was I when I heard about the crash of the space shuttle?), and about beliefs (Should a man open the door for a woman?). People do not know how they find the answers to such questions, but they know that they can find them if they only ask.

Perhaps equally important is the fact that people know, again implicitly, what questions not to bother asking themselves because they know they cannot easily find the answer. These include questions about forgotten past history that has never come up again (What was the name of the little girl who sat next to me in the second grade?), things that no one remembers if they are asked in the wrong way (What picture was on page forty-two of your science text in high school?), and things that we know were never stored away in the first place (Tell me five word analogies that were on the SAT test that you took to get into college).

Why are some questions answerable and others not? The answer is indices. Certain concepts, and the words that name those concepts, are indices in memory and others are not. George Washington is an index. So is ice cream, the space shuttle, and etiquette. But book is not an index, at least not by itself. Page numbers are almost never indices, and SAT may be an index, but curiously not to the SAT itself. In any case, while it is clear that most beliefs are indices, not all concepts are.

Even a superficial reading that results in the recognition of a story as one of your own stories can differ from person to person. Consider the next subject:

SUBJECT 5:   You're right. You got married very young. When you're young like that you are very preoccupied with sex. I remember the time before I got married, going over to a friend's apartment in order to have a liaison with my wife-to-be because we couldn't at the home of my parents. That wasn't accepted.

Here, Subject 5 recognizes a story from his own life, not about what else you do besides sex, but about the complexity of getting sex.

INDEX 8:   Young people must go to extremes to find places to have sex.

Subject 5 did get divorced from the wife he refers to, so perhaps he is also making a prediction about what will happen to Shrevie. Perhaps he is saying that interest in making arrangements for sex can provide the interest in a relationship. Yet, even here, Subject 5's view is that young people find things to do and talk about that do not relate to what marriage will be like. Subject 5 saw Shrevie's story as a story about himself. Here too, understanding means finding a story you already know and saying, "Oh, yeah, that one."

The last subject did not see this story as being about sex or marriage. For him the index was quite different than it was for the others:

SUBJECT 6:   Well, that reminds me of the qualifying exam in Artificial Intelligence actually. It reminds me of the phenomenon where you're spending time thinking about one particular thing going on in your life, and then when that thing is over you are supposed to be happy because you have passed through this barrier. Before you get married, your main goals are having a place to have sex and having sex, and then when you're married, that's taken care of, and then, all of a sudden, all sorts of other problems start to creep in. That reminds me of the qual. You're focused on how your whole life is going to be okay if you just pass the qual; but when you pass the qual, then other aspects of graduate school start sweeping back in. All of a sudden, you're upset that your room is a mess, and your social life starts to seep back in, and you have to find a way to do research.

Subject 6 is referring to the qualifying examination in Artificial Intelligence that graduate students spend months preparing for in their second year at Yale. If they fail, they are asked to leave graduate school. This particular subject had passed his exam three years earlier, but his office mate had taken the exam a month before this story was read to him. For Subject 6, certain ordeals in life cause one to lose the forest for the trees. He sees that the trials involved in sex and marriage can prevent one from seeing that life goes on. He believes that focusing on immediate problems causes one to lose sight of the larger issues.

INDEX 9:   Putting aside all your goals in order to achieve one major
           goal only works for a short time. Eventually real life
           reappears.

And, of course, here again, Subject 6 already believed this, prior to hearing Shrevie's story.

An important question, therefore, is, How did each of these subjects manage to find his own story in Shrevie's story when each story is so different? How does this kind of very subjective understanding actually work? The key point is that there is no one way to understand this story. When someone hears a story, he looks for beliefs that are being commented upon. Shrevie's story has many possible beliefs inherent in it. But how does someone listening to Shrevie's story find those beliefs? He finds them by looking through the beliefs that he already has. He is not as concerned with what he is hearing as he is with finding what he already knows that is relevant.

Picture it this way. An understander has a list of beliefs, indexed by subject area. When a new story appears, he attempts to find a belief of his that relates to it. When he does, he finds a story attached to that belief and compares the story in memory with the one he is processing. His understanding of the new story becomes, at that point, a function of the old story. The key point here is that once we find a belief and connected story, no further processing, that is, no search for other beliefs need be done. We rarely look to understand a story in more than one way. This process explains why each person understood Shrevie's story quite differently. The mind cannot easily pursue multiple paths.

Let's pursue this way of looking at story understanding while considering a number of responses to a story taken from *The Breakfast Club:*

TIME: 1985
PLACE: Shermer High School, Shermer, Illinois

Five high school students, Brian, Andy, Alison, Clair, and John, must spend Saturday in detention at the school library. Their assignment is to a write a thousand-word essay describing who they are. They all come from different cliques in their school and are described by one of the group as being "a brain, an athlete, a basket case, a princess, and a criminal." Although they don't know each other as they start the detention, by the end of the day each has revealed something about himself, and all five become friends. Andy, "the athlete," explains why he got detention.

ANDY: Do you guys know what I did to get in here? I taped Larry Lester's buns together. Yeah, you know him? Well then, you know how hairy he is, right? Well, when they pulled the tape off, most of his hair came off and some skin too. And the bizarre thing is is that I did it for my old man. I tortured this poor kid because I wanted him to think I was cool. He's always going off about, you know, when he was in school all the wild things he used to do, and I got the feeling that he was disappointed that I never cut loose on anyone, right? So, I'm sitting in the locker room and I'm taping up my knee, and Larry's undressing a couple lockers down from me, and he's kinda, kinda skinny, weak, and I started thinking about my father and his attitude about weakness, and the next thing I knew I, I jumped on top of him and started wailing on him.

Then my friends, they just laughed and cheered me on. And afterwards, when I was sittin' in Vernon's office, all I could think about was Larry's father and Larry having to go home and explain what happened to him. And the humiliation, the fucking humiliation he must have felt. It must have been unreal. I mean, how do you apologize for something like that? There's no way. It's all because of me and my old man. God, I fucking hate him. He's like, he's like this mindless machine I can't even relate to anymore. "Andrew, you've got to be number one. I won't tolerate any losers in this family. Your intensity is for shit." You son of a bitch. You know, sometimes I wish my knee would give in, and I wouldn't be able to wrestle anymore. He could forget all about me.

Subject 1 makes a comment and not a story.

SUBJECT 1:   I always wondered what the assholes who beat up on me in junior high school were thinking. It's sort of nice to think that they were actually humans and that they did it for some reason.

There must be a story, however, behind the comment. Subject 1 got beaten up in school and never understood why. The particular stories are probably not interesting stories or else Subject 1 didn't feel like telling them. Nevertheless, he was reminded of them. How?

One possibility is that *bullies who beat up smaller kids in high school* is an index which Subject 1 has used to label one or more stories in his memory. He first had to construct that index from the story he heard. Next, he had to find the stories in memory labeled by that index. Then, on listening further to the new story, he had to recognize that his story in memory had no reason listed for why someone was beating him up. As he hears a reason in the new story, he finds that he has no old story to match it against. Thus, he can, if he wants to, learn something from this story. Namely, he can add a possible reason derived from Andy's story to explain the actions of the actors in his own story. Therefore, understanding a story in order to learn from it means finding an old story in memory that matches the new story but then enhancing the old story with details from the new.

Now let's look at the next subject:

SUBJECT 2:   You have to be your own person. You can't keep trying to please someone else. You should develop to the best you can be, and your father will have to learn to like it.

Here we have another comment that seems to reflect an untold story. Somewhere in memory, Subject 2 probably has an opinion about this story that he is not revealing. Notice that the index is something like *When deciding what kind of person to be, trying to please someone else never works (Index 11).* Again, the two subjects have heard very different stories.

In Subject 3's story, we have another case where the subject has understood Andy's story by reliving his own version:

SUBJECT 3:   Part of the problem is that you are trying to prove yourself by doing things you don't want to so that you can appear cool. When I was in eighth grade, I went to visit friends of the family in the countryside, and they had a boy about my age. He had a shooting rifle. So we went hunting, and he made a big point of having this special privilege of the gun. He wouldn't let me use it, and I was basically acting like a scout. But I really wanted to fire his gun. He said that if he killed one of the chipmunks which we were hunting then I would get the gun. Eventually, up comes the chipmunk. I pointed it out to him, and he shot and killed it. We walked over to the chipmunk—it looked so pathetic. It was still sort of twitching. It was such a pointless killing. I felt really bad because I felt responsible. I tried to be cool. You do something for no reason, no reason at all. You don't even stop to think about it. You just act, and, then afterwards, you feel terrible.

After telling his story, he then uses it to have better insight into Andy's story. The process seems to be like this. First, Subject 3 found an index from Andy's story which he states in the beginning as *Trying to prove yourself may cause you to do things you don't want to so you can appear cool (Index 12).* But as he tells his story, he begins to think about his own story rather than Andy's and realizes that his own story is labeled in an additional way by something like *Guilt follows the rush of the moment when you do something against your own value system (Index 13).* He then realizes that this is a better analysis of Andy's story. Still, in the end, what he has understood is really his own story although remembering it this additional time may have allowed him greater insight into it. We dwell on our own stories, not those of others.

Subject 4 is almost a classic case of not paying attention to someone else's story any more than is necessary for being able to retrieve your own:

SUBJECT 4:   When I was in the seventh grade, I was in the locker room, and one of the guys who was a lot bigger than me, for no apparent reason, started jabbing and popping me. Everyone was standing around in a circle watching, as people tend to do. Then finally, even though he was so big, finally, I stood up and started wailing on him. Immediately everyone jumped on my side, and he was chased out of the place. So that was sort of a victory for me even though we didn't get into a bloody knockdown fight. All I had to do was stand up for myself and wail on him to get everyone else on my side.

The index *getting beaten up in school* caused Subject 4 to recall his own experience, and he found nothing else to think about. Certainly understanding in this case may seem to be something quite different from what constitutes understanding in the other examples, but the difference here is really a question of degree and not of kind. Understanding means searching memory. Sometimes we have less memory to search, and sometimes we have fewer indices available with which to search. An understander is, in some sense, in control of both of these variables. He decides how much attention to pay to the world around him and how much to remember about what he has previously processed. Attention and memory are strongly related.

Subject 5 has resonated to an index that he found in Andy's story about how *the efforts to please an unsuccessful and demanding father can lead to bad decisions in life (Index 14)*.

SUBJECT 5:   A friend of mine had an older brother who ended up on drugs. Looking at his family situation was always weird to me. His father was an alcoholic sportswriter who seemed to have big expectations for both of his sons. The older son had been a stellar athlete and a great student in high school. In college, he just came apart and ended up a drug addict and wasted his mind one way or another. At one point, he was in a mental institution, I think. I was friends with the younger son, and I always wondered if the same thing would happen to him because he seemed to be very successful and very oriented towards doing well somehow or other where his brother had fucked up—but it seemed like he was on the same road his brother was on. So I don't know, I can sympathize with this guy.

The recalling of his story from memory caused Subject 5 to recognize Andy's story as one he had seen before, and no more really came to mind.

Subject 6 saw Andy's story as showing that *sometimes you act irrationally in a group when you wouldn't if you were alone (Index 15).*

SUBJECT 6:   Yeah, I don't know. Everyone does all sorts of shit because of who they think they're supposed to be and because their parents told them who they thought they were supposed to be. Actually, it happens just as much from who your friends think you should be. I'm reminded of my undergraduate days, being in the band, an incredibly obnoxious and rude bunch of people. And in that gang, you felt safe doing things that you wouldn't do otherwise. You'd get up in the middle of a football game and do a series of Humpty Dumpty cheers: "Humpty Dumpty sat on a wall, Humpty Dumpty had a great fall, all the king's horses and all the king's men raped the queen." It's like you scream it at the top of your lungs in the middle of a football game. It's still an open question for me to what extent you sort of surrender yourself to something which seems like a bad thing to do. Or to what extent is it reasonable to let yourself try out things you wouldn't do otherwise? Basically, you can rationalize what you do in a lot of different ways. The question is to what extent are you rationalizing? When have you really done something that shouldn't have been done?

As in the case of Subject 3, Subject 6 evaluated his own story again, and this time constructed an index from a different point of view: *Trying new (bad) things with the encouragement of a group is probably the only way one can safely try them (Index 16).* Subject 6 is not sure of his beliefs and thus might see Andy's story as more evidence to be considered. When our own beliefs about a situation are in a state of flux, however, we can learn from paying attention to other people's stories.

This aspect of story understanding is, in some sense, what we really mean by understanding although, as we have seen, it is not really the most common form of story understanding. We would like to imagine that we learn from the stories of others, but we really only do so when the stories we hear relate to beliefs that we feel rather unsure of, ones that we are flirting with at the moment, so to speak. When we are wondering, consciously or unconsciously, about the truth, about how to act or how to understand some aspect of the world, then the evidence provided by others can be of some use. We can extract evidence from a story, supporting or refuting a given belief that we are considering. This extraction process is an important form of understanding which serves as input to various thinking processes.

Subject 7 has seen Andy's story as a story about change. He has constructed an index such as *Part of growing up is selecting the groups that you want to belong to and trying their value system for a while (Index 17)*.

SUBJECT 7:   I am reminded of two people I knew in high school. One guy I had known since kindergarten. He was a jock, and he was a very popular guy. He hung out with everyone, and the girls all liked him. Toward the end of high school, he became more and more sensitive and less and less of a jock. He was a very smart guy. And I remember toward the end of high school, somebody told some crude joke, and Terry objected to the language. I thought this was strange coming from a jock, but he'd really turned around. And then I had another friend who I had also gone to school with since kindergarten. He was an artist, and his father was an artist as well. This guy was very talented and sensitive. The opposite thing happened to him. Toward the end of high school, he kind of stopped being smart and decided he wouldn't study much anymore. He started hanging out with all the jocks. That was much more fun, and he decided that he just wanted to become a regular guy. So I think of these two people's paths crossing. They both wanted acceptance by some group that hadn't accepted them before.

Subject 7 had seen the movie and probably remembered that Andy was making an uncharacteristic admission to a group of kids that were not at all macho. So for Subject 7, the index was quite different

from those constructed by the other subjects. His index was constructed from more information than was provided by Andy's story.
He was also recalling the story of the movie itself from his memory
and "reading" that story as well. He was like the others, however,
in that he was simply reminded of an old story and then let the old
story take over the comprehension of the new story.

Index Construction and Understanding

We tell stories for many reasons, one of which is to indicate to our
listener that we have understood what he has said to us. Assessing
understanding by assessing the relevance of a story that we hear in
response may be the only avenue open to us. If we choose to measure
understanding by the ultimate impact of a story on our permanent
memory structures, we may be very disappointed. To the extent that
people do understand anything at all, we can identify three different
features of understanding:

1. matching indices for story retrieval
2. adding aspects of a new story to empty slots in an old one
3. seeking further evidence for stories that were only
   tentatively held as having been correctly understood

Thus, the strong hypothesis is that most of the time we are merely
looking for stories to tell back. We do this by extracting indices from
what we hear and by using these indices to find stories we already
know. When we find them, processing stops, and we wait to tell our
story. We only incorporate what we have heard into memory when
we feel that our own stories are inadequate in some way, for example, if a story is missing a piece. Such pieces can be supplied by other
people's stories. We may find a story inadequate when we use it to
exemplify a belief that we are not quite sure we hold. We are willing
to consider new stories as evidence for or against those beliefs and,
therefore, to record and to remember better the stories of others.

By this definition, understanding means the incorporation of aspects of what you have understood into some permanent memory

store. People as diverse as reading comprehension testers and Artificial Intelligence researchers agree upon this standard definition of understanding. My argument is that precious little of this kind of understanding actually takes place. A more accurate measure of understanding is the one that people use on a daily basis, namely a subjective evaluation of the story that we get back in response. If it is a great deal like our own story, we feel that we have been understood. In this case, then, understanding means clever indexing. But it should be clear, index extraction is a highly subjective process with no prescribed way of finding indices.

Learning Something New

We all understand differently—this much is obvious. The reason that we understand differently is that our memories are different. My experiences simply aren't yours. In order to understand anything, we must find the closest item in memory to which it relates. As Chapter 3 notes, the concept of the script simplified the understanding process for stereotypical situations. In the book *Scripts, Plans, Goals and Understanding,* Abelson and I claimed that understanding required one to find the correct knowledge structure and to use that structure to create expectations for what events were likely to take place so that new events could be understood in terms of what was normal. Thus, when a story about a cocktail party was being told, an understander brought out his cocktail party script which told him about what ordinarily happens at cocktail parties, and he used that script to guide his understanding of the story that he was about to hear.

In my book *Dynamic Memory* (Cambridge, 1982), this concept was extended to allow a more idiosyncratic view of understanding. The concept of a dynamic memory was proposed, one that changed in response to what it had understood as time went on. The conception of understanding developed there was that one's knowledge structures were more idiosyncratic than just standard scripts. Each of us has his own conception of a restaurant, formed after numerous restaurant visits. Although we all know what kind of standard expectations there are and what information is shared across a culture about restaurants, we also know that sometimes what we expect to happen next comes entirely from our own personal experiences. We get reminded of past experiences by current ones, and we use those past experiences as a kind of guide to help us process new experiences.

The reason that we get reminded while processing something new is to help us by providing the most relevant knowledge that we have in memory. If knowledge of restaurants in general is useful when you enter a restaurant, then it follows that knowledge of Taillevant is useful when you enter Taillevant and that knowledge about prior circumstances in which you have taken a date to a fancy French restaurant in order to impress him or her is especially useful when you are about to try the same thing again.

Reminding is very useful for planning and therefore for understanding the plans of others. When someone tells you a story, however, he is talking not only about plans but often, as we have noticed, about beliefs. And for this reason, we tend to respond to stories with stories.

The premise behind our conception of a dynamic memory is that we try to help ourselves in understanding by finding the most relevant information that we have in our memory to use as a guide. But when what is to be understood in a story is about beliefs, the kind of guidance that we need changes. We don't need to know what will happen next. We are not trying to assess someone's plan so that we can plan against it. We are not trying to find the right thing to do to help us get what we want. When we hear stories like the ones from *Diner* and *The Breakfast Club,* all we are trying to do is understand them. If we are passively viewing the movie for example, understanding the movie means being able to follow what is going on by relating what we are seeing to what we know—learning something from the movie, in a very weak sense of learning. In a conversation, understanding means being able to respond to a story. In both of these cases, then, understanding means attempting to extract indices such that old stories can be related to new ones. For movies the intent is recognition; for conversation, the intent is to be able to respond.

When stories are about ideas rather than plans, the problem for the hearer is to respond to the ideas. But ideas are much harder to get a grip on than plans. We may all agree on the plans a murderer was following when we finish a mystery novel, but such agreement is more difficult to come by when we attempt to discuss the key ideas in a novel that is about people and their relationships. A murder mystery has a plot, which means an involved set of plans, so when the understanding process involves plan extraction from a text, the process is fairly straightforward and not especially idiosyncratic. But when a novel has no plot, when no clear plans are being stated and followed, finding the ideas that are being expressed becomes a problem of belief extraction. This extraction of beliefs can be especially difficult because often actors and even the writers who create fictional actors don't know what their beliefs are. Actions can express beliefs, and so as understanders, our job is to find the beliefs that are inherent and implicit in a given action.

What this means, in the end, is that when the understanding process gets complicated, the primary mechanism that we have available to us to guide understanding, namely reminding, must work especially hard on rather scanty evidence to find something to get reminded of. The main fodder for reminding in such circumstances is beliefs that have been extracted from a text. Such beliefs cause our own personal stories to come to mind when those beliefs also happen to be indices in our own memories. But then a funny thing happens—we feel compelled to tell those stories. Why we desire so strongly to tell our own stories is something we have already discussed in part and to which we shall return later. The point here is that once we have found our own story, we basically stop processing.

The reason for stopping is partially based upon our intentions in the first place. Since most of the time we were really just looking for something to say back in response, having found something, we have little reason to process further. But more important, what we have found usually relates to an arguable point, an idea subject to challenge, a belief about which we are uncertain. As understanders, one of our goals is to gather evidence about the world so that we can formulate better beliefs, ones that will equip us better to deal with the real world. Once we have found a match between someone else's experience and our own, we are excited to begin thinking about the connections so that we can add or subtract beliefs from our own personal data base.

There is a funny side effect to all this. We really cannot learn from other people's stories. In getting reminded of our own stories, ones which of course have more poignancy and more rich detail than the ones we are hearing, we tend to get distracted into thinking more about what happened to us. The incoming story can get recalled in terms of the story of which we were reminded, but in the end, we rarely recall the stories of others easily. More often than not, other people's stories don't have the richness of detail and emotional impact that allows them to be stored in multiple ways in our memories. They do, on the other hand, provide enough details and emotions to allow them to be more easily stored than if the tellers had simply told us their beliefs.

So we are left with an odd picture of understanding. Real communication is rather difficult to achieve. We do not easily remember what other people have said if they do not tell it in the form of a story. We can learn from the stories of others, but only if what we hear relates strongly to something we already knew. We can learn from these stories to the extent that they have caused us to rethink our own stories. But mostly we learn from a reexamination of our own stories. We hear, in the stories of others, what we personally can relate to by virtue of having in some way heard or experienced that story before. Understanding is an idiosyncratic affair. Our idiosyncrasies come from our stories.

□ 4 □

Indexing Stories

□

IT IS all well and good to say that understanding means telling good stories and to say that we respond to stories with stories, but this leaves out a key question: *How do we find the stories that we wish to tell?* And from this question there follows another key question: *How does one know that one has a story to tell?* The answer to both these questions is one word: *indexing*.

No matter how the story of Artificial Intelligence is told, no matter whose point of view is adopted about how the mind works or how a computer mind might work, the problem always reduces to search. A mind must be able to find what it needs to find, and it must know that it has found it. To tell a story, you must have labeled it properly, stored it away with a name that will allow it to be found, possibly many years later, when some process calls its name. If there is no way to find a story, it might as well not exist. If it cannot be found by reference to its content rather than by reference to a number or unrevealing name, for example, then it might as well not be there.

It is likely that the bulk of what passes for intelligence is no more than a massive indexing and retrieval scheme that allows an intelligent entity to determine what information it has in its memory that is relevant to the situation at hand, to search for and find that information.

A Canonical Form for Belief-based Indices

Earlier, we saw a number of potential indices derived from looking at subjects' reactions to two stories. Now let's consider those indices as a group, leaving out those that were not formulations of beliefs already held by the people who understood the two stories.

Index 1: Marrying too early can lead to a dull and pointless life.

Index 2: Blindly following scripts that are chosen for you in life can cause you to raise questions when it is too late.

Index 3: You desire things you can't have, and then when you can have them you don't desire them so much.

Index 4: Desiring sex clouds your judgment about whether you really like and want to spend time with the person you desire.

Index 5: Good relationships depend upon intrinsic interest in a person, not sex.

Index 9: Putting aside all your goals in order to achieve one major goal only works for a short time. Eventually real life reappears.

Index 11: When deciding what kind of person to be, trying to please someone else never works.

Index 12: Trying to prove yourself may cause you to do things you don't want to so you can appear cool.

Index 13: Guilt follows the rush of the moment when you do something against your own value system.

Index 14: The efforts to please an unsuccessful and demanding father can lead to bad decisions in life.

Index 15: Sometimes you act irrationally in a group when you wouldn't if you were alone.

Index 16: Trying new (bad) things with the encouragement of a group is probably the only way one can safely try them.

Index 17: Part of growing up is selecting the groups that you want to belong to and trying their value system for a while.

One way to look at these indices is to reduce them to a form independent of the words used to express them. If we are going to discuss indices, we must find a language in terms of which they can be discussed. All of these indices have a basic structure in common—they all have themes. In the language of *Scripts, Plans, Goals and Understanding,* themes are general life topics that tend to generate goals related to those topics, and the results of those goals relate to the overarching theme. Indices all discuss goals with the obvious intended results of those goals that relate to the overarching theme. They all discuss actual results that were not part of the original intended results of the goal being pursued. Finally, indices all provide a lesson that is the new belief or point of view that is the point of the index, namely what is supposed to have been learned from whatever experience this index relates to.

Viewed in this way, the indices above can be characterized as follows.

Index	Topic	Goal/Intention	Actual Result	Lesson
Marrying too early can lead to a dull and pointless life.	early marriage	stability/ normality	pointless life	Avoid early marriage.
Blindly following scripts that are chosen for you in life can cause you to raise questions when it is too late.	script following	normality	questions raised too late	Sometimes it can be too late to change.
You desire things you can't have, and then when you can have them you don't desire them so much.	achieve difficult goal	happiness	didn't make happy	Be suspicious of your goals.

Index	Topic	Goal/Intention	Actual Result	Lesson
Desiring sex clouds your judgment about whether you really like and want to spend time with the person you desire.	need for sex	sexual satisfaction	spending time with someone you don't like	The need for sex can cloud thinking.
Good relationships depend upon intrinsic interest in a person, not sex.	male/female relations	have good relationship	achieve it	You must have something in common with a love object besides love.
Putting aside all your goals in order to achieve one major goal only works for a short time. Eventually real life reappears.	goal suppression	achieve major goal	old goals reappear	Achieving major goals doesn't make minor goals go away.
When deciding what kind of person to be, trying to please someone else never works.	self-definition	please father	make self unhappy	Be yourself.
Trying to prove yourself may cause you to do things you don't want to so you can appear cool.	group acceptance	appear cool	feel lousy	Be yourself.

Index	Topic	Goal/Intention	Actual Result	Lesson
Guilt follows the rush of the moment when you do something against your own value system.	adventurousness	try something new	feel bad and guilty	Evaluate what you are about to do before you do it.
The efforts to please an unsuccessful and demanding father can lead to bad decisions in life.	self-definition	please father	made self unhappy	Be yourself.
Sometimes you act irrationally in a group when you wouldn't if you were alone.	group acceptance	appear cool	feel lousy	Be yourself.
Trying new (bad) things with the encouragement of a group is probably the only way one can safely try them.	personal growth	try something new	unknown	Groups provide the security to allow growth.
Part of growing up is selecting the groups that you want to belong to and trying their value system for a while.	self-definition	join an affinity group	might not be right	Try many paths before deciding who you are.

Now, let's look at these indices with a bit more rigor in the choice of vocabulary. The vocabulary we shall use is from *Scripts, Plans, Goals and Understanding*. In the scheme proposed there, high-level themes about life circumstances generate goals that need to be achieved that in turn generate plans of action. In that book, we said people followed goals that gave rise to plans that in turn gave rise to standard courses of action which were the embodiment of those plans. We sought to analyze carefully the kinds of goals people could be expected to have and the life themes that gave rise to those goals. For example, if someone robbed a bank (a plan), it might have been to get money (a goal that generated the plan) in order to live luxuriously (a theme that generated the goal). This scheme helped us represent the actions and motivations behind those actions that we found in stories.

These same elements are the stuff of indices. This has to be so, in fact, or else it would be impossible to ever get reminded of a story. When one is processing a story, one must attempt to understand it. This means, according to *Scripts, Plans, Goals and Understanding*, that one must construct a representation of that story in terms of themes, goals, plans, and actions. The representation that is constructed for a story, while understanding it, must be in terms of the same elements in terms of which it is to be stored. That is, we store stories in memory in terms of the elements in which we have represented those stories. It follows, then, that the indices for retrieving a story would be exactly those that were used to represent it. In this way, we could be reminded of a new story by an old story simply by storing the new story in terms of the same elements we have used to understand both stories, namely the themes, goals, plans, and such that characterized what was going on in each story.

We have added an additional element to this index composed of theme-goal-plan connections by using a predicted result (to which one usually has a story attached that exemplifies circumstances under which one has seen such a result) and a lesson that the storyteller has drawn from that story. Let's look at the same indices with this structure in mind.

Index	Theme	Goal	Plan	Result	Lesson
Marrying too early can lead to a dull and pointless life.	lead normal life	marriage	marry early	pointless life	Avoid early marriage.
Blindly following scripts that are chosen for you in life can cause you to raise questions when it is too late.	lead normal life	follow normal goals	follow normal plans without thinking	questions raised too late	Sometimes it can be too late to change.
You desire things you can't have, and then when you can have them you don't desire them so much.	general happiness	achieve difficult goals	work very hard	goal achieved, but not happiness	Be suspicious of your goals.
Desiring sex clouds your judgment about whether you really like and want to spend time with the person you desire.	sexual stud	sex; love	find someone, no matter if you like her	sex achieved; happiness not achieved	The need for sex can cloud thinking.

Index	*Theme*	*Goal*	*Plan*	*Result*	*Lesson*
Good relationships depend upon intrinsic interest in a person, not sex.	love	good relationship	spend time with person of opposite sex	boredom unless there are shared interests	You must have something in common with a love object besides love.
Putting aside all your goals in order to achieve one major goal only works for a short time. Eventually real life reappears.	metagoals (about goals in general)	achieve major goal	suppress minor goals	minor goals reappear after major goal is achieved	Achieving major goals doesn't make minor goals go away.
When deciding what kind of person to be, trying to please someone else never works.	self-definition	please father	follow father's plans	make self unhappy	Be yourself.
Trying to prove yourself may cause you to do things you don't want to so you can appear cool.	be accepted by friends	look cool	follow "cool" plans that please others	feel lousy	Be yourself.

Index	Theme	Goal	Plan	Result	Lesson
Guilt follows the rush of the moment when you do something against your own value system.	lead adventurous life	adopt new goals	try new plans	feel bad and guilty	Evaluate what you are about to do before you do it.
Trying new (bad) things with the encouragement of a group is probably the only way one can safely try them.	personal growth	adopt new goals in a group	try new plans in a group	unknown	Groups provide the security to allow growth.
Part of growing up is selecting the groups that you want to belong to and trying their value system for a while.	self-definition	try new goals	join group with new goals	might be wrong group	Try many paths before deciding who you are.

Structures and Indices

We asserted, in *Scripts, Plans, Goals and Understanding,* that in order to understand a story, it needed to be broken down into the conceptual actions underlying the events. These actions were then understood in terms of the scripts, plans, goals, and themes to which they referred. It is not surprising, therefore, that memory uses such structures as indices to find the stories it had already understood. In *Dynamic Memory* we pointed out that memory structures and processing structures had to be one and the same in order for reminding to take place. Indices that are outer contextual, that is, ones that transcend contexts, are organized around themes, and were called Thematic Organization Packages (TOPs) in *Dynamic Memory*. Such high-level indices come from juxtapositions of plans, goals, and themes.

My contention here is that when results, especially unexpected results, are added to the package of themes, goals, and plans, an inherent prediction is added that allows a story to be found by looking at the structures that were involved and the results that were obtained. Attached to this package is a lesson—in essence, the abstraction of the contents of a story uniquely derived from that story. When the same lesson comes up frequently, however, the lesson itself becomes a type of structure, and it can be understood apart from the story which originally gave rise to it. This structure becomes, in essence, a skeleton story.

The important question, then, is *What can constitute an index?* The answer is that, while nearly anything can be an index in principle, certain features of a situation are more likely to be used as indices precisely because they are the features that are likely to be extracted from a situation as it is being understood. So, we are likely to be reminded of something with yellow polka dots by something with yellow polka dots, but little in the way of theory is necessary in order to explain this phenomenon. On the other hand, themes and lessons of the kind that we mentioned above are much less obvious phenomena with a much bigger role to play. One important question to answer then is: *What is a theme?*

Themes

Here are the themes that we used above:

lead normal life
general happiness

sexual stud
love
metagoals (about goals in general)
self-definition
be accepted by friends
lead adventurous life
personal growth

What characterizes this list is the focus on personal preoccupations. When people talk to each other about their "problems," when they have "heart-to-heart talks," the subjects on this list are what they are talking about. Not surprisingly, then, such subjects, as amorphous and indefinable as they may seem at first glance, are an important part of the indexing process. If these are the subjects people talk about, then we not only have information about but also are prepared to hear about and respond to these subjects.

The problem for an understander is to ascertain which of these or other themes is being discussed. This process is by no means simple or straightforward. It depends upon, among other things, the themes prevalent in the life of the hearer. You cannot understand very well what you neither know about nor have any experience of. The primary problem in understanding someone else's story, then, is determining the theme that is being implicitly discussed. When some determination has been made about the overriding theme, the story-based understanding process begins.

Indexing Our Stories

One thing that we have seen is that indexing is an idiosyncratic affair: One person's indices are not another's. We are reminded of what we are reminded of. We cannot get the wrong reminding. We may not get a particularly useful reminding, but whatever one we do get will be the one that the indices we computed from the input led us to.

When we examined Shrevie's story before, we saw that different listeners computed different indices; so clearly a given story has no right index. Nevertheless, a right way to compute indices—that is, a vocabulary and method of construction—is common to us all. We construct different indices because what we pay attention to and what we know of the world are different, because the stories that we have already processed are different, not because our indexing schemes differ in principle.

This having been said, let's now go back and look at the indices that might label some of the stories told in this book. The question we shall ask is: *What index might have labeled a given story so that the particular story told came to mind?* One thing we must continue to bear in mind while asking such a question is that no right answer exists, only possible answers.

We could tell any story at any time. Presumably, we tell stories with some point in mind, some reason for telling them. These points are attached to the stories in some way. We find these points by constructing an index derived from what we have heard or thought. The index is constructed by observing events outside our memories ordinarily and by labeling them in such a way as to correspond to labels we have previously constructed for our own stories. Thus, a given story in our memory can have many possible labels, and a given event in the outside world can cause us to construct many possible labels. Sometimes, then, we will not tell the same story in response to the same input each time we receive that input. It is possible, but, as it happens, unlikely. We are standard enough in our labeling or else we have so few stories to tell that, rather than tell different stories each time we receive similar inputs, we tend to tell the same stories repeatedly, even in response to different inputs. Thus, to some extent our indexing schemes are more functions of the stories we have to tell rather than of the stories we hear.

With this premise in mind, let's reconsider some of the stories we have already told. Here is one that we discussed in Chapter 1:

Recently, I attended an informal talk by a leader of the sixties counterculture. These days he describes himself as a performer, a kind of comedian.
In the sixties, he was also a performer. His humor was part of what made
the counterculture so appealing. I was rather surprised, however, that he
now saw himself as a performer. True, he got paid for performing, but he
still cared deeply about the same issues he had always cared about. I told

him that he reminded me of Jimmy Swaggart, the television evangelist. Naturally, he was curious as to why I thought this. I said that Jimmy Swaggart was only masquerading as a righteous man, getting paid well for performing when he was trying to hide the sinner that he really was. The sixties leader was also getting paid for performing as a clown when he was actually hiding the political reformer that he really was. In both cases, the masquerade was easy to see through; what was odd was that the performers seemed unable to see through it themselves.

How might this story have been indexed in memory? The first problem here is that the story actually consists of two stories: The first story is the actual story; the second story embedded in the first story is the one that I told to the sixties comedian. Each has a different index. Let's start with the second story.

In order to recognize Jimmy Swaggart in the sixties comedian, I had to have labeled them in the same way. In other words, I had to derive an index, based upon my observation of the comedian's behavior, that caused me to think about Jimmy Swaggart and then to think about why I had thought about Jimmy Swaggart. To do this, I had to make some observations like:

He's a radical, but he pretends he's a performer.

and

He is so caught up in being funny that he seems to care more about being liked than he does about changing the world.

Observations such as these—generalizations—are the stuff of which indices are made.

The next step, then, is to translate these generalizations into indices. To understand what that translation process looks like, we need to examine the end result, namely my indices for Jimmy Swaggart. Now, Jimmy Swaggart at the time of this story had recently lost his television ministry because he was caught taking nude photos of a prostitute. This event made me wonder why people who were into such kinky sexual things were the same people who ranted and raved the most about sin. (A similar event had happened a year earlier with another television evangelist.) Considering that books and movies on this general theme had been written, I thought something was to be learned here, some generalization to be drawn.

And draw it I did. I concluded that an interest in various sexual obsessions, combined with a feeling that these obsessions were evil in some way, had probably convinced these evangelists to spend their lives telling people not to refrain from sinning but rather to believe that sin could be forgiven. Their preaching forced them to cover up their own obsessions. In other words, one might think about Jimmy Swaggart as a person who used his role as a public performer to conceal the type of person he really was. My index, then, for discussions of television evangelism, Jimmy Swaggart, and the Bible Belt mentality in general, evolved as: *Use your public role as a performer to conceal from others and possibly from yourself what's going on in private.*

Now obviously many other things can make me think about Jimmy Swaggart. For example, the concepts of preaching, fundamentalism, the power of television, and even the name "Jimmy Swaggart" can make me think of Jimmy Swaggart. But making or encountering the generalization that public performance can be used to conceal private obsessions, i.e., the index itself, can also get me to think about Jimmy Swaggart.

In this case, the above index called the Jimmy Swaggart story to my mind by translating:

He's a radical, but he pretends he's a performer.

and

He is so caught up in being funny that he seems to care more about being liked than he does about changing the world.

to

Use your public role as a performer to conceal from others and possibly from yourself what's going on in private.

This translation is really no translation at all, however. Although these sentences are very different in English, they are not likely to be very different assertions to the mind. What we need to express these kinds of sentences is a language that would render them identical. To do this, we can attempt to use the format we developed above. The question arises, then: What in this story fits into this format? The theme here is to be loved despite something that makes you unlovable. This theme generates the goal *to be highly visible in order to be loved by many people,* which in turn generates the plan *to perform in public in some way that will make people like you.* The lesson I derived from this—this is *my* index after all—is that to hide one's true nature from oneself is really very difficult. The reason I was reminded of Jimmy Swaggart is that I had constructed this representation of the comedian's actions and previously had constructed the same representation of Jimmy Swaggart's actions.

The first story here illustrates the points that (1) not everyone sees the same experiences the same way and (2) stories are a very good way to express one's ideas. That story, namely the story of telling the comedian my observation about him, was indexed in my mind as follows:

Theme: explaining how reminding and indexing work
Goal: find a story that illustrates the point about different coding
Plan: tell sixties comedian story
Result:
Lesson:

Notice that the indexing process here yields no result and no lesson. In fact, there really is no story here. The outer story is simply a story about a story. It has no point. Nothing happened. In some serious sense, it is not a story at all. Then why did it look like a story when I told it in Chapter 1? The answer is that the story inside the story looked enough like a story to carry the outer story, so that when I said I was going to tell a story, it seemed that I had. But had it been a real story then something interesting would have had to have occurred as a result of my telling it or I would have illustrated some point to be learned from the story. Instead, the story is pedagogical, its point to illustrate a phenomenon. As such, it has an interesting status in memory that sets it apart from real stories. Real stories are remembered because they have lessons that are derived from them that serve as indices to memory. Without a lesson, we have difficulty remembering something. We can tell the story of what happened to us yesterday, for example, but if we didn't learn a lesson from what happened to us, we won't remember a year later what we said or much of what occurred. Not every story that we tell is really a story in the sense of being a memory entity. In fact, I wrote about the sixties comedian the day after our encounter. If a few more days had passed, I probably would not have recalled the event well enough to make it into a story.

Let's consider another story from Chapter 1:

A friend and I were discussing stories and then moved on to a discussion about Jewish attitudes toward intermarriage. He said that two Jewish friends of his mother had gone out when they were young women, and when they'd returned home, their mother had asked them what they had done that day. They'd responded that they had played tennis. Their mother had asked whom they had played with, and they had said, "Two guys." The mother had then asked what kind of guys, and they had responded, "Italian," to which the mother had said: "Another day wasted."

In hearing this story, I asked my friend what he thought would have happened in our discussion of Jewish attitudes if instead of telling this story he had said, "I knew someone who thought that playing tennis with Italians was a waste of time," or "Some mothers don't want their daughters to spend time with non-Jews."

Is this a story? In the sense of story that I am referring to here, a story must have a lesson. Otherwise, retrieving the story in a domain-independent way would be impossible. Some stories can be retrieved easily enough in a domain-dependent way: Stories about Jimmy Swaggart can remind you of stories about Jimmy Swaggart or preachers or television—anything that is specifically in the story. But in order to get reminded of a story independent of the surface features of the current topic, the lesson provides the central part of the index. In other words, lessons can be domain-independent.

So the question here is: Does this story have a domain-independent lesson? Let's use the model presented to analyze this story:

Theme: getting married
Goal: find husband
Plan: play tennis with a boy
Result: no marriage—not a proper candidate
Lesson: Young girls should spend time with marriageable boys.

What is wrong here? The problem is that this index is one the mother might have used to tell the story—it describes the story well enough—but clearly my friend did not use this index to retrieve the story from his memory. He doesn't believe in the lesson of the story at all but just believes that this story is a funny way of explaining Jewish attitudes toward intermarriage. The question still remains, then: What index could he have used?

Observations and Advice

The stories from Chapter 3 that we started with were the personal responses of my students to a problem presented in the stories read to them. Their stories all had lessons because they were stories derived from real experiences and meant as advice for a person with a problem. The students found lessons from their own lives to tell in response because such stories were appropriate to tell. These *advisory stories* are certainly retrievable via obvious means such as names, places, and various concrete objects; but they are also retrievable by the lessons that they tell about. Thus, for advisory stories, lessons are an important index.

The two stories we just looked at were not advisory stories, and, consequently, forcing a lesson on them was difficult. Instead, they were stories meant to illustrate some truth in the world, where that truth was not offered as advice but as observation. Such stories we can call *observation stories*. The observation in this last story was that Jews have funny attitudes toward intermarriage and the importance of getting daughters married off. My friend did not offer this story as advice, nor did he remember the story by looking for a lesson that he had learned. Similarly, my story about the comedian was not offered as advice either to the comedian or the reader. Rather, to the reader it was offered as an observation about the various ways that experience can be coded and to the comedian as an observation about certain human behaviors. Thus, we clearly need a different indexing scheme for observation stories.

To find an observation story, we can retrieve either the behavior that is being observed or the observation itself. The behavior is retrieved through the goals and plans that describe the behavior, as we discussed earlier. But now there is no lesson, just an observation. Furthermore, since this is a story about something we have observed, we do not generate goals for ourselves or have a theme that generates such goals, but instead we have a topic. The topic, therefore, is the most important part of the index because it causes the observation to come to mind. So the correct representation of the tennis story is:

Topic:	Jewish attitudes toward intermarriage
Goal:	find husband
Plan:	play tennis with a boy who isn't Jewish
Result:	no marriage—not a proper candidate
Observation:	Jewish mothers believe that young girls should spend time with marriageable boys.

And here is the Jimmy Swaggart–sixties comedian story reconsidered in this light:

Topic:	explaining how reminding and indexing work
Goal:	be highly visible and mask true self
Plan:	be a loved performer
Result:	planner effectively hides his true nature
Observation:	Sometimes people hide their true nature by performing in some other role in public; different people can view things in different ways.

You can see that we have different intentions in telling each type of story, and therefore we have different ways of finding stories to tell. Within certain topics, we can find stories to illustrate an observation that we have made. However, when someone seeks advice that relates to a life theme, you may refer to valuable lessons derived from experiences revolving around the same theme. Therefore, in indexing, the kind of structure that dominates a conversation is very important.

Obviously, advisory conversations give rise to advisory stories, and conversations focused on a given topic lead to observation stories. These two types of structures are really quite similar. The life themes central to advisory stories are, in essence, topics; similarly, lessons are also observations. Thus, the latter structure that we have outlined is the more general one for indexing. In other words, before you can find a good story to tell, you need to know the nature of the conversation and the ideas you have to contribute. The story is simply what happened—the goals and plans and results. The index is what surrounds the story—what reminds you of the story and what you want to add to it. Thus, an index has two parts. Something said in conversation brings an observation to mind. The observation is the index to the story itself whereas the topic is the index to the observation.

With this idea in mind, let's reexamine some of the stories from Chapter 2. Consider this one, for example:

I know how you feel, Miss Kubelik. You think it's the end of the world—but it's not, really. I went through exactly the same thing myself. Well, maybe not exactly—I tried to do it with a gun. She was the wife of my best friend, and I was mad for her. But I knew it was hopeless—so I decided to end it all. I went to a pawnshop and bought a .45 automatic and drove up to Eden Park—do you know Cincinnati? Anyway, I parked the car and loaded the gun—well, you read in the papers all the time that people shoot themselves, but believe me, it's not that easy—I mean, how do you do it? Here or here or here [with cocked finger, he points to his temple, mouth, and chest]. You know where I finally shot myself? [Indicates knee.] Here. While I was sitting there, trying to make my mind up, a cop stuck his head in the car, because I was illegally parked—so I started to hide the gun under the seat, and it went off—pow! Took me a year before I could bend my knee—but I got over the girl in three weeks. She still lives in Cincinnati, has four kids, gained twenty pounds—she—Here's the fruitcake. [Shows it to her under Christmas tree.] And you want to see my knee?

Whatever brought this story to mind is the topic, and what the teller had in mind to say is the observation. To the extent that the teller had in mind to give advice about a life theme, then we would be talking about an advisory story rather than just a simple observation story. Where does this story fit? But, of course, this isn't an advisory story. It is a cathartic story intended to make both the teller and the hearer feel better. It comes up because the topic of killing oneself comes up, and the index to the story is clearly the reasons why one might kill oneself and the validity of those reasons. So here again, indexing is a two-part process, and again we have a topic that relates to the subject at hand and that calls up the observation, but in this context the observation is not a lesson.

One thing that seems to be true is that any aspect of life can be a topic. But one question is: What kinds of things can a topic call up? This question is important because, in order to understand how stories are indexed, we must know the form that these lessons, observations, or whatever can take. In other words, the elements that comprise lessons and observations are the elements that comprise indices.

Proverbs

Here are some English proverbs, some more well known than others:

Too many cooks spoil the broth.
Many hands make light work.
A runaway monk never praises his convent.
A stranger's eye sees clearest.
It is the last taste of things that gives them the name of sweet or
    sour.
Better reap two days too soon than one day too late.
In a calm sea every man is a pilot.
If you buy meat cheap, when it boils you will smell what you have
    saved.
Grasp all, lose all.

Milk the cow but don't pull off the udder.
Double charge will split a cannon.
The cats that drive mice away are as good as those that catch them.
A hook is well lost to catch a salmon.

What do these proverbs have to do with what we are talking about here? For one thing, they look a lot like the observations and advice extracted from the story representations we have seen. Of course, proverbs are couched in a more poetic language than people use today, more reminiscent of the farm or the sea than of modern urban culture. But don't be confused by the tone of the language used in these proverbs. The concept of indexing is strongly related to the formation of a proverb.

A proverb is, quite often, a piece of advice. Since human beings find themselves in only so many situations, these situations repeat themselves. People today are faced with the same kinds of decisions, however different the context, that their counterparts in other centuries faced. They still must protect those they care about, save for tomorrow, make plans for today, achieve goals, deal with dilemmas, and so on. Proverbs are advice for these human concerns, much the same as the stories we have considered. Proverbs are what we have called culturally common stories, but the culture in the case of most proverbs is really just the culture of being a human being. No matter what language you speak, what century you live in, or how civilized you are, certain situations and the choices arising from those situations are universal.

So the elements that make up proverbs are precisely the same elements that make up mental indices. In other words, stories are stored in memory, represented in some internal representation scheme in terms of the same elementary units that comprise the basis of many proverbs. Let's look at the above list again, this time with an eye toward isolating the elements of which they are comprised:

Too many cooks spoil the broth.
    (planning when multiple actors want to direct the plans)
Many hands make light work.
    (planning when multiple actors want to be the workers)

A runaway monk never praises his convent.
  (observation about the trustworthiness of other people's
    judgments)
A stranger's eye sees clearest.
  (observation about the trustworthiness of other people's
    observations)
It is the last taste of things that gives them the name of sweet or
    sour.
  (observation about the trustworthiness of other people's
    observations)
Better reap two days too soon than one day too late.
  (advice about putting plans into effect)
In a calm sea every man is a pilot.
  (observation about estimation of other people's abilities)
If you buy meat cheap, when it boils you will smell what you have
    saved.
  (observation about the long-term effects of short-term planning)
Grasp all, lose all.
  (observation about the effects of bad planning)
Milk the cow but don't pull off the udder.
  (planning advice about carefulness)
Double charge will split a cannon.
  (planning advice about trying to do too much at once)
The cats that drive mice away are as good as those that catch them.
  (observation about making judgments about value)
A hook is well lost to catch a salmon.
  (observation about trade-offs when you want something)

As we have asserted, proverbs are, to some extent, composed of
the same elements as the indices discussed earlier. They are intention-
ally more domain-independent than the indices, however, because
they were not garnered from real situations with personal stories
serving as the basis of the advice being given. The same kinds of
categories, nevertheless, are being used. Consider, for example, some
of the categories with respect to planning.

how to choose the right plan
when to plan

the side effects of certain plans
difficulties with who helps
difficulties with who is in charge
sequencing plans properly
understanding their causes and effects
understanding how certain plans obviate other plans

This kind of analysis is true for goal-oriented proverbs as well. With respect to observations, the form seems to be: *When this happens, that happens.* Many of the *thises* and *thats* have to do with planning, but sometimes they simply have to do with what people say or do under certain circumstances and with how seriously they should be taken. Sometimes—although not with proverbs since proverbs transcend individuals—observations are simply about oneself. The next story from Chapter 2 is that type.

My first day as a copyboy I was sixteen and wearing my only grown-up suit—it was cream colored. At two-thirty, the head copyboy comes running up to me and says, "My God, haven't you washed the carbon paper yet? If it's not washed by three, it'll never be dry for tomorrow." And I said, "Am I supposed to do that?" and he said, "Absolutely, it's crucial." So I run around and grab all the carbon paper from all the desks and take it to the men's room. I'm standing there washing it, and it's splashing all over me, and the editor comes in to take a leak, and he says, "What the fuck do you think you're doing?" And I said, "It's two-thirty. I'm washing the carbon paper."
I'm beginning to feel like I never stopped.

In this story, the teller makes an observation about himself. Could it have been a proverb? Sure. Maybe a proverb could be invented like: *Once you let them get to you, they never stop.* It really doesn't matter whether an observation or lesson of the kind we have been discussing is a proverb or not. The fact of the matter is that we can find all the indices we need by looking at proverbs or by looking at the observations and conclusions people draw about life. Proverbs and such conclusions differ only in their universality across a culture.

A Canonical Form for Indexing

What form do indices take? Indices have a domain-dependent part and a domain-independent part. The best way to discuss this is to begin with a story, of course.

A friend of mine was describing the problems he was having with his current girlfriend. He was thinking of marrying this woman. He felt that he loved her, and he thought that she was a good candidate for marriage. Her one problem was that she yelled and screamed at him a lot, but he thought that he might be able to make that go away or minimize it over time.

While discussing his problem, I was reminded of a time when I had to choose an employee. I found a candidate who seemed perfect. As we got to know each other during the interviewing process, the talk turned to personal issues. He frequently bragged about how he had recently won his divorce case. What this meant was that he kept all the money and the children. His wife was devastated. He had spent tremendous amounts of time and money in attempting to win this case and was very proud of himself. I wondered at the time how someone could be so vicious to someone he had loved but did not see this as a reason for not hiring someone who otherwise seemed so perfect.

After time, we had a falling out, and I watched this man become more and more vicious toward me. Of course, I was reminded of what he had done to his wife. I told this story to my friend with the admonishment that he should learn to read the signs. People tell you what they will be like to deal with over the long term. You just have to learn to listen.

I drew a conclusion from my friend's story that expressed a belief that indexed a story of my own. He was hoping that his future relationship with this woman would not include the behavior in her that he saw and disliked. I believe that the signs you read in people early in a relationship foretell the future of the relationship. The story I told further emphasizes the gravity of this point by adding that: *Even if the things you notice and dislike about a person seem to have nothing to do with you, the attitudes that produced the behavior that you dislike are likely to manifest themselves in behaviors that will affect you.*

The story I told, therefore, had to be encoded mentally in terms of the lesson that the story expressed. That lesson would look something like: *In deciding whether to enter a long-term relationship with somebody, assume that the behavior you dislike in the person will continue to manifest itself, and make sure that you are willing to live with that behavior.*

Now, let's try to put this unwieldy rule of thumb into a form that the mind might actually use. First, let's look at the index for the story that my friend told.

> **Theme:** establish long-term relationship with another person for a purpose
> **Goal:** get married
> **Plan:** choose wife whom you love but who exhibits a bad behavior
> **Result:** bad behavior causes new problems
> **Lesson:** Learn to read the signs better.

Next, let's consider the index for the story that I told.

> **Theme:** establish long-term relationship with another person for a purpose
> **Goal:** find employee
> **Plan:** choose person whom you like but who exhibits a bad behavior
> **Result:** bad behavior causes new problems
> **Lesson:** Learn to read the signs better.

Obviously, these two indices are very similar. If the mind uses such indices, finding a match here would not be surprising. When listening to my friend's story, I had to ask myself how the result of making a bad choice about long-term relationships, a result that could have been foretold, related to some story I knew. Clearly, the question retrieved the story from my memory. Had I asked myself the same question but included relationships with girlfriends as the subject instead of long-term relationships, I would not have been able to find the story I told.

Theme-goal-plan-result-lesson indices can be considered at a variety of levels of abstraction. The result, when considered with a goal that is generalized in a useful way, will provide an index that can be used for retrieval.

Military History

What is an expert? An expert, for our purposes here, is someone who has a great many stories to tell in one particular area of knowledge and who has those stories indexed well enough to find the right one at the right time. We interviewed an expert on military history ostensibly to get him to tell us some stories about various battles but actually to see how he had labeled the stories, how he accessed them, and how he saw them. He proved to be, as one might expect, a repository of stories about various episodes in military history. The interesting question became then: How do people find each of the relevant stories to tell that they know? Or, to put this another way: What are the indices that they use?

The interviewer tried three different methods of extracting stories from the expert. The first was to restate the essence of the stories that had been told earlier in the day in a kind of indexlike form to see whether the same stories would be told again, that is, to see whether these were, in fact, actual indices. The second was to permute the indices that had been uncovered in the early part of the interview and to ask questions to see whether any stories would be retrieved that way. In addition, standard proverbs restated in military terms were formulated as questions to see whether they were useful indices as well. All three methods worked.

INTERVIEWER: Can you think of a battle which was won by using deception by making your war plans look like normal activities?

EXPERT: Well, sure, the campaign of 1940 comes to mind. Not so much normal activities as the activities that the enemy is expecting. The '73 campaign also fits what you just said.

INTERVIEWER: Do you know some case where the plan was too complicated for execution because the troops were not good enough to execute the plan and this caused them to lose?

EXPERT: Well, Germantown. That's the one that usually comes to my mind in that case.

INTERVIEWER: How about where a commander is trying a plan which might work for some commanders, but the commander himself is not able to execute it?

EXPERT: Chancellorsville is a good example of that because his concept of getting behind Lee was not a bad concept.

INTERVIEWER: How about the opposite of what you said, where the planning is so detailed as to compensate for any weakness that the troops might have?

EXPERT: Well, the planning is detailed and rehearsed; the actions are rehearsed. The best example of a set piece battle that I can think of offhand is the Egyptian crossing of the Suez Canal in 1973. They rehearsed it in crossings of the Nile River. They rehearsed it in crossings of a branch of the Suez Canal that was still in Egyptian hands, north of Ismailia and south of Port Said, and they practiced there time after time.

INTERVIEWER: Does that remind you of any other battles where it is not necessarily the skill of the troops but where any plan is too complicated. For example, where a plan would have worked if only you had more firepower . . .

EXPERT: The German offensives of 1918 most certainly fall into that category. The German offensive of 1914, when von Moltke reduced the strength of his right flank, contrary to von Schliefen's dying admonitions, and so the resources on the right flank were not enough to carry out the concept of Schliefen's plan.

INTERVIEWER: Can you think of a battle where a trap was set up by forcing the opposing troops to follow you into a land barrier that sets you up for ambush?

EXPERT: Canei of course is the classic example of that. There are other examples of that also. The next best that I can think of is Montgomery at Alanhalfa, where he set up a plan, hoping Rommel would attack. Rommel did attack.

Rommel didn't have enough strength. So then Rommel
tried to play more similar games by withdrawing, hoping
that he could entice Montgomery to pursue.
Montgomery didn't pursue.

Another very good example of this sort of thing was
the battle of Hastings. Some of you may recall that
William of Normandy had been repulsed all day in his
attacks against the Saxon line on the high ground of
Hastings and finally made an attack and pretended to
withdraw in confusion. And it was just about this time
that Harold was hit in the eye by an arrow that had
been fired up in high-angle fire. And the Saxon troops,
seeing the Normans apparently withdrawing in
confusion, pursued, and Harold was in no position to
hold them in line. Once they got out of their position,
the Normans turned and then cut them to pieces.

Our expert was full of these stories. If you asked the right question, you got a new story. He went on for hours and certainly could
have gone on much longer. For our purposes here, the interview
raises a central question: Will the index format that we have suggested in this chapter work for military history also?
Consider as an example the indices:

1. a battle that was won by using deception by making war plans
   look like normal activities
2. a plan that was too complicated for execution because the troops
   were not good enough to execute the plan, and this caused them
   to lose

These indices were very clear labels for our expert and fit very
easily into the format we discussed earlier.

1. Theme:	win battle
Goal:	lull enemy to sleep
Plan:	disguise war plans by making them look like normal activity
Result:	enemy goes to sleep
Lesson:	Deception wins battles.

2. Theme: win battle
  Goal: envelop opposition
  Plan: complex envelopment using deception
  Result: troops cannot carry out plan because it is too complex
  Lesson: Plans have to be realistic for the troops involved.

Indexing is a major problem that lies at the heart of intelligence. No intelligent system is likely to function effectively if it cannot find what it knows when it needs to know it. One can easily imagine many possible schemes that would work as labels for stories that would allow their retrieval at the right moment. Two things seem certain, however. First, a vocabulary of labels is necessary in order to talk coherently about a given subject. Our military historian taught us his vocabulary as soon as he began to discuss his stories. (His vocabulary is to be found in *Understanding War* by Col. T. N. Dupuy; New York: Paragon, 1987.) Second, the vocabulary must be employed in a description of themes, goals, plans, results, and lessons. These are the stuff of indices, the way in which we understand the applicability of a story. The major problem in finding a story to tell is understanding how it relates to what we are currently hearing or talking about. We reach this understanding by assessing what themes, goals, plans, and results exist in common between what we are hearing and what we know. When we can match at this level, we can find and tell our story.

An interesting question to ask here is: Is our informant an intelligent man? Another way to ask this is: If a machine had produced these answers, would that machine be reasonably judged to be intelligent? The answer to this question strikes at the heart of what we have been discussing here.

My claim is that storytelling strongly reflects intelligence. Telling a good story at the right time is a hallmark of intelligence. One right time is when you are asked a question. Another right time is when someone says something to you and you respond with a relevant story. To be able to tell stories at the right time one must either be very lucky, have very few stories to tell and only be in circumstances where those stories are relevant, or else one must have a massively indexed memory, reflecting nuances of difference between stories and allowing one to detect those differences in examining the inputs that one is processing. Knowing a great deal about a subject means being able to detect differences that will reflect themselves in differences in indexing. In other words, intelligence depends upon clever indexing.

Our expert is intelligent about military history. He sees nuances where others would not. He analyzes new stories well enough to be able to relate them to old stories that might not obviously be the same. He can see military stories in a variety of different ways because he has created for himself a set of complex indices about military history. A machine that used those indices would seem quite intelligent. But we probably would not want to grant it real intelligence until it had made up those indices for itself. No one teaches us how to index, after all. We make up our own way of seeing the world, following generally accepted parameters, of course. Intelligence implies the creation and use of indices.

□ 5 □

Shaping Memory

□

WHY, when something important happens to you, do you feel compelled to tell someone else about it? Even people who are reticent to talk about themselves can't help telling others about events significant to them. It's as if nothing has happened until an event is made explicit in language.

We have mulled over this question in our lab from time to time, but not until our work on stories did an answer begin to take shape. Why do we tell stories? We have discussed a variety of reasons in earlier chapters. However, we can find an additional explanation by considering the well-known expression "How can I know what I think until I hear myself talk?" We often talk in order to tell about, comment upon, and analyze our own personal experiences. Imagine, for example, that you have just returned from a vacation or that you meet someone who knows that you have recently been on a date that you were especially looking forward to. In either of these situations, when you are asked how it went, you can respond with a short pithy sentence or two, or you can begin to tell a story that captures the essential parts of the experience.

Now imagine that another person asks you substantially the same question. How different is your second story likely to be from the initial story? Of course, the time you have to tell the story or differences in intimacy with the person you tell it to may affect the telling, but the likelihood is that, on a gross level, the subsequent stories you tell will leave out and emphasize the same things. The stories will be, from a gist point of view, substantially the same. In other words, while telling about a trip to a great restaurant, if you don't tell about the lovely park where you ate lunch, the park episode will eventually cease to be part of the story.

The process of story creation, of condensing an experience into a story-size chunk that can be told in a reasonable amount of time, is a process that makes the chunks smaller and smaller. Subsequent iterations of the same story tend to get smaller in the retelling as more details are forgotten. Of course, they occasionally get larger when fictional details are added. Normally, after much retelling, we are left with exactly the details of the story that we have chosen to remember. In short, story creation is a memory process. As we tell a story, we are formulating the gist of the experience which we can recall whenever we create a story describing that experience.

We need to tell someone else a story that describes our experience because the process of creating the story also creates the memory structure that will contain the gist of the story for the rest of our lives. Talking is remembering. It seems odd, at first, that this should be true. Certainly, psychologists have known for years that rehearsal helps memory. But telling a story isn't rehearsal, it is creation. The act of creating is a memorable experience in itself.

In order to remember an experience, then, we must tell it to someone. If we don't tell the story soon enough after the experience or often enough immediately after the experience or if we don't tell the story at all, the experience cannot be coalesced into a gist since its component pieces begin to mix with new information that continues to come in. We cannot remember a great restaurant if we keep eating in ones quite like it day after day.

In other words, while parts of the experience may be remembered in terms of the memory structures that were activated—a restaurant may be recalled through cues having to do with food or with a place or with the particular company—the story itself does not exist as an entity in memory. Thus, without telling a story, any generalization that might pertain to the whole of the experience would get lost. We could remember the restaurant, but we might forget that the entire trip had been a bad idea. We might be able to reconstruct generalizations about the trip as a whole, but this process would require doing exactly what one would have had to do in the first place. That is, reconstruction with an eye toward generalizations creates gists which are then relayed as stories. In other words, we tell stories in order to remember them.

The opposite side of the coin is also true. We fail to create stories in order to forget them. When something unpleasant happens to us, we often say "I'd rather not talk about it" because not talking makes it easier to forget. Once you tell what happened to you, you will be less able to forget the parts of the story that you told. In some sense, telling a story makes it happen again. If the story is not created in the first place, however, it will only exist in its original form, i.e., in a form distributed among the mental structures used in the initial processing. Thus, in the sense that it can be reconstructed, the experience remains. When the experience was a bad one, that sense of being in memory can have annoying psychological consequences. If we encounter a particular setting or prop, unhappy remindings may well occur when not expected.

When you begin to tell a story again that you have retold many times, what you retrieve from memory is the gist of the story itself. An old man's story that he has told hundreds of times shows little variation, and what variation exists becomes part of the story itself regardless of its origin. People add details to their stories that may or may not have occurred. Why should they be able to remember? They are recalling gists and reconstructing details. If, at some point they add a nice detail, not really certain of its validity, telling that story with that same detail a few more times will insure its permanent place in the story gist. In other words, the stories we tell time and again are identical to the memory we have of the events that the story relates. Stories change over time because of the process of telling, because of the embellishments added by the teller. The actual events that gave rise to the story in the first place have long since been forgotten.

But what about a story that is told for the first time? After it has been told once, what is remembered: the story or the events behind the story? Why is it impossible to remember anything that you haven't told someone else?

Let's imagine a day in the life of a man living alone in a city. He works by himself and for himself. He sees and talks to no one about his particular experiences during the course of one day. He gets a haircut. He buys some groceries. He shops for new shoes. He fills out tax forms at home and watches some television. At work, he reads some material that has been sent to him, but he writes down nothing about that material. The next day he resumes a more normal life, interacting with people and talking about his experiences, but for some reason he never speaks to anyone about the day we have just described. Now, the question is, what can he remember about that day?

The answer to this is complex because we don't know two things. First, how unusual is this day for him? And, second, how much rehearsal has occurred? Let me explain why each of these questions matters.

What makes an event memorable is both its uniqueness and its significance to you personally. For example, we easily remember the first time we do anything of significance. So if this man has never spent a day alone or if he was deliberately trying out such a life-style, he would probably remember the day. Or would he?

At first glance, it seems probable that he would remember such a unique or significant day; therefore, how easily can we imagine the man never telling anyone about it? If people are incapable of not telling others about significant events, then this man, too, feeling that the day was important, would be likely to mention it to some-one.

This brings up the question of rehearsal. One phenomenon of memory is that people talk to themselves, not necessarily aloud of course, but they do tell themselves stories, collecting disparate events into coherent wholes. So let's imagine that, while this man talked to no one about his day, he did talk to himself. What might he have said? If rehearsal entails storytelling, he would have had to compose a story with some pertinent generalizations or observations drawn from the day. Moreover, he would have had to keep retelling himself that story in order to remember it.

What happens if he fails to tell anyone, including himself, about his day? Does he fail to recognize the grocery store where he shopped when he sees it again next week? Does he fill out his tax forms again? Must he reread the material that was sent to him at work? Of course not.

Obviously, we can remember events that we have not discussed with anyone. But how? How are events like going to the grocery store remembered? Certainly such events never become stories, so they are not maintained in memory by repeated telling. How, then, are they maintained? The answer is that memory has two separate capacities often referred to by psychologists as the semantic-episodic memory distinction. This distinction, however, misses the point considerably.

Psychologists have long noted that memory must be organized hierarchically because certain information seems to be stored around general concepts that help us understand more subordinate concepts. So for example, if someone asks whether a flounder has gills, you can easily answer without ever having considered the question before, and, more important, without actually having that information in your memory at all. All you need to know is that a flounder is a fish and that fish have gills. Similarly, you know that a Buick has wheels because it is a car and that a female horse has teats because it is a mammal. The idea behind semantic memory is simply that this kind of information is shared hierarchically. We store the information that female mammals have teats and infer that therefore horses have teats because they are mammals. Clearly, people must have information organized at least to some extent in this way because they know a great deal more than they have ever actually experienced.

An episodic memory, on the other hand, would be one in which we stored actual events that have occurred in our own lives. So, visiting Grandma's house on Thanksgiving is an episode in memory. Such episodes don't seem to be organized hierarchically. Are *Grandma visits on Thanksgiving* stored under *visits to relatives, holiday get-togethers,* or *wild parties I have attended*? Or have so many *Grandma visits on Thanksgiving* become a central category of their own? And, if so, what would the creation of such a category mean? Would it mean that the answer to what you ate that day was always turkey? It would if what you ate *were* always turkey, but the time that you ate duck instead might be remembered as well.

The distinction between semantic and episodic memory is a matter of some debate to psychologists largely because the issues are not at all well defined. A neatly organized hierarchy of semantic concepts is easy to imagine, but the world is full of oddities and idiosyncratic events that fail to fit neatly into a preestablished hierarchy. For example, we may "know" from semantic memory that female horses have teats, but we may more readily access this fact from an episodic store if we witnessed our pet horse giving birth and then suckling its young. Our first memories of playing ball may very well come to mind when the word "ball" comes up, and the properties we ascribe to "ball" may well be ones that a particular ball we remember actually had. In short, the nature and structure of memory remains at the frontiers of research.

A more useful distinction can be drawn between story-based memory on the one hand and a generalized event-based memory on the other. To understand this distinction, let's go back to the question of where our hero's grocery store, tax-form-filling, and reading experiences are stored in his memory.

We know that he can recall what he did in each instance, so how is this ability to recall different from his ability to tell a story? Probably he cannot tell the story of his day, while he can recall certain aspects of his day. This difference reflects itself in a kind of abstract idea of "place" in memory.

To "recall" the grocery store visit means he knows he has been there. Had something interesting happened there, especially something that taught him something new about the operation of grocery stores, for example, we can feel sure that he would remember it. But how can we make this assertion when he probably won't be able to recall this day if he never talks about it to anyone? We seem to have a paradox here, but in fact we do not.

When people have an experience in a grocery store, they update their knowledge of grocery stores. If this were not the case, people would never learn where the milk was or how much things cost or when to take out their check cashing card or whatever. When these things change, people change along with them. Sometimes it takes a few trials—they still look for the milk where it used to be, but eventually changes in memory follow changes in reality. So people learn from their experiences, but where does this learning take place in the mind?

People need a file of information about grocery stores that includes specific information about where their favorite grocery store keeps the milk and what it wants from them in order to cash a check. This file must also include general information about grocery stores apart from their favorite, however. When we enter a new grocery store, we want to be able to use expectations about our favorite store that will help us in the new one. For example, we want to predict that the milk will be near the cottage cheese in any grocery store and that a new one might not take our check. In other words, we are constantly drawing upon our file of knowledge about grocery stores and adding to that knowledge when new experiences teach us something worth retaining.

What we are decidedly not doing, however, is updating our memories on what we might call a daily unit basis. That is, we are not making note that on October 16, we bought a quart of milk and six oranges. We could try to do this, of course, but we would have to try very hard. We might make up a poem about what we bought on that day and then memorize the poem, for example. But if we do not take some extreme measure like that, we will simply fail to remember the experience unless something rather strange or important occurred at the same time. Why can't we remember what we bought in the grocery store on October 16, 1982?

Humans are intelligent rememberers. We remember an experience to add to a storehouse of knowledge that might be useful later on.

We are looking for knowledge that tells us something about the nature of the world in general.

This storehouse of knowledge is analogous to the psychologist's notions of semantic memory: that we must have a way to store knowledge so that it can be used again next time, knowledge that teaches us about the world in general, knowledge that is rather similar from human being to human being. Although this notion that a part of memory should be devoted to such general knowledge seems inherently correct, the notion seems equally wrong that such knowledge would not have at its core a seriously idiosyncratic component. We may all know that a flounder is a fish and that a fish has gills, but we do not all know that our father used to eat flounder every Tuesday, and therefore, so did we, and we refuse to eat it ever again. Yet, this latter fact is just as much a part of the definition of flounder for us as is the fact that a flounder has gills—maybe more, since one fact is far more real to us than the other.

Any general storehouse of knowledge, then, is likely to depend very strongly upon the expectations about various objects and situations that have been gathered over a lifetime of experience. Thus, when a new experience occurs that speaks to what we already know about something, perhaps updating it, perhaps overriding it, we add that experience to our memories. This is why we remember filling out the tax form. We add the experience of filling out the tax form to our general storehouse of similar experiences. That experience then becomes part of our general knowledge of tax form filling and updates what we already know.

Similarly, when we read something, the facts we garner from our reading go to particular places in memory, to the structures we have that are repositories of information about those subjects. Information about restaurants updates what we already know about restaurants, stories about travel to exotic places cause our memory to add new information about those places to existing knowledge about those particular places and to general information we may have about exotic places. Of course, the actual updating of knowledge structures is much more complex than this. In *Dynamic Memory* I discussed how pieces of memory structures, once altered, updated those same pieces as instantiated in other structures. Thus, for example, if you learn something about paying with credit cards in a restaurant, that new information needs to update how to pay in a department store and at an airport as well. The way this happens is through sharing of standardized smaller knowledge structures of which "paying" would be one, and "credit card paying" would be another even smaller structure.

Through such structures, and through the sharing of smaller structures by larger structures, we build up generalizations about the world. Every time we use a particular body of knowledge in our interactions with the world, that knowledge gets altered by the experience. We cannot fill out a tax form without using the prior experiences we had in filling out tax forms as a guide to help us through the experience. But because that knowledge is being used as a guide, it changes. We add new information about tax forms, about the experience of filling them out, that overrides what we previously knew. When we are finished doing anything, therefore, our memories are altered by the experience. We don't know what we knew before.

One consequence of this dynamic nature of memory is that, because actual experiences are constantly being broken up into their component pieces and are being added to general event memory bit by bit in different places, no coherent whole remains. Breaking up our daily experiences into their component parts is terribly important. If we did not, we would never learn anything cross-contextually. Let me explain.

Suppose that you had trouble paying your bill at the doctor's office. You went to a new doctor, one you had never seen before, and he asked you to pay him at the end of the visit. You were surprised by this as you expected him to send a bill, so you offered him your credit card. He looked at it, handed it to his nurse, but later came back saying he had to have cash. You paid him all you had with you. The next day, however, when you went to pay for a purchase at a local store, you realized that you had lost your credit card.

Memory has to be constructed so that, at the very least, you have updated your store of knowledge: The next time you visit this doctor, you must remember to bring enough cash; the next time you visit any doctor for the first time you must recall this incident so that you will have both the cash and the memory available to test whether your generalization—new doctors demand cash—is correct. Moreover, the next time you visit any professional office for a one-time visit, you will do the same. The visit to the doctor will have been added to what you know about paying by credit card so that whenever you consider where you might have left your credit card, this incident will come to mind.

Learning from experience, then, means learning a great many different kinds of things. Whole experiences must be broken up and analyzed in order to learn from them and to place the new information that has been learned where it can be found later when needed. In this incident, we need to learn things about paying and things about doctors, both at a specific and general level. Therefore, in order to find these things when we need them, this visit to the doctor must be decomposed into its many component pieces and added to the storehouse of information associated with those pieces in memory.

We should not imagine that this acquisition and storage of new information is in any way conscious, of course. When a doctor asks for cash, we don't think, *How odd, I'll have to remember this incident as an example of an augmentation of expectations in the professional office visit script.* Rather, we consciously note the oddity, and our memory takes care of the rest, updating and altering expectations in a variety of places in memory that might need this new information. We will not be surprised a second time when a doctor asks for cash. In addition, that lack of surprise means our expectations have been altered in a variety of different places as well: expectations about credit cards, payments in general, doctors, professional office visits, and so on. Our mind unconsciously decides what expectations this new event relates to and updates those expectations, searching for them in a variety of places in memory.

The process of updating our general knowledge base every time we have a new experience that relates to an aspect of that knowledge base has an odd side effect, however. The construction of a memory that organizes information around generalized events destroys the coherence between the particular instantiation of those events. The dynamic nature of the general knowledge base that comprises memory causes the experiences of walking to be placed with prior ones of walking, those of shopping to be placed together with others of shopping, and so on. Constant updating of a memory for events in general, one that houses expectations about what happens in various situations in general, causes a general storehouse about typical events to be built up by destroying the connectivity of one particular event to another particular event. A particular event of walking, therefore, becomes disconnected from its intended purpose of enabling one to go shopping at one particular time, for example, thus rendering our hero useless when asked how he got to the grocery store. His only recourse is to make an educated guess: *I must have walked; it's not far, and I usually walk if it's a nice day, and it was June after all.*

Because of this need of memory to effect a constant disconnection of events from those that follow, we feel a need to undo this process when something of significance occurs. We can stop the dynamic disconnection from taking place and remember events in sequence by consciously giving our memories an event to remember that is a unit, specifically, a unit that we have rehearsed, sometimes frequently. In this process, the role of stories in memory comes into play, and hence the concept of *story-based memory* arises. Stories are a way of preserving the connectivity of events that would otherwise be disassociated over time. One reason we tell stories, therefore, is to help ourselves in remembering them.

For stories to be told without a great deal of effort, they must be stored away in a fashion that enables them to be accessed as a unit. If this were not the case, stories would have to be reconstructed each time they were told, a process that would become more and more difficult with time as a particular event faded from memory. Telling a story would require a great deal of work to collect all the events from memory and to reconstruct their interrelation. Further, stories would be quite different each time they were told. Reconstruction would not be the same each time, and instead, different stories would result depending upon what parts of memory were looked at during the time of telling. This kind of storytelling does occur, of course, especially when stories are being told for the first time, but most storytelling requires so little work and is so repetitive, each version so much like the other, that many stories must be stored and re-trieved as chunks.

A different type of memory process, then, must be active here. Our hero who fails to tell one or more stories from his isolated day will understand and remember what has happened to him in the sense that the facts will be available to him. But they will be available to him only when the various segments of his day are accessed for some reason, when someone asks him about his favorite grocery store, for example. What he will lose is the ability to tell a story about that particular day. The day will disappear as a unit from memory, as will various aspects of the day. In other words, events of the day will no longer be accessible by asking oneself about what happened today, but after a while can only be found in the other parts of memory which will have subsumed them. What is remembered, then, will be in terms of what one knows about grocery stores, not a story in and of itself arising from the events of that day. To find that kind of story in memory, one must have put it there consciously in the first place, either by telling it to somebody or to oneself.

Story-based memory, then, is a different kind of memory from the memory that contains general world knowledge. Story-based knowl-edge expresses our points of view and philosophy of life and, as it comes from experiences, is closer in spirit to what psychologists have meant when they have spoken of episodic memory. Story-based memory, however, depends upon telling and gets built up by telling. The consequences of this process are interesting when one considers what we tell and why since we are, quite unconsciously, making decisions about what to remember.

Sharing Stories

But what if you have no one to talk to? In the view of storytelling and memory proposed here, the accuracy and extent of childhood memories depends upon having someone to tell one's stories to at the time of occurrence and having someone who shares those stories who will understand when you refer to them throughout life. One prediction, then, is that an only child might have less vivid childhood memories for things that one cannot easily discuss with one's parents but might have more vivid memories if the parents were the sort that discussed everyday events in great detail. Two siblings of the same sex and of similar ages who were not rivals might have the best memories of all.

This same view of storytelling as memory has its effect in the area of divorce as well. When a couple is divorced, their shared stories might tend to disappear, there being no one to reinforce those memories over time. One of the horrors of divorce is the sense of loss that one feels. Part of that feeling of loss is explainable by the actual loss of memory that continues to worsen over time.

The opposite side of this coin is illustrated by friendship between people of the same sex. In what is often called "bonding," people swap stories of their various escapades that make the escapades more real, more important, and more memorable in the telling. Knowing that someone knows your stories gives them a reality apart from your own mind. The events become real as you tell them and assume that someone else remembers them, which in turn enables you to refer to them from time to time and thus to reinforce their existence. Clearly, memory over a lifetime is very affected by whom you talk to and whether you keep talking to them.

Dreaming

An interesting aspect of storytelling is the telling of dreams. Here again, we seem to have a tremendous need to tell others dreams that were especially frightening, exciting, or confusing. Why the need to tell them? Given what we have already said about why people tell stories, this problem seems to have two aspects. First, telling the dreams is a way of attempting to remember them. Certainly, without telling them to others, remembering dreams becomes quite difficult since they simply retreat into the morass of unexamined memories. In fact, the only alternative method of remembering them would seem to be telling them to oneself, either by writing them down or rehearsing them verbally in one's head.

A second interesting aspect revolves around the fact that, as dreams often fail to make a lot of sense in the usual view of that term, telling them forces a kind of coherence on them. This coherence tends to distort the original dream and to make it more storylike than it originally was. By reconsidering the dream more cogently, the teller must, in part, interpret the dream. The telling, then, is a kind of evaluation that enables one to think about the dream in a new way. Thus, for dreaming at least, the creation and telling of stories is a vital part not only of memory but also of critical thinking processes.

But this question has another side, of course. What if the dream was a bad one, a nightmare? In this case, we might ask what is the good of telling it? The standard answer is that getting it out verbally can be cathartic. We need to tell nightmares to someone close to us so that we can make sense of them and reassure ourselves that they were only dreams. Recognizing what we have said about stories, however, we may have another aspect of dreaming to consider.

If the telling of a dream makes it into a story, then, telling also makes the dream more memorable. Thus, in telling a nightmare, we open the possibility of remembering the nightmare as a coherent unit. This remembering would have both a good and a bad effect. The bad effect is fairly obvious; namely, we now have a story that is unpleasant in memory. The good effect is somewhat less apparent and depends upon our conception of memory.

In *Dynamic Memory* we proposed a theory of memory composed of Memory Organization Packages or MOPs. A MOP covers a context-dependent aspect of memory, such as taking a trip or going on a date. Any MOP is composed of a set of scenes, each of which covers visually defined boundaries that might occur in a variety of different MOPs, such as the waiting room scene that can occur in the doctor visit MOP as well as in the lawyer visit MOP. In this view of memory, episodes that occur get stored in terms of the scene in which they took place and can be connected to the larger context by reconstruction.

A dream might take place in many scenes. Recalling part of a dream, therefore, would depend upon activation of a scene in which the dream took place. Thus, new information about restaurants that came from a dream might be indistinguishable from information on restaurants that came from real episodes. For example, if a monster bit you while you were riding in a train, that episode would be stored in terms of the scene of railroad car riding. In a normal situation, we would have to reconstruct a coherent memory piece that would allow us to recall that this had taken place during a visit to Aunt Martha. In attempting to put this episode in memory as a dream, this same reconstruction would have to be done. In other words, reconstruction ties the scenes together to make a coherent whole. But reconstructing dreams is very hard to do after sufficient time has elapsed. Reconstruction relies upon principles of coherency, and dreams are often incoherent.

The story creation process is a reconstructive process whose end result is a new memory entity that can be stored as a unit independent of the original scenes. Now in most cases the new story probably creates a kind of redundant memory. We should, in theory, be able to go back to the original sources and to reconstruct a new story; but, in fact, most episodes get lost over time. We don't recall every time we were in a waiting room. We recall only odd events that may have taken place in a waiting room. The normative events get mushed together to form processing structures that help us know what to expect the next time we enter a waiting room. Nevertheless, we can, and do, remember odd occurrences that took place in a waiting room.

This latter feature of memory, the ability to recall exceptions to our normal processing expectations in a scene, causes us to get reminded of prior experiences when we reenter a similar situation. Although this feature of memory has many positive benefits, especially enabling the ability to learn and to modify your expectations, it can have an important negative effect: You may get frightened upon reentry into a scene because something bad comes to mind. Being frightened is not too terrible if you know why you are frightened, that is, if you can recognize precisely what the memory is that was stored in that scene. But sometimes you can be frightened without knowing why. To use our example, trains may frighten you because you had a nightmare about being bitten by a monster on a train.

To get back to our original point, then, telling the story of the monster on the train would make that story more memorable. Therefore, one positive effect of constructing this story would be to render any future undifferentiated fears less likely. The story would remain in memory to make recognizable the source of the fear about riding in trains. So even when the story is bad in some way, story creation can have a value if it helps to identify new information about a given subject as having come from a dream and not from reality.

Many people have posed the question about why we dream at all. The major player in this issue was, of course, Freud. Freud observed strong sexual feelings in both his male and female patients at a time when women were perceived as immune from such drives. Freud came to the conclusion that many of the memories of his patients were, in fact, fantasies that had become real and that two levels of reality exist: objective reality and psychological reality. For any individual, psychological reality is as potent a force as perceptions of objective reality. His patients, thus, were suffering from a conflict between their conscious minds and the irrational forces of their unconscious. Freud saw dreams as the means to communicate with these forces and as the link between the conscious and the unconscious.

A simplified model of Freudian theory posits that humans are animals with instincts, but these instincts conflict with the requirements of the society we live in. The conflicts that arise are repressed but remain in the unconscious and continue to reveal their power particularly in dreams when the conscious mind is vulnerable in sleep. Freud believed, then, that the purpose of dreaming was to preserve the state of sleep and to keep the ego from understanding the message of the dream. As a result, dreams disguise any threatening messages likely to wake the sleeping person.

Clinical experiments indicate that everyone dreams and that the number of dream periods people experience is the same. What differs, however, is people's ability to recollect dreams. Investigators refer to two categories of individuals—recallers and nonrecallers. Ann Faraday points out in *Dream Power* (New York: Coward, McCann, and Geoghegan, 1972), that nonrecallers need a stronger stimulus to wake them up than recallers; therefore, nonrecallers must sleep more deeply than recallers. Recallers, then, are those who wake up more often during the night and, consequently, remember more dreams in the process of waking. Nonrecallers, however, also tend to have duller, blander dreams—perhaps dreams that are more difficult to remember than the more interesting dreams of recallers. Moreover, nonrecallers share certain personality traits. Nonrecallers are likely to be more inhibited and conventional than recallers; the reluctance of nonrecallers to remember dreams seems to parallel their denial of negative experiences in daily life. Faraday asserts that "nonrecallers banish or repress dreams from conscious memory because they contain distressing wishes and thoughts and [nonrecallers] are afraid of what interpretation might reveal."

Another interesting aspect of forgetting dreams concerns volunteer subjects who normally recall dreams at home but who are resistant to remember their dreams in a laboratory setting. Faraday believes their anxiety arises from the fear that their dreams will reveal too much to themselves or to the experimenter.

Similarly, repression also plays a part in the forgetting of a once-remembered dream. Faraday recounts how Freud recalled that when awaking from a dream he set about interpreting it immediately, but in the morning he sometimes had forgotten both the dream and his interpretation although he remembered having had a dream and having interpreted it. Freud also observed that many of his patients in the process of telling about a dream suddenly recalled forgotten incidents in the dream. Freud asserted that these "forgotten" parts were the most significant to understanding the dream.

Researchers such as Faraday and Witkin and Lewis have found that writing down a dream if one is awakened in the middle of the night will help catch the dream. Freud, on the other hand, believed that writing down the dream set the forces of repression to work. Interestingly, those subjects asked before sleep to try to remember their dreams the next morning remembered more dreams than those who were not instructed to do so. What are the implications of these findings for the purpose of this discussion?

From the point of view of a dynamic memory, dreaming would appear to play the role of expectation validation. When we experience something new, we need, as I have said, to update the relevant memory structures. Updating our memories about how doctor's office visits tend to proceed is not especially interesting stuff. Nevertheless, how certain can we be about this new expectation that we have added to memory? Are all doctors suddenly going to expect all patients to pay in cash? Maybe it's just you who will always have to pay in cash? Maybe no one trusts you anymore.

We seek explanations of odd behaviors precisely because we need to update our expectations about what will happen next. If we explain the new event by the fact that this doctor doesn't trust first-time visitors who are not expected to return, then we can create expectations accordingly. On the other hand, if we feel it's the clothing we wore, we can alter our behavior or update our expectations for when we wear that clothing again. In either case, we must explain to ourselves what is going on.

We know, however, that our explanations are really only hypotheses. We cannot be certain that these hypotheses will ultimately turn out to be correct. And we do not, of course, want to cast into stone an expectation that we have garnered from one experience. So what do we do? One possibility is to think about our expectation. This solution presents two problems. First, we are not always aware of the expectations that we have just decided upon. Expectation creation, as I have said, is by and large not a conscious process. How can we carefully examine something we do not know that we did? Sometimes, of course, we are aware that new events have had an effect on us. We can think out the consequences of decisions that we have made, for example, or we can imagine what it would be like to travel someplace if the expectations that we have are realistic and if things can conceivably turn out as we would like. In other words, when we have the time and inclination and when we are conscious of our expectations, we can test them in a dry run to see whether they are consistent, sensible, and, in the case of plans, workable.

Dreaming performs precisely this role for memory when it is not possible, for whatever reason, to test expectations consciously. One of the primary reasons is, of course, that most of the time we are unaware of the expectations we have newly acquired. To put this another way, evidence from REM sleep strongly suggests that animals dream. If we are not inclined to grant animals consciousness, we can safely assume that, if animals are testing out expectations, they are not aware of their expectations. So as we acquire expectations throughout the day, we need to check them out, to see whether they disagree strongly with previously acquired expectations, for example, or to see whether the consequences of certain actions that we now expect are altogether desirable.

To perform this expectation check, the mind seems able to run simulations of various situations without regard to serious reality checks. In other words, if the primary issue is to check whether a set of expectations is valid or the consequences of a plan are desirable, one need not be too concerned with whether the simulations that are run to check them out are very realistic. If the person for whom a new expectation is most apt is dead, why not bring him to life? If he needs to get somewhere in a hurry, letting him fly is okay. One reason why realism is of little importance here is that so much more can be accomplished without it. Let me give you an example.

When my son was in the eighth grade, he was editor in chief of his school newspaper. He told me the following dream that he had: Keith Hernandez, the first baseman for the New York Mets, enrolled in his school. My son felt obligated to offer him the job of editor in chief, because my son idolizes Keith Hernandez. Hernandez took the job but did not run the paper at all, allowing my son to continue running it. All in all, my son was pleased with this outcome.

My son asked me about what this dream meant. I asked if there was someone he admired that he wanted to get to work on the paper and he responded that his best friend had been talking to him about the paper and that he did want him to get involved but he didn't know in what capacity. He was worried about who should work for whom since he respected his friend's writing ability a great deal.

So why did my son select Keith Hernandez in his dream rather than his friend? One possibility is that his need was to think about how to deal with someone he respected a great deal and, when he asked his memory to provide such a character for his dream, his memory found someone for whom the respect was complete, making clear that the real problem was how to deal with someone he respected. After all, his friend was someone whom he respected only a little in comparison to Keith Hernandez. Further, the issues were much more clear-cut with Hernandez; they had no other relationship to complicate matters. The dreaming thus allowed a simplified view of the expectations in the situation. Such extremes cause the expectations that are being tested to be really tested. In this way, generalizations that are drawn from the dreams may be more significant than just serving as solutions for immediate problems. My son was, after all, trying to solve a problem that he knows will come up again in a different form on another day.

The important thing is to check out the performance of relevant expectations that you may be using for many years to come. If you are concerned about how you might behave under adverse conditions, then a dream allows you to create those conditions and find out. Dreams are simulations, ready to be run any given night. If you are concerned about your real feelings toward someone, your expectations about how you will act and how you think he will act are reasonable to check out. Dreaming seems such a good idea for memory that to imagine computers equipped with dynamic memories but unable to dream seems almost ridiculous. How would they know whether their most important expectations were right? You can't always wait for the occurrence of actual events that happen to relate to yesterday's expectations.

But dreaming has a hazard connected with it. Why should we assume that dreams are processed any differently by memory than actual events? When a sequence of actions occurs in a dream, these actions have been created from memory and then must be comprehended and stored away in memory in a new form. The sequence of events that comprise the dream are understood no differently than a sequence of events in the real world. In each case these events must be comprehended and stored away in memory. What is the difference? In each case, we have events that need to be understood, and, therefore, in each case relevant pieces of events will need to be related to the events in memory that most closely match them. And, in each case, those pieces will be integrated into memory as updates on prior expectations. Thus, memory, in testing out expectations, also creates expectations.

How does memory know the difference between reality and fantasy? In fact, it doesn't. Since the role of most dreams is to check out expectations already in memory, and since we acquire these expectations from reality, our conclusion, although perhaps derived from fantasy, is rooted in the mind's conception of reality. In other words, when we test out an expectation by dreaming it, we either conclude that it was right and thus incorporate it more firmly in our memories, or else we decide to exclude it from what we know. Either way, the input was from reality, and the end result was our own version of reality.

Dreams, however, as we all know, can take on some very unrealistic forms. Or, perhaps more important, dreams can relate to things that are quite realistic that our memories might want to record in the memory store, but dreams, of course, only chronicle mental (and fictitious) events. In those cases, separating fantasy from reality can be quite important. Certain dream events are obviously fantasy, but others are close enough to reality that we need to reexamine them when we wake. You wouldn't want to assume intimacy with someone you had been intimate with only in your dreams, for example. You might want to check out your expectations about your interest in and desire for such intimacy, however. So while dreaming can be useful, it can be hazardous as well.

So where does storytelling come in? As we have noted, telling a story tends to make a unit of a sequence of events, and this unit can be remembered more easily. On the other hand, failing to create this unit is simply likely to leave its individual pieces in memory disconnected from their preceding and following events. So we are left with a paradox. Telling a story that is derived from a dream tends to reinforce that dream as a memorable unit. Further, telling a dream as a story forces a coherence on that story. On the other hand, not telling the story causes the events in that story to be remembered just as if they had happened, which can be psychologically confusing on occasion.

Under this view, the value of telling one's dreams is clear enough. We tell dreams in order to ensure that we understand the events in them—first, as dreams, and second, as personal stories that allow us to think about and reevaluate the dream material. But more important, telling dreams separates their content from memory, allowing us to see the elements that are fantasy as fantasies, not as realities. So we dream to test expectations, and we tell dreams to make sure that our expectations are realistic. The major value of telling dreams as stories is to prevent confusion, i.e., to remember the dream as a dream and to increase the likelihood of learning something from the dream.

When we cannot tell a dream, we forget it—we lose it as a memory unit. But we are likely to remember its component parts by storing them in various places in memory as if they were events that actually happened. In this case, we cannot consciously learn from the dream, but we can inadvertently learn from it. Unfortunately, this kind of learning by adapting existing knowledge structures does not easily allow us to separate dreams from reality. Dreaming is a double-edged sword.

Some Comments on Therapy

We have seen that the effects of telling stories can be alternately useful and destructive depending upon the situation. One such ambiguous situation is the therapeutic treatment of various psychological disorders by the means of conversation with a therapist. Let's look at the process of the psychoanalytic dialogue in light of what we have been saying here.

Of course, a variety of interactions take place in therapy. An important one is the telling of stories. Patients tell stories to therapists. Therefore, one question to ask is whether the telling of stories is of therapeutic value to a patient. When discussing the storytelling process in therapy, two clearly different types of storytelling behavior are worth noticing. One can tell new stories or old stories.

Human beings are collections of stories. They accumulate stories over a lifetime, and when they are given the opportunity, they select an appropriate story and tell it. They determine appropriateness by a variety of measures, primarily familiarity, emotion, the potential for shared viewpoint, and seeking approval. As we have seen, the gist of a story can be altered to use a story for a variety of different purposes. The stories we tell are strongly affected by whom we are telling them to. In any situation where we find ourselves telling an old story, we might reasonably wonder why we have chosen to tell a particular story. As we have seen, we have many reasons for telling a story.

In a therapeutic situation, patients are asked to tell stories that define themselves to the therapist. The process of selecting and telling stories to a therapist is not terribly different from selecting and telling stories to the person in the next seat on a long airplane flight. In either case, one must decide on the appropriateness of a given story, and one seeks the approval of the listener for the encouragement either to elaborate or to tell another story.

Listeners, then, perform a very important role for storytellers. Listeners reveal, usually implicitly, which stories they want to hear. They may like ones that show how important or powerful the teller is, or may think such stories are exaggerations or simply ought not to be told. They may want to learn some specific thing from the stories, or may simply want the storyteller to finish up so they can tell their own stories in response.

Therapists are also listeners, of course, and in many ways, they are rather typical listeners. They do not usually tell their own stories in response, but they, too, reward some stories and criticize others. They also do this implicitly, at times. Tellers have a sense of whether their stories are meeting with approval while they are telling them, and they can alter them during the telling to regain the attention or approval of the hearer. Thus, therapists who are especially interested in sexual stories, for example, are likely to get such stories from their patients by encouraging their telling.

The trick for any listener is to send out the right signals, those that encourage the telling of the stories that the listener wants to hear. Which stories, then, does a therapist want to hear?

In the selection and evaluation process, eliciting the listener's approval is very important. We want to please our listener, but pleasing is a fairly complicated idea. If we know that we are our listener's hero, we might tell stories about our successful exploits in the world. If we know that our listener admires sensitivity, we might alter our stories to reflect that sensitivity. In a therapeutic situation, we attempt, of course, to please the therapist. What pleases the therapist, however, may not be good for us in the long run.

For example, stories that indicate that we do not need a therapist's help would certainly not please the therapist. Therapists are unlikely to agree with this assertion, but they must certainly want their patients not only to have problems, but to have problems that they themselves feel competent to help with. Also, therapists, like any other people, tend to notice aspects of a story that interest them and to respond to those aspects while ignoring others. Interactive story-tellers, who tell their stories in parts while being interrupted by their listeners, alter their stories according to the interruptions. Thus, when listeners make it clear by their reactions that certain kinds of stories interest them more than others, tellers are likely to alter their stories accordingly. Tellers try to tell the stories their listeners want to hear. This process is as true of storytelling to therapists as it is of normal storytelling, maybe even more true.

The telling of one's old stories is a process not without conse-quences. The outside world determines which of our stories are worthy of telling by the way it listens to them. These stories then become our own definition of self. We are the stories we like to tell. If we surround ourselves with people who agree that certain kinds of stories are wrong to tell, clearly, we will tell those stories less frequently. Stories that make us feel good to tell need willing listen-ers if we want to feel good. Similarly, those stories that put the teller in a bad light may well find willing listeners, but the effects may be quite harmful in the long run. Being defined by a set of negative stories is deleterious to one's mental health.

New Stories

Of course, we don't only tell stories we have told before. Which events we choose to make part of our stories is important to how we define ourselves: When new stories are constructed for telling, the process of constructing those stories changes memory signifi-cantly. The storytelling process relies very heavily upon evaluation rules that tend to reflect very strongly one's view of the world, oneself, and the events that have occurred in one's life. Thus, two people might be expected to relate events quite differently depending upon their individual perspectives on what was worth telling, what was significant, what the listener was interested in, and what the events revealed about themselves. This last dimension alters the story composition process most profoundly. In order to tell a story that reflects well upon oneself, one might select quite different episodes to relate than if one wanted to tell the same event in a way that might lead the listener to feel sympathy.

The story composition process reflects very strongly the view that the teller has of himself combined with the view that he wants others to have of him. Any listener who really wants to know the person he is talking to, would, of course, want to hear the person's favorite stories. Similarly, any teller who really wants his listener to know him would want to tell his favorite stories. The more we desire intimacy, the more intimate the nature of the stories we tell. This pattern is true of the therapeutic situation, as well. For this reason, therapists want their patients to tell stories about the events in their lives. By listening to patients' stories, the therapist can see how these people view themselves. There is another side of the coin, however.

From the point of view of memory, the process of telling a story is significant because of the subprocess of composing the story that telling entails. In order to compose a story, one has to search memory for relevant episodes to relate and discard episodes that one chooses not to relate. Thus, the composition of a story requires both a search and an evaluative process that selects and discards items found during the search.

Once a story has been composed, it tends to stick around. As we have observed, when you tell the story of your vacation, you concentrate on certain details and leave out others; relating the same events in a different way becomes more and more difficult. Each subsequent telling of the story is likely to get shorter, and to enhance the second or third telling of a story so that it is much different from the first becomes much more difficult. Therefore telling—or more important, composing—stories affects memory profoundly. Memory tends to lose the original and keep the copy. The original events recede, and the new story takes its place.

Why does memory work in this way? The story composition process requires a great deal of work; therefore, repeating the process every time for each additional telling of the story is quite costly. Moreover, in a composed story the number of episodes to remember is much smaller than the number of original events themselves. Further, these episodes have a coherency to them that allows reconstruction of missing or loosely connected details. Remembering less is simply easier, especially if what we are trying to remember is all located in the same place in memory and we don't have to search for it again. A story, remembered as a story, is a unit that can be easily found, easily told, and be made useful for a variety of purposes.

On the other hand, collecting events from the various MOPs in which they were stored is a sloppy process at best. You might find something different each time. You would certainly lose information or at least fail to find it some of the time. Further, the attention to detail required would be staggering. It would never be safe to forget something just in case it might be found useful later. Retrieving an entire short story that is stored in only one place in memory is much simpler. It makes retrieval easier. It makes memory work less hard, it allows forgetting, and it provides a constancy of lessons to be learned that needn't be constantly reexamined.

In other words, memory works to preserve the way we first compose a story, i.e., to preserve our original viewpoint vis-à-vis the listener. To put this another way, if the first telling of a story reveals one's problems in dealing with a situation rather than showing oneself in the best possible light, we will remember the story that way.

Telling stories in a way that expresses our problems or our lack of ability to cope in the real world poses a serious hazard, then. Of course, therapists encourage exactly these kinds of stories. The questions *What is your problem?* or *What can I help you with?* or even a much more neutral *What did you want to talk about?* all elicit a story that reflects poorly on one's ability to cope. So the very telling of stories whose emphasis is negative reinforces the kinds of problems that therapy is supposed to address by adding new, negative stories to one's repertoire of stories.

To look at this from another vantage point, we can imagine that the storytelling aspect of therapy might work better if it were completely reversed. People who are encouraged to tell stories for the first time in a way that puts themselves in a positive light should begin to see themselves more positively as their memories fill with positive stories. So instead of telling one's troubles to someone who is likely to be sympathetic, our memories would be better served by being forced to tell only happy stories like those a father might tell a child. Telling one's troubles to a best friend or therapist may feel good, but we may need to worry about the long-range negative effect on our memories. In fact, some therapists do encourage patients to retell negative stories in a more positive way, but even these therapists cause yet another telling of the negative story.

Not Telling

At this point, we might reasonably ask what the effect of not telling a story might be. Suppose we have a bad experience. Is the best strategy to keep it quiet, to suppress it? Therapists would certainly argue that to suppress such an experience is a bad idea. What does the storytelling model of memory predict about suppression?

First, the model does *not* predict that leaving a bad episode in memory untouched and forgotten is a great idea. As we noted with the monster-on-the-train dream, fears can develop which will be associated with particular scenes in a MOP if a frightening episode is simply left in the scene in memory where it occurred. On the other hand, we have said that telling a bad story reinforces it in memory, making it easier to remember and more likely to be recalled. So which is it? To tell or not to tell?

The answer here is rather obvious actually. We tell stories in order to create records in memory that will coalesce a complex experience into a coherent whole. The story composition process creates that coherent whole which the storytelling process reinforces in memory. When a bad event that one does not want to dwell on occurs, we should tell someone about it, nevertheless, in order to start the composition process going. Recall that a side effect of the composition process allows memory to forget the details not collected in the composition: After composition, details not collected for the story become harder to remember than they would have been had no story been told at all.

Once the story has been composed and told, a memory structure is created, linked to the MOPs that were used, and the forgetting process begins. Of course, memory maintains the newly created story. But, and here is the key prediction, a story must be told fairly often to retain its status as a viable, that is, findable memory structure. In other words, if you have a bad experience, you should compose the story, tell it once, and never tell it again. The sooner you tell a story, the sooner you can begin to forget it—by never telling it again. If you want to remember the story, on the other hand, keep telling it. Telling stories is fundamentally a memory reinforcing process. The more you tell, the more you remember. The areas you dwell on when you talk are the areas your memory wants to, and does, reinforce.

Repression

What happens, however, when the negative story you want to tell has no listener available, but you can't stop thinking about it? Or, alternatively, what happens when a negative event occurs, no story is constructed at all, and the negative event doesn't actually disappear? Of course, we really do not understand a great many mental phenomena very well. High among these is what we commonly refer to as repression.

Sometimes we create stories that we never tell. These may be stories about why we are always doing something wrong, or they may be stories about dark events in our past that we don't really want to admit actually happened. Stories that remain untold have a variety of properties that differentiate them from more normal stories. The major difference is that certain incoherences are allowed to exist in untold stories. When we tell a story, we make sure it is both coherent and relevant to some point that might interest the listener. When we fail to tell a story, we don't need to examine the story for consistency or point. We can tell it to ourselves and reinforce it just as we might reinforce a story we actually tell by telling it; but, as we have said, our listener modifies our story by the very act of listening. Ordinarily, this modification does not occur for stories we tell only to ourselves. Here again, we see why it is important to tell one's stories. Therefore, if you can't easily forget disturbing events and insist on telling stories to yourself, you would be better off telling them to someone else, a therapist if need be.

The phenomenon of repression relies upon this idea of the un-wanted and untold story. When we have no one to tell a story to, we tend to bury it. It may well go away; indeed, without rehearsal, it should go away. Certain events, however, are too important to go away simply because we fail to tell their story. Stories about the grocery store will go away if we don't tell them partly because they are not so interesting or important and partly because we replace such stories with similar ones. But stories about significant episodes in our childhood, for example, do not go away so easily, partly because our childhood doesn't keep recurring, and partly because significant episodes are, by definition, different from the norm and thus unlikely to repeat. Episodes that define a situation will tend to remain in memory, looking for a repetition that will allow us to make the appropriate generalizations. Just as we need to know whether the doctor made us pay cash because of who we are, we need to know whether we have explained other unusual events correctly. But, we cannot easily check out our generalizations and explanations if the events we are concerned with don't replicate. Furthermore, child-hood explanations are childish. Since explanations are often the indices or labels for stories, bad explanations may not easily find another situation to match against.

Thus, untold stories tend to stick around when they are unique in some way, waiting for a similar story to occur to see whether gener-alizations can be made. If such stories are very negative stories and remain untold, they can indeed affect a person's thinking. Here again is an important use of therapy.

Nevertheless, the idea behind repression is probably wrong. Peo-ple are probably not consciously trying to repress a story. Rather, they are unconsciously trying to remember it so that they can match it to another story like it—should one ever occur. Usually, such a story is unlikely to occur on a conscious level; therefore, the memo-ries remain in various knowledge structures and will cause havoc from time to time. Thus, telling stories in such situations is quite therapeutic.

Some Comments on Therapists

Let's reverse this discussion a bit and look at the psychoanalytic dialogue from the point of view of the therapist. Given what we have said so far about storytelling and understanding, therapists must be very peculiar kinds of understanders. According to most psychiatric schools of thought, therapists are not supposed to tell their own stories; but if they cannot tell their own stories, how can they understand?

Psychoanalytic training emphasizes, in a sense, the suppression of the normal instinct to relate what you have heard to what you know from your own life. Therapists often try to relate what they have heard from the patient to what they have previously heard from the same patient. In other words, telling the patient one of his or her own stories is considered to be good psychiatric technique, especially if the previous story is at odds with the current story or in some way explains the current story.

Now, while this technique is probably a good one for the patient, what exactly does it do to the therapist? The learning processes of a therapist who behaves in this way must be quite strange. Learning, after all, depends upon clever indexing. One cannot compare one story to another—one cannot get reminded of one story by another—unless one has indexed them in a similar fashion. And what does this reminding buy? It buys generalizations. Seeing the similarity between two stories can cause us to recognize patterns of behavior that repeat themselves. The therapist knows this when reminding a patient of the patient's own similar stories. But in order to do this, the therapist must fail to be reminded, must actively inhibit, the recognition of similar situations in his or her own life. In other words, a therapist must actively avoid learning from the stories of patients.

Therapists do not do something that is quite natural to do, after all: They rarely tell one patient about the problems of another patient. Yet if therapists are thinking about their patients they should constantly notice parallels between patients and should use the situation of one patient to help him or her understand and make predictions about the situation of another. They must suppress this natural instinct, however. They can't say that the last time they heard anyone talk like that the person committed suicide. Certainly, in such a significant situation, a therapist is likely to be reminded of one patient by another. But, remember, the therapist is actively trying to suppress such remindings, and he or she does not dwell upon them nor tell about them, which is, after all, a way of understanding them better. Thus, during a therapy session, a therapist is suppressing the very instincts that would allow a greater understanding of a patient's situation in general. The therapist *is* attempting to gain insights into each patient in particular, but is unlikely to learn anything more cosmic in the process.

Can a nongeneralizing therapist do a good job? Of course. Some people need to hear themselves played back to themselves. They don't categorize or index their stories in such a way as to make useful generalizations or to recognize the repetitions of patterns. The therapist becomes, in a sense, their memory. He or she may use a different indexing scheme than the patient would have used, since indexing schemes are often quite idiosyncratic. Nevertheless, when someone else listens carefully to your stories, so carefully that he or she can play them back to you the way your own memory should have done, such a person can be quite helpful in providing insights into your own behavior simply by employing a different indexing scheme than you did.

Therapists become alter egos, so to speak—differently organized versions of what is ideally the same set of stories. For this service, two prices are paid—one by the patient and one by the therapist. In telling stories to the therapist, the patient is solidifying personal memories in a way that is being rewarded by what feels good to tell about and what the therapist rewards the patient for telling.

The price paid by therapists is being unable to learn globally from the totality of all the situations they encounter. As they compartmentalize the stories of each patient in their own memory box, not intertwined with the stories of the other patients or with their own stories, they lose perspective. The loss of insight into the human condition might be too heavy a price to pay for being a therapist precisely because therapists are in a unique position to attain such insights.

Self-Organizing Memories

A goal of computer scientists who worry about how to create artificial intelligence is the self-organizing memory. Certainly the hardest part of the creation of an intelligent entity is not finding information that it should know. We can easily figure out things to tell it. The problem is finding a way for the intelligent entity to know where to look in its own memory to find what is in there. One solution to this problem is the self-organizing memory. Scientists wouldn't have to decide where to put each piece of information in memory; rather, the memory would do the job itself. This idea seems fantastic yet also seems to beg the question. How would the system know where to put things itself? By and large, we don't know the answer to this, but we do know that people do this fantastic job quite naturally. Human memories self-organize. We don't consciously think about where to put the new experiences that we have each day. They simply find a happy home somewhere in memory. Moreover, we don't think about how to find them again; we just find them when we want them.

Actually, the problem isn't all that simple nor all that automatic. We do influence what gets put into memory, and we also influence how what is put into memory is retrieved. Retrieval depends upon how we view what we have experienced, what labels we have assigned to an experience while we are considering that experience. These twin powers—initial selection and initial viewpoint—determine what we know and how we can see the world through what we know. We remember, in this way, what we choose to remember and how we choose to remember it. Because of the need to tell stories and to hear our own stories as we tell them, what we remember and what we are able to remember determines who we are and determines how others see us. Human memory doesn't entirely self-organize. We control the process more than we realize. By labeling cleverly, we cause stories that would seem dissimilar to others to appear in our minds at the same time, thus enabling us to compare them and learn from them. Telling stories and, more important, creating stories to tell is an important part of the learning process and hence of the process of memory organization. We tell stories in order to make a conscious check on how memory organization is going. It helps us to find out what we are currently thinking when we tell a new story, what we used to think when we tell an old one, and what we think of what we think when we hear what we ourselves have to say.

□ 6 □

Story Skeletons

□

Communication via Stories

THE stories we tell each other, we also tell ourselves. This has the odd effect of causing us to see our own lives in terms of preestablished, well-known stories that can obscure the ways in which our actual situation differs from the standard story. Consider the following statement made by someone commenting upon the relationship of two friends of hers.

He used to admire her. She was a rising star in her profession, and he thought that she was terrific. He was willing to make sacrifices for her because he respected what she was doing. He made choices about having children, household chores, and his own career, based upon his attempt to let her be whatever she could be. He believed in the women's movement, and he believed in her. And then she betrayed him. She stopped caring about her career. She competed with him for the children's attention. She eventually gave up working altogether and spent her time jogging or hanging around in women's support groups. He is tremendously angry at her because he feels betrayed. What were all his sacrifices for—so she could goof off?

The teller of this story has decided that the marriage of her two friends was an example of a betrayal story. In effect, once she decided to see their situation as one of betrayal, she didn't need to see it any other way. Aspects of the relationship between the two people unrelated to betrayal, or that contradicted the notion of betrayal, were forgotten. Seeing a particular story as an instance of a more general and universally known story causes the teller of the story to forget the differences between the particular and the general. In this instance, the teller of the story can use the word "betrayal" as a very short story for telling on other occasions when time is more dear. In other words, the concept of betrayal becomes what she knows about this situation. It controls her memory of the situation so that new evidence of betrayal is more likely to get admitted into memory than contradictory evidence.

We have a great many words and phrases in English that are really the names of complex stories and thus serve to standardize particular situations. These words are stories or more accurately the names of stories. Although useful for telling stories quickly, they are very dangerous because we have standard sets of reactions to them. For example, we all believe that betrayal is bad. Is this relationship, however, an example of betrayal? Certainly, the teller relates the story so that betrayal is an accurate description. But betrayal was used as a skeleton story around which the actual story was constructed.

In other words, by using a skeleton story for betrayal, the teller could only construct a story of betrayal. All other aspects of the story were left out. But why, for example, could the teller not have told a story of "devotion?" Only small changes would be needed to make this a story of devotion—a statement that he still loves her and hopes she will return to her former self or one that shows he values and will support her in her role as mother. Often the truth or falsity of these additions is not so easy to determine. We cannot always know every aspect of a situation that we describe. This story could easily have been a devotion story if the teller had chosen to see it that way.

Thinking in terms of standard stories poses a serious danger, although doing otherwise is not so easy. We want to see the situations that we encounter in terms that are describable to others. We often have only a short time in which to tell these stories. So, even if the fit with those stories is not exact, seeing and describing complex situations in terms of standard stories provides an easy shorthand method for communication. But a problem can arise when we see our own lives that way. That is, if we react to our own situations by understanding them in terms of general standard stories, we can make some serious mistakes.

Cultural Norms in Language

Standard stories, like the *I Ching,* for example, have been around for centuries. We take the standard stories of our culture and interpret what happens to us in terms of such stories. In other words, often the stories we rely upon to help us reason and remember are not even our own. Knowing a culture means knowing the stories that the culture provides and observing how people interpret their own experiences and construct their own stories in terms of the standard stories of the culture.

The language of the culture also reflects the stories of the culture. One word or simple phrasal labels often describe the story adequately enough in what we have termed culturally common stories. To some extent, the stories of a culture are observable by inspecting the vocabulary of that culture. Often entire stories are embodied in one very culture-specific word. The story words unique to a culture reveal cultural differences.

When we describe a word or expression in one language as being untranslatable, the story to which the word refers is either unique to the culture that the language reflects, or else a well-known story exists in that culture to which that word refers. To explain the word in another language, however, would require telling the skeleton version of that story.

One of my favorite Yiddish words is *rachmones.* The most direct translation in English is "mercy" or "charity," but these words fall way short of expressing what *rachmones* means. A better translation might be expressed by the phrase "give me a break." But, best of all, we need to hear a skeleton story. *Rachmones* means being able to give somebody a break who may not really deserve it or to be charitable emotionally when hatred is called for. *Rachmones* means being kind at any time and in any way to those who need it.

Often, the best way to explain these "untranslatable" words is by a story. For example, a story I have often heard to explain the well-known Yiddish word "chutzpah," meaning "colossal gall," is this:

A boy who is mean and ill-tempered goes through years of fighting with his parents until finally one day he kills them both. He is brought to court and asked how he pleads. He states that he is guilty but that the court should have mercy on him since nobody cares for him because he is an orphan.

This story illustrates "chutzpah" better than any definition could.

If you did not know the meaning of "chutzpah" before, when someone now uses the word, you may be reminded of this story and can use it to understand what was meant. I have given you a story from which you can construct the skeleton version of the story that underlies "chutzpah."

Of course, what I have just done may seem rather artificial. People don't usually give you stories to illustrate the meanings of words; they give you dictionaries. Well, actually, this isn't entirely true. When we learn to speak our own language, we don't know how to read. Dictionaries are the province of the educated adult. When people learn to speak, they learn what each word means because they have heard the stories connected to these words first. Children learn complex words because these words are used to describe situations that they have observed or taken part in. When children are told that they have been "inconsiderate," they have no idea what that word means. They only know what they have done. In order to learn the word, they must construct a story that describes their own actions to themselves. Then, when they hear the word again, they must compare the former story with the new story that is unfolding before them. So they learn the skeleton story that underlies the word "inconsiderate" by comparing the two versions. In fact, we do learn the meaning of complex words through stories.

Understanding via Skeletons

This book is not about language but about stories: The key issue here is not how we learn to talk but how we learn to understand others. The understanding process, however, involves constantly misunderstanding one another to the extent that the words we use refer to skeleton stories that we don't quite agree upon. Consequently, my version of "inconsiderate" is probably different from yours. We almost certainly don't agree on what the word means.

Earlier, in discussing how conversation is the same as mutual reminding, I presented a conversation about "being suckered" that had four reminding stories in it. Let's look at the beginning of that conversation for a moment.

John and Sam went to a university cafeteria for lunch. Sam got into the sandwich line, where the server, a young woman, was slicing roast beef, ham, corned beef, etc. Sam saw a nice looking piece of meat on the side of the cut roast beef and ordered a roast beef sandwich. However, the server had previously cut some beef off, and she put this previously sliced beef into the sandwich. It wasn't nearly as nice as the meat that was still unsliced. When they got seated at their table in the dining room, Sam turned to John and said, "Boy, have I ever been suckered!" And he explained what had happened.

John said, "No, you haven't been suckered, because my impression of the word 'suckered' is that it implies serious attempt to defraud. You want a real suckering experience? On our trip to Spain, we were driving across the country, and we came to this tiny village. We went into a little store run by someone who looked just like a Gypsy lady. We bought some cheese and great bread and really nice looking sausage and some wine. Then we had it all wrapped up, and we drove out of the town. We parked in a secluded location, found a hill with some trees, climbed up to the top, and sat down, looking out over the beautiful countryside. Then we opened the wine and unwrapped the food. Garbage. All there was was garbage, carefully wrapped garbage. Now that was a suckering experience. The Gypsy lady suckered us."

The argument here was about what "suckered" means. Who was right, John or Sam? Well, John's meaning was right to himself and

Sam's to himself. Each has a different skeleton story that underlay the particular story he was telling. In other words, the skeleton story is their "definition" for the word; the actual story, the one they are telling at any given moment, builds a new story around the skeleton. In this situation, John and Sam disagree slightly about the meaning of the word "suckered." This fact should not be very surprising since, in a sense, we should always expect such disagreements. We are all unlikely to have identical skeleton stories or to agree on the situations to which a given skeleton story best applies. In fact, such disagreements generate points of view. More important, such disagreements form the foundations of political discussion in its most general sense. We see events in terms of skeleton stories so that we can use those events as ammunition to support our cause. To see how this process works, let's look at some skeleton stories as used in real life.

Some Skeleton Stories

If we construct our own version of truth by reliance upon skeleton stories, two people can know exactly the same facts but construct a story that relays those facts in very different ways. Because they are using different story skeletons, their perspectives will vary. For example, a United States Navy warship shot down an Iranian airliner carrying 290 passengers on July 3, 1988. Let's look at some different stories that were constructed to explain this event. All the stories that follow are excerpts from various *New York Times* reports in the days following this incident:

Mr. Reagan smiled and waved at tourists as he returned to the White House. But in speaking to reporters he remarked on what he had previously called "a terrible human tragedy. I won't minimize the tragedy," Mr. Reagan said. "We all know it was a tragedy. But we're talking about an incident in which a plane on radar was observed coming in the direction of a ship in combat and the plane began lowering its altitude. And so, I think it was an understandable accident to shoot and think that they were under attack from that plane," he said.

In this quotation from Ronald Reagan, the use of skeletons to create stories can be easily seen. Mr. Reagan has chosen a common skeleton: *understandable tragedy*. The skeleton looks something like this:

Actor pursues justifiable goal.
Actor selects reasonable plan to achieve goal.
Plan involves selection of correct action.
Action taken has unintended and unanticipatable result.
Result turns out to be undesirable.
Innocent people are hurt by result.

In essence, what Mr. Reagan has done is to select this skeleton and to interpret the events of the shooting down of the airplane in terms of that skeleton. Had he been asked to tell the story of what happened, he would simply have had to fill in each line above with the actual event that matches it. As it is, he merely had to recognize that that skeleton was applicable and to use the phrases "terrible human tragedy" and "understandable accident," which are well-known referents to that skeleton.

Now let's look at some other comments on the event:

After expressing "profound regret" about the attack, Mrs. Thatcher said: "We understand that in the course of an engagement following an Iranian attack on the U.S. force, warnings were given to an unidentified aircraft. We fully accept the right of forces engaged in such hostilities to defend themselves."

Mrs. Thatcher has used a much more specific skeleton, namely the *justifiability of self-defense*. This skeleton proceeds as follows:

First actor pursues unjustifiable goal.
First actor selects plan.
Plan has intention of negative effect on second actor.
Second actor is justified in selecting goal.
Second actor selects justifiable plan.
Plan causes action to take place which harms first actor.

Let's look at the other side of the political spectrum now:

Libya's official press agency called the downing "a horrible massacre perpetrated by the United States." It said the attack was "new proof of state terrorism practiced by the American administration" and it called Washington "insolent" for insisting that the decision to down the plane was an appropriate defensive measure.

Here, two different skeletons are invoked. The first is *state terrorism* and the second is *insolence*. The insolence skeleton is an amusing one to invoke, but we shall ignore it and concentrate on the terrorism skeleton:

Actor chooses high-level goal.
Country blocks high-level goal.
Actor chooses secondary goal to harm citizens of country.
Actor endangers or actually harms citizens of country.
Actor expects blockage of high-level goal by country to go away.

"State terrorism" supposedly means that the actor is a country too. But "state terrorism" is not exactly a well-known story skeleton for an American. In fact, Arab leaders refer to this skeleton quite often and we can figure what it must mean and why Arab leaders use it to justify their own actions. Other people's story skeletons, ones that we have not heard before, are usually best understood by analogy to skeletons we already know.

Notice that the events under discussion fit as easily into the state terrorism skeleton as into the above two skeletons. The art of skeleton selection is exactly that—an art. No real objective reality exists here. One can see and tell about events in any way that one wants to. In each case, certain aspects of the story being transmitted are enhanced and certain elements are left out altogether.

The real problem in using skeletons this way is that the storytellers usually believe what they themselves are saying. Authors construct their own reality by finding the events that fit the skeleton convenient for them to believe. They enter a storytelling situation wanting to tell a certain kind of story and only then worrying about whether the facts fit onto the bones of the skeleton that they have previously chosen. This method has almost comic qualities to it when various interpretations of an event are so clearly interpretations independent of the event itself. For example, consider the following comment:

A newspaper in Bahrain, *Akhbar Al Khalij,* said: "No doubt yesterday's painful tragedy was the result of Iran's insistence in continuing the Iran-Iraq war. The United States as a great power does not lack moral courage in admitting the mistake. This will help contain the effects of the accident."

The remarks above refer to two skeletons: the *justifiable bad effects of war on the aggressor* and *moral courage.* Both of these skeletons could have been used to describe nearly any event in the Middle East that the newspaper wanted to comment upon.

The use of new events as fodder for invoking old skeletons is the stuff of which international political rhetoric is made. In the *Times* of the same period, we have another reference to how Reagan commented on a similar situation some years back:

President Reagan, in a speech after the Korean plane was shot down after straying over Soviet airspace above Sakhalin Island, said: "Make no mistake about it, this attack was not just against ourselves or the Republic of Korea. This was the Soviet Union against the world and the moral precepts which guide human relations among people everywhere.

"It was an act of barbarism," Mr. Reagan went on, "born of a society which wantonly disregards individual rights and the value of human life and seeks constantly to expand and dominate other nations."

While the Americans used the *barbarism* skeleton, where the Koreans were the victim and the Russians the actor, to describe the shooting down of the Korean airliner, the Russians, in describing the Korean Airlines attack, used the *military aggressor* skeleton, where the Koreans were the actor and the Russians the victim. This same discrepancy occurred in the Russian statement about the Iranian airliner:

The Tass statement said the attack Sunday was the inevitable result of the extensive American military presence in the Persian Gulf.

"The tragedy, responsibility for which is wholly with the American command, has been far from accidental," the agency said. "It has been, in effect, a direct corollary of United States actions over the past year to increase its military presence in the gulf."

It added: "The Soviet Union has repeatedly warned at different forums that the path of military actions cannot lead to a normalized situation. If the warnings had been heeded, the July 3 tragedy would not have occurred."

International politicians are not alone in telling stories by selecting their favorite skeletons and fitting the event to the skeletons. The candidates for president also had something to say:

Mr. Jackson said there was "no evidence that the U.S. ship was under attack by that plane." But he added, "The issue is not just failed technology, but failed and vague policy for the region." Mr. Jackson argued that the United States should not be in the gulf unilaterally, but as part of a United Nations peacekeeping effort that would have as its prime goal a negotiated settlement of the Iran-Iraq war.

At a Fourth of July address at the Charlestown Navy Yard in Boston today, Mr. Dukakis described the incident as a "terrible accident," adding: "Clearly we have the right to defend our forces against imminent threats. And apparently, the shooting down of the airliner occurred over what appears to have been an unprovoked attack against our forces."

For Mr. Jackson, the appropriate skeletons were *bad technology causes errors,* and *vague policy causes problems.* Mr. Dukakis, on the other hand, looked suspiciously like Mr. Reagan, indicating that he was already acting presidential. Mr. Jackson had already realized that he was not going to be president at this point, but he was still campaigning to be taken seriously. Therefore, he was still raising issues. The Iran incident reminded him of two of his favorite issues, so he chose to see the Iranian airplane event in terms of those issues.

Last, we should look at the Iranian point of view. They, too, have their favorite skeletons in terms of which they can look at this event. First, let us look at the remarks of an exiled Iranian official:

"It must be clear that much of the policies in Iran today are dictated by the internal struggle for power," said Abolhassan Bani-Sadr, the first president of Iran. Mr. Bani-Sadr, who spoke in an interview, lives in exile in Paris and opposes the current regime.

"In that sense," Mr. Bani-Sadr said, "this American act of aggression will increase pressure to steer away from conciliatory policies in favor of radicals inside Iran who want to crush all talk of compromise. I am sure the trend now will be toward more mobilization for more war, although it will get nowhere."

Mr. Bani-Sadr was trying to predict the future rather than retell an old story. Nevertheless, he still relied upon a skeleton to create his new story. The skeleton he chose was *fanatics find fuel to add to fire*. Now look at a comment from inside Iran:

Hojatolislam Rafsanjani, who is the commander of Iran's armed forces, warned today against a hasty response to the American action. In a speech reported by the Teheran radio, he told Parliament, "We should let this crime be known to everyone in the world and be discussed and studied."

The Speaker, who has emerged as Iran's most powerful figure after Ayatollah Khomeini, went on to say that the Americans might "want a clumsy move somewhere in the world so that they can take the propaganda pressure off America and transfer it somewhere else."

Hojatolislam Rafsanjani added that Iran retains the right of taking revenge, but that "the timing is up to us, not America." He called the downing of the airliner "an unprecedented disaster in contemporary history" and said it should be used by Iran to "expose the nature of America," statements indicating that for now the Speaker favors a measured response.

Here again, we have a story about the future. Two skeletons are invoked as possible candidates for the basis of this story. One, *force opponents into bad move*, refers to the intentions of the U.S. as seen by the Iranians and is really a part of a continuing story of conflict between the two countries. The second, *avoid revenge to show up opponent*, is more or less the other side of the same coin. In both cases, we have a kind of conscious admission by Mr. Rafsanjani that the real question is which story skeleton will be followed in the creation of the next set of events. The only problem with this assertion is that Mr. Rafsanjani naively seems to assume that some audience is waiting to see the next act in the play. A more accurate assumption is that, no matter what happens next, all the viewers of the play will retell the story according to skeletons that they have already selected; i.e., they will probably not be moved to reinterpret any new event in terms of some skeleton that they do not already have in mind.

Skeletons and Memory

Story skeletons can have an important effect on memory. Since we see the world according to the stories we tell, when we tell a story in a given way, we will be likely to remember the facts in terms of the story we have told. This effect on memory has an interesting offshoot. When we select a particular skeleton because we have no real choice from a political point of view, we, most likely, will begin to believe the story we find ourselves telling. Consider the following statement, for example:

Iran Air's senior Airbus instructor, Capt. Ali Mahdaviani, ruled out the possibility of pilot error in the tragedy. He said it was possible that the airliner's captain, Mohsen Rezaian, failed to respond to signals from the American cruiser *Vincennes* because at that stage in the flight he was busy receiving air controller instructions off two radios and from four control towers, Bandar Abbas, Teheran, Dubai, and Qeshon Island in the gulf.

He insisted that the airliner would not have been outside the flight corridor and certainly would not have been descending, as early Pentagon reports said. He attributed the incident to a panicky reaction from the American cruiser, but did concede that the decision to fire the two surface-to-air missiles was made in difficult circumstances. "I think the decision to shoot down the plane was taken in very nervous conditions," he said.

And now consider an opposing statement:

"We have in this briefing all the facts that were made available to the captain when he made his decision," said Senator John Warner, a Virginia Republican and former Navy Secretary. "We are all of the same view, that he acted properly and professionally."

Senator Sam Nunn, the Georgia Democrat who is the chairman of the Armed Services Committee, agreed. "I find nothing to second-guess him on, based on his information," Mr. Nunn said.

He was quick to add, however, that the information that Capt. Will C. Rogers 3d, the commanding officer of the *Vincennes,* was working with might be contradicted by information on the computer tapes, which are believed to have recorded every action taken by the ship's operators, every bit of data picked up by its sensors, and every communication heard in the region during the encounter.

"It is an entirely different matter to second-guess a decision that had to be made in three or four minutes, to second-guess it over a two-week period," Mr. Nunn said, referring to the deadline for Navy investigators looking into the events.

Each of these statements is what might have been expected from the people who made them. Yet how were the memories of the spokesmen affected by the stories they told? In some sense, they told stories that they had to tell. Neither of these spokesmen was necessarily one hundred percent sure that the pilot and/or the captain weren't somewhat wrong in what they did. Situations are rarely that black-and-white. But having made a statement to support his man, each spokesman probably believed more in his man after defending him.

One issue in story understanding, then, is to determine which story skeleton is the right one to choose. Moreover, this issue is important in storytelling and, therefore, in memory as well. We can see an event in so many different ways that we must understand how we decide which story skeleton is applicable. In politics, this decision is easy. Russians or Iranians don't have to debate about which skeleton to choose. Rather, they make choices on the basis of political positions adopted before any story is heard. But for individuals who must decide how to look at a given situation, the possibilities are much larger.

One of the oddities of story-based understanding is that people have difficulty making decisions if they know that they will have trouble constructing a coherent story to explain their decision. In a sense, people tell stories to themselves to see whether they are comfortable enough with telling them for a while. You need to believe your own story in order to tell it effectively. Thus, decision making often depends upon story construction.

Divorce Stories

In order to understand an episode in our lives, we must construct a story that makes the episode make sense. We do not like to believe of ourselves that we act randomly or without reason. When we make a decision or take an action, we like to believe in our choice, especially if that decision or action is a significant one. In a sense, then, we must construct a story before we take an action to ensure that the action we are about to take is coherent. Further, if the action is in any way incoherent, we make it more sensible by putting it into a framework that is acceptable to those who hear the story. In other words, if what we do fits into a well-known, socially acceptable story skeleton, then we can believe that we have acted properly.

One of the most significant actions someone can take is to get divorced. This decision can often be quite emotionally wrenching, especially when children are involved. Anyone who has been divorced probably has a story to tell about that divorce. Further, one would expect these stories to fit into some well-known and socially acceptable story skeleton. If the actual events were too complicated for a standard story skeleton and confusion remained about whether or not the divorce was a rational decision, the story would probably reflect this fact only by inference. In other words, we expect that coherent stories that rely upon a standard story skeleton may well mask, in varying degrees of effectiveness, a less coherent set of events which do not fit neatly into a story skeleton.

We interviewed people who had been divorced and asked them to tell us the story of their divorces. The subjects were all teachers. The stories shown here are edited from longer versions. Let's look at the first story:

A: I was divorced actually two years ago. I probably would have stayed married for much much longer had Peter stayed working, but he decided to take retirement from his job and start his own business, and I wasn't really thrilled about the idea, but it's not the sort of thing you can talk a man out of. He said, "You know you can work with me." I said, "No chance, we'd be divorced in a week." He took it as a joke. He said, "We work so well together," and I thought, That's because I do it the way you want to, not the way I like. So, I went out and got a full-time job teaching, and gradually it started to dawn on me how very unhappy I was with having him around. He was a guy who felt that he was always right, and he was a perfectionist.

He was extremely hardworking, very demanding of himself, and extremely demanding of everyone else. Sometimes he'd be critical; sometimes, if I'd take him to task about it and say, "You know you're always so critical," he'd say, "You're the most wonderful, you're the best person I could have married, etc. etc." I realized he was saying to me on the logical plane that I was the best wife he could have had. He certainly wouldn't want to trade me for someone else, but at the same time, I could improve just a few things.

Then I went back to work, and I started saying to myself, Wait a minute, I don't have to spend the rest of my life being squashed. I realize I think I was afraid of him in a way, not that he physically abused me or attacked me in any way except verbally. And I think he undermined my ego to a certain extent, and after I started working, and he was home, I really found I didn't like to be home. I didn't like to be around.

One summer, I took a job at a tennis camp just to see how it felt to be away. I was a computer teacher at the tennis camp—it really was a lousy camp and not a very good experience except that I realize that I really was happy about myself.

Then when I came down here, he started thinking he'd look for a job down here, and I was hoping he wouldn't find one. He didn't, and when he'd come down to visit every couple of weeks, I found I was really not looking forward to seeing him. And he began to realize that he wasn't being particularly welcomed by the people here, and I think the poor man really was quite hurt. When we'd go up to visit him, we'd arrive so tired and find a list of things he wanted us to do. We realized this is not much fun, and we stayed here, and he stayed there and then after about a year, there were a couple of other little incidents with his family and what have you, and he one day said to me, "Maybe we should get a divorce."

You know, my mother always looked upon divorced women as some sort of fallen women and fast-living, loose women. "She's divorced, you know." I can't be one of those people whom people point out and say, "She's a divorcée, you know, what can you expect. And children, what can you expect of him, you know his parents are divorced." Divorce really has a very bad press, and it took me a couple of months to get into my little head that this was the eighties, and this was the United States, and plenty of people I liked and respected got divorced, and they hadn't turned into scarlet women, so gradually it dawned on me that this is not such a bad idea.

I phoned Peter, and I said, "You know you're right, we should get divorced," and I think it totally took him by surprise. He didn't obstruct it, but he would occasionally call and say, "So you really want to go ahead with this?" and I'd say, "Yes, I do." Peter thought that it would shake me up if he said maybe we should get divorced. I'd say I can't lose this marvelous man, and what have I done wrong. Let me shape up a bit and we'll keep the marriage going.

In fact, once I made the decision, it was a wonderful feeling. I remember going out running one day and thinking, Oh, I feel free, I feel as if a sort of load has been lifted. I think what it was was that I no longer had this person standing over me and criticizing whatever it was that I was doing. The longer we were separated with the divorce coming, the more I felt the sense of incredible freedom, and life was almost poetic. Once I made the decision, I never had a moment's doubt. I was thinking one night, Well, so it's easy for me to divorce him now. Here I am, I have the kids with me. What am I going to do in two or three years time when they leave? I'll be on my own. Then it struck me, if I was married to him, I'd be with him, and I'd rather be on my own. You know, at least if I were on my own, I could do my job, I could run, I could play tennis. I could go to lectures or whatever, and I basically could enjoy myself on my own. So it was a good feeling to get divorced.

What kind of story is this? The first problem arises from the story skeleton it uses. A fairly standard story skeleton that women use to describe their marriages runs as follows: *man oppresses woman who in turn demands more independence.* For the woman who is telling this story, this skeleton conflicts with another one from her childhood: *woman leaves man and turns to wanton life.* She clearly had a conflict between which of these two skeletons would be her story, and one can guess that she decided to test herself by getting a job in another state away from her husband. The odd thing here is that we can only guess at her motivation because she says almost nothing about her decision to move out. She just uses the phrase "then when I came down here" to refer to her leaving her husband and getting a job elsewhere prior to any talk of divorce. Notice that no standard socially acceptable story skeleton really exists for her sort of separation, and for this reason, she might not have told that part of the story. What made her decide to split up her family for a job? This behavior is not common and would have to be explained—but she barely mentions it. When no standard story skeleton is available, telling stories is difficult.

People need to make sense of their own lives. One way of feeling that you have made sense is to tell your story to other people and hear them respond in positive, supportive, ways. To make sure that you have expressed your story in terms that others understand, you must use the right skeleton. You wouldn't use the word *rachmones* while talking to someone who you knew would not know the word. Similarly, you would not talk about *man oppresses woman who in turn demands more independence* unless you had reason to believe that your hearer knew that skeleton. You could, of course, try to instruct your listener about the meaning of the skeleton, but you would not get the empathy you were looking for. To avoid this feeling of isolation, of lack of understanding, when talking to someone from whom one wants support, people naturally use skeletons that they know will get them that support. When people want to make a case for themselves or when they want to describe a situation to others in order to get a certain kind of reaction, they choose a well-known and culturally agreed upon skeleton, one to which they can predict the reaction of others.

To do all this, it is sometimes necessary to distort the facts some-what. A teller will make the story fit into the skeleton and will tend to leave out the parts that do not quite fit. To see some of this in action and to get a feel for what other kinds of skeletons there are, let's consider another divorce story:

B: I got married when I was twenty-two. I grew up in Colorado in a fairly traditional Western home, had a great college experience, went off to graduate school and stayed in a Ph.D. program. I was in Pennsylvania, an environment that was foreign to me, and I met this man who was older and much more sophisticated, had been married. And in some intuitional ridiculous feminine way sought him out to help support me and get me through this. I was tired of school by that time, and that was disintegrating. I more and more clutched to this individual. I couldn't possibly imagine life without somebody telling me what to do and how to do it. So I was Catholic, he was Jewish. I was Western, he was New York City. Many opposites, so we ended up getting married.

And what happened is, I grew up. It sort of was forced on me to become my own person after I became a mother. For the first time, I really had to be conscious of myself and my own motives and how I was doing things because I had this child to take care of, and I also had a full-time job and had to get all this stuff done. I did not need or want to have this oppressive atmosphere created by this person that I married who resented every step of my independence and personal growth.

I found a lot of development of self coming in the classroom relationships with kids, and he would tell me that my relationships were sick. He once said to me, "I've created you, and I want to instill this sort of debt." Interestingly, I ended up in counseling because he said I had a problem. The therapy helped me put some objectivity on this relationship which was really tortuous, very stultifying, very oppressive, as you can imagine. So it began, I think, on a suggestion on his part, I think, to get me to think right. Right thinking, you know, ended up backfiring because I was able to establish some distance from the relationship and finally realize in the long process that I couldn't survive. I was dying in this relationship, and I had to get out. We were married five years. It seemed like one hundred fifty.

Surely, I would have gotten divorced if I hadn't fallen in love with C. It was going to happen. I had already sort of semi-separated but had gone back. I'd been through therapy, but I think even the moments I spent with C. taught me what it was like to be with a real human being male; you didn't have to feel threatened and horrible. It gave me a real glimpse as to what it could be really like, and I was sure that was the impetus. We had seen each other from the start of the affair only once before the lawyers. So it wasn't as though that was the cause. I often think people think, Well, you've fallen in love, and that's the cause. I have often believed that whatever's wrong is wrong, and you're attracted to other people because things are so wrong.

This story relies upon two standard story skeletons. The first is *young woman marries older man because she wants guidance; he wants her to remain a child, but she grows up and changes and doesn't need him anymore.* The second is *partner in bad relationship finds lover to use as means to effect final separation from spouse.* The teller of this story wants the hearer to believe that the first skeleton is operating and that the second is not. Her story is simple and clear and obvious according to her rendition of it. It is quite natural, she is asserting, that a young woman would marry an older man for guidance and then be prevented from growing up by a man who liked being married to a young woman. By relying on this old standard story skeleton, one she can assume that her listener has heard before, she can assume that her divorce will be seen as having been socially acceptable, reasonable to do, in other words. But things are rarely this simple, of course. In this case she mentions a second skeleton, which people normally disapprove of, and which she asserts was not really operating. The reason she mentioned it at all, one can assume, was that C., the man she had her affair with and was now married to, was present and about to tell his story.

C: My first marriage took place within hours literally of my graduation from college. I graduated from college at two o'clock in the afternoon and was married at seven o'clock that evening. I promised my father I'd wait until I graduated. I'd not had a lot of relationships with different women. The woman that I'd married I had met in the summer after my sophomore year in college. I was working in a summer camp in upstate New York. We were both on the staff together. It became one of those summer kinds of counselor things that—we got very serious in the course of six weeks. I was going to school and living in Ohio. She was living in Albany, New York. For the next two years in the relationship, we saw each other only at vacation times which were, I think, artificial at best. There are all the festivities that surround vacations, and we never had any sense of each other in day-to-day living, which proved to be one of the fatal flaws in the marriage.

My mother had died when I was nine years old—I'm the youngest of three children—two older sisters. My sisters were old enough so by the time I was in junior high and high school, it was just my father and me by ourselves, two men. And I grew up doing lots of the household chores, cooking, cleaning, all the rest of that sort of stuff, sort of envying classmates and friends who had moms, who came home from school, everything was done. So I really feel that there was some chunk of my psychological development that just was missing, and I think a great force operating pretty subconsciously in my search for a spouse was someone who was going to mother me. Do all of those things, and clearly, that's what Sara, my first wife, was all about. I would say for the first year or so I was having everything that I did not have growing up. I had this woman who really was taking care of me, and it was great, and I think that masqueraded as a deep relationship. There wasn't much what would I say emotional, intellectual exchange between the two of us. I felt I did not have any grand feeling of emotion toward Sara, but I was thinking, well, this is just the way marriages are.

Then, we moved to a much larger independent boarding school in Illinois which represented the very best of independent education in that it was a very intellectual community, very diverse, lots of fine minds, and I continued to grow professionally myself there. Found myself very very comfortable in that community, increasingly comfortable, while Sara was finding herself increasingly uncomfortable with that. And it was at that point that I began to feel that the marriage was not only very empty but was going to continue to be very empty simply because we were two very very different people. The directions that I wanted to move not only professionally but personally and the sorts of people I was attracted to on a social level were not people that Sara was comfortable with.

At the very end of my relationship with Sara, B. and I did in fact begin a relationship in which I was discovering what it meant to have the full range of deep feelings for another human being, and that just confirmed my belief that this relationship wasn't going to work, so we separated.

This story relies upon a few skeletons at the same time. The first is *married too young and tried to imitate the idyllic image of a fifties suburban marriage* (the "Leave it to Beaver" skeleton). The second is *man tries to replace mother with wife and then decides that's not what he wanted.* And, a third is *one partner grows while other stays the same.* These three are all rather related, and, of course, they are tied together with *partner in bad relationship finds lover to use as means to effect final separation from spouse,* which was convenient in this case since he found a woman (B.) who had exactly the same story as the one he wanted to tell. In his case, too, he denies that this last relationship was the cause of his divorce. We tell the stories that we want to believe, after all.

Now, look at the next story:

D: The relationship started. My sister was married to this person's brother. But what I should have known in hindsight is there were certain qualities to this person that I should have known in terms of his attitude toward women and his commitment to one person. We were married in August, and we were divorced August three years later, so it was very short. And, as it turns out, there was someone else, another woman involved before we got married, and there were women involved all the way along. But I didn't know this. I guess I didn't want to know this. So it was definitely something that I had a hard time getting over. I think that because I was very young and I had a feeling that divorce meant failure. What I know now is that the failure was not on my part, the failure was on the part of this person toward relationships in general. Matthew came in at a point, and I almost felt guilty that he had come into my life. I knew I wanted out. I knew something was wrong, but I didn't know how to get out of it. I'd just made a move to a new location, and all of a sudden my whole life was changing again. I was seen at that point as being, or I perceived that I was being seen, as the one who had found somebody else and so was running off, but, of course, what people didn't realize was that he had somebody in the wings for a long time. So I think that produced a feeling of guilt in me that we had a moral contract. I look back on it as more of a relationship that didn't work as opposed to a marriage that failed, but that's seven years after. I certainly didn't feel that when I first was getting out of it.

Here we have a very standard story skeleton: *man has affairs and cannot commit himself to a relationship, thus he leaves wife to terminate it.* And, here again, the teller notices that the skeleton *partner in bad relationship finds lover to use as means to effect final separation from spouse* could be inferred from the actual events, so she insists that it was not the dominating skeleton in this story.

Humans cannot easily digest the complexity of the world they live in and the actions that they and others take in that world. We look for explanations of our own behavior and of the behavior of others that seem to make sense. But what does it mean to make sense of a behavior? When we tell about a series of events that have occurred over a ten-year period, as in a divorce story, we look for overall patterns rather than attempting to relate every event that ever happened. We look for generalizations to make. But what kinds of generalizations can we make? First and foremost, we look for generalizations that we have seen before and that we believe others have seen before. We speak in generalizations that our listener can understand.

Earlier, we discussed the problem of trying to explain the actions of others. If we look at explanation as the need to explain everything we see and hear about on the basis of first principles, the process may be somewhat more complex than people are prepared to handle on a daily basis. But if we have available to us a set of standard explanations in the form of story skeletons, we can explain the behavior of others by trying to match their behavior to the standard skeletons. In other words, we try to understand events by reference to events we have already understood. An available set of skeletons, of old favorites as it were, helps us to impose a uniformity on an otherwise incomprehensible world. We know what patterns to look for, and we insist on finding them.

This same process goes on in reverse when we tell a story. If we tell a story that is really brand-new, in the sense that none of the behaviors has been seen before, then both the teller and the hearer have a great deal of work to do. The teller must relate almost all the events that took place. He cannot take shortcuts and assume that his hearer will infer the details because his hearer has no basic everyday story to use as a guide. The hearer is trying to match what he is hearing to what he already knows about, but if he cannot find explanation patterns that work to explain the behaviors he is being told about, he must try to explain things without reference to previous related events. This is very difficult to do.

So tellers of stories and listeners have an implicit agreement. Tellers will only tell standard stories, stories that are easy to understand. When tellers find some events to relay that are incomprehensible, they will not relay them, or they will force them into a format that makes them look comprehensible. In fact, tellers have no other choice. They cannot easily remember events that are incomprehensible except as a series of isolated occurrences. They use explanation patterns themselves to understand the events that they are about to relate.

When people decide to tell about their divorce, they are telling about the situation the way they understand it and the way they hope their hearers will understand it. They are thus forced, in some sense, to make their story acceptable and easily comprehensible both by their initial attempts to understand the events themselves and by their prior attempts to tell others their story. To achieve this goal, they choose a standard story to tell—a story skeleton—and force the facts to fit the skeleton. If parts of the story do not fit the skeleton, they ignore them. If the story also fits a skeleton that is not favorable to tellers, they acknowledge the superficial parallels and then dispute the accuracy of that skeleton in their case.

A storyteller might be more accurately described as a story-fitter. Telling stories of our own lives, especially ones with high emotional impact, means attempting to fit events to a story that has already been told, a well-known story that others will easily understand. Story-fitting, then, is a kind of deceptive process, one that creates stories that are not always exactly true, that lie by omission. These lies, however, are not necessarily intentional.

A true story could be told but would take much more time. So time, in many ways, is the villain here. Your listener doesn't have hours to listen to your story, so you create a short version that looks more standard, that fits a well-known story skeleton. The problem with this solution, as we have seen, is that the teller himself begins to believe his story. In short, storytelling is a very powerful process. We remember our own stories. Stories replace the memory of events that actually took place. So when people tell the kinds of stories we have seen in this chapter, they usually believe them.

Married couples often comment on a sequence from the Woody Allen movie *Annie Hall*. The sequence involves two scenes, where first the female lead and then the male lead discuss their sex life as a couple with their respective therapists. The woman complains that her boyfriend wants to have sex all the time—two or three times a week. The man complains that they almost never have sex together—only two or three times a week.

This movie scene expresses the essence of story construction. We take the facts and we interpret them in such a way as to create a story. In order to facilitate communication and to allow easy conversation, we use standard story skeletons that we share as a culture. The choice, however, of which skeleton to use is, in essence, a political choice. We choose to see the world according to a view that we find convenient, and we communicate by adopting standard points of view. The stories we tell communicate this view both to others and to ourselves. In the end, we become shaped by the skeletons we use.

Which of the *Annie Hall* characters is right? This question is, of course, absurd. Both characters are right, as are all the politicians quoted earlier. The skeletons we use indicate our point of view. Storytelling causes us to adopt a point of view. With this adoption comes a kind of self-definition, however. We are the stories we tell. We not only express our vision of the world, we also shape our memory by the stories we tell. As we come to rely upon certain skeletons to express what has happened to us, we become incapable of seeing the world in any other way. The skeletons we use cause specific episodes to conform to one another. The more a given skeleton is used, the more the stories it helps to form begin to cohere in memory. Consequently, we develop consistent, and rather inflexible, points of view.

Story Processes

Although it is a convenient metaphor to imagine that the mind is a collection of thousands of stories all properly stored away and waiting to be told, the situation is considerably more complicated than that. When you tell a story, one of the reasons that you feel as if you are thinking of what to say is that that is precisely what you are doing. The *gist of a story* is what is held in memory, not the particular words that comprise the story itself. When we tell a story, we are transforming the gist into a story in a particular language with particular words, suitable for telling to the person who is listening.

We can tell the same story in different ways in order to satisfy different goals. We can, of course, tell a story in different languages, if we speak different languages, so obviously the language itself is not part of the gist. Also, we can tell a story at different intellectual levels, for example, one version for a child and another for an adult—so obviously gists do not include the way that a story is told. We can even tell the same story with different points in mind, depending upon our audience, so even points are not part of the gist of a story. Clearly, storytelling activates a set of processes that operate on the gist of a story in various ways depending upon many factors that are part of the storyteller's environment. The gist and the number of possible stories that can express that gist are very different entities indeed. Therefore, a set of mental processes that transform gists into stories must exist.

Transforming the Gist: Some Examples

Let us look at some stories created with different intentions in mind. I asked a student with considerable acting experience to tell a story of something that had happened to him in a variety of ways. What follows are two basic stories that he told, each in a very different way, depending upon the intention that he was trying to get that story to satisfy.

The first two stories are the basic stories told from the memory of this student with the intention of having a cathartic effect.

STORY 1: I was at a gas station this morning. I have this Volvo. It is a tank. I backed into this planter, this big concrete made-out-of-mortar thing and knocked the thing apart. I felt like such a zero. They called the police, and the cop came over, and he didn't give me a ticket because I was on gas station property. But I can't believe I did that.

STORY 2: I've always had, well always had, our family has always been very, I have the kind of family that is very formal in some way or another. We always—we're not the kind of family that never talks to each other about emotional things I guess the way some families do, but when we talk about things like that, it's always in a very very rational framework. My family always had a lot of rules; it was always a very rational family. So last summer, my sister got married, and my sister is a lesbian, and so she was marrying another woman. And this is something that—it wasn't a shock to my family—we've known that for a long time, but I came to the ceremony without knowing how exactly it was going to go, what was going to happen. And there was a lot of ceremony and a lot of women's kind of rituals and things like that. And I knew that potentially it was going to make my mother and my family uncomfortable, but I remember at one point in the ceremony we had to go around the circle—the audience participated all through the ceremony—and invoke people that were not there that we might wish were there or might have wished to be there if they could have been there, and I remember wondering who that might be, who I would invoke who wasn't there, and I invoked my own partner who I'd been living with for years, and that seemed like a good thing, and then it got around to my mother, and she invoked our father who passed away when I was twelve. And it was just like a flash because I broke into tears. I had not thought of my own father. Somehow, that seemed like such an obvious and evident thing, and it seemed as if perhaps he was there in some very real, very emotional sense at that point. And my mother's hitting on that somehow brought that out and brought that forward, and I just realized how tightly bound up we all were with each other and how much, and how in the midst of this very bizarre circumstance, somehow what had happened was a stripping away of what had covered things up before and not any kind of perversion of them. It was quite a revelation.

The next version of the first story was told with the intention of illustrating a previously made point about his vision problems and of describing himself in the process:

STORY 1:   I was driving my Volvo once into a gas station, and what must have happened is that I was traveling forward, and I hit this big square concrete thing. It was high enough that I should have seen it, but it was over here in my right visual field. It was just another one of those cases where there is missing field here and I bashed right into it. I mean it was bright daylight, and I drove into it. Sometimes I just don't see stuff.

The next version of the second story was told with the intention of trying to illustrate a point:

STORY 2: My sister got married last summer, and I went to the wedding, and it was a nontraditional wedding. The audience participated in the different things that happened at the wedding, so at one point we all went around and invoked people who we thought should be there and weren't or thought would want to be there and weren't, and then at another point, we were supposed to come forward and sort of offer our blessing to the couple and talk about what they meant to us personally. And of course, one of the people in the wedding was my sister, and so I felt like I'd have something to say, and each time the turn had come round to me in the circle before, I had something moving to say, and so I felt like I was on a roll and that I was impressing everyone with how compassionate I was and the insight of my comments. And I remembered when my turn came around again, I was going to talk about how my sister and I always played imaginary games together when we were little kids and to make some point about how this kind of force used to create imaginary games could be used to forge something in real life too. But when my turn came up, I couldn't speak—I was so choked up that I couldn't speak. I blathered on in half-completed sentences and walked away thinking, They're just going to think I'm nuts, they're going to just think I can't talk. And then after the ceremony, everyone came up to me and said to me, "I was so moved when you talked about your sister. I couldn't believe the love that you felt for your sister, and it was so genuine and so heartfelt." And they said, "What a kind human being you are," and I was astounded, and afterwards I thought to myself, Well, I guess sometimes it isn't performance in the end that counts, that there is such a thing as just genuinely coming through at one time or another. So that we succeed sometimes at our best intentions despite our best intentions.

In the next version of the first story, the teller tried to make the listener fall in love with him by making himself seem vulnerable:

STORY 1: I had this old Volvo a few years ago. It was my first car, and people always have a certain special relationship to their first car, and I had one to this. I am not the type of guy that ever thought that I was really fast, the way some people do in a car, but when I was in this car I thought I was invulnerable. One day I drove the car into a gas station and drove right smack into a concrete planter, knocked it to pieces, and broke my right headlight. I wasn't injured, but I was so embarrassed. I, I felt like, I felt, I felt just completely devastated. I talked to the guy that was working at the gas station, and he told me that I was an idiot. I was going to have to pay him $10,000 to have the thing installed—it was brand-new. I realized that there was a lot more to being safe than being in a car that I wouldn't get killed in; that I was still just as vulnerable and just as potentially damaged as anybody out there. My Volvo wasn't really going to protect me at all in some way or another.

In the next version, the storyteller was instructed to recount the events as if he were a teenager telling the story to his mother:

STORY 1:   Mother, uhh . . . I hit a cinder block planter with the car today in a gas station. Didn't do any serious damage to the car. Uh, I damaged one headlight. I am fine. Uh, the guy at the gas station on the other hand is very angry. I will take care of it. I will pay for getting the car fixed, and if it turns out there is some damage to the gas station, then, that needs to be taken care of, I will take care of that, too.

The next version was produced when the teller was asked to make believe that he was applying for a job as a driver and had to explain a problem on his driving record:

STORY 1:   As I recall, I was in a big hurry. I was coming back into town, and at the last minute, I decided to stop for gas. As I was coming in, something happened at the gas station where the cash register and that junk is. I looked over—I must have been coming in about three miles an hour—and I nudged this planter about two feet high sitting right out in the middle of the runway where you get gas. I pushed bricks off of it with the front of the car, and the guy comes out screaming bloody murder and says that he has put his life savings into there, and he won't have customers anymore because some of the bricks are missing from the planter and that people will think that the station is run-down and that he is going to sue me for every penny I am worth. So that is why we called the insurance company at all—otherwise, it was nothing.

The next version of the second story was told with the intention of offering advice to a friend:

STORY 2:   Well, once I had to participate in my sister's wedding, and my sister is a lesbian, so this was a lesbian ceremony, and it was also an alternative feminist ceremony, and I know almost nothing about lesbians, and I know very little about alternative feminism, and I'm also a man. So I didn't know what the heck I was going to do. I was the only man participating in the ceremony besides her intended's five-year-old son. And so here I was at the practice that morning—the only man in a houseful of fifteen women, fourteen of whom were lesbians, and I didn't know what to do. I didn't know what I was supposed to say to people. Flirting was out of the question. It was hard to figure out how to relate, but I realized a couple of things. I talked about my sister, and it so happened that I had on one other occasion been to another, for completely different reasons, another alternative feminist ceremony where they had invoked the goddess and done all these other mystical things, so I talked about that, and mostly I listened. And as soon as I started doing that, these people came forward, and I realized very soon that they knew as little about how to treat the sixteenth person in the house who was a man as I did how to treat the other fifteen who were women, and that no one questioned my right to be there. I was her brother, and everyone was glad to have me there, but no one knew what to do with me. I mean flirting was out of the question, and so it was as rough for them as it was for me, and I think that the key was finding some kind of common element and listening.

Actual stories are produced from a gist that is stored in memory. That gist may include a skeleton at its base with some extra elements thrown in. Or it may include no standard skeleton at all, being a truly unique story. Each of the stories shown here was produced by transforming either the gist of story 1 or the gist of story 2. The teller did not have multiple versions of each story stored in memory. Rather, when told with a particular intention, the story which is stored in memory changes form. This transformation of the gist uses a variety of mental processes, each of which is trying to get a particular intention accomplished. Consequently, the resulting stories are different because the intentions are different. In other words, stories can differ in intention but be identical in content. Gist, therefore, is a conception about events, not a conception about the communication of those events. Communicative intent, however, has the effect of transforming gists into stories. Memory for events is unrelated to communicative intent, but as soon as we begin to tell a story we also begin to transform the memory gist into a story that we think relates

to what our listener should hear. In other words, we can fool ourselves into believing that something actually happened by transforming what really happened for the purposes of telling about it.

Communicative Intent

The first versions of each story were told upon instruction from me
to tell stories that were cathartic. Thus, we can assume that each
story was composed by taking its gist and transforming it according
to the intention of expressing catharsis. However, for the sake of
argument, let's assume that each story is identical to the gist that is
stored in memory. What is wrong with such an assumption? The first
problem is that each story had many more events than the ones that
were explicitly related. The Volvo has a color, a year, a condition.
The gas station has a certain look and feel to it. It is modern or old,
in a city or on a country road. It sells a particular kind of gas, and
so on. The policeman said some things; the station owner said some
things; the teller of the story said some things. All of these have been
left out. The wedding had guests who were dressed in a certain way;
various foods and drinks were probably served. These facts were also
left out.

In the first telling of a story, a teller decides what to leave out. This
decision is based upon a number of factors that include whom he is
telling the story to, why he is telling it, and how he now perceives
what has happened to him. After all, one cannot say everything that
has happened. A story about a two-week vacation could take two
weeks to tell. A teller must decide what aspects of the gist are likely
to be of interest to the hearer.

On subsequent tellings of the story, details that have been consis-
tently left out tend to get forgotten, although they can be reconstructed in some instances. The gist itself can be changed by the
telling of a story over time. Pieces of the gist that are never told tend
to disappear from the gist itself. The location of the gas station is
never mentioned in any of the versions of this story, but if this event
took place while the student was at Yale, then the gas station was
probably in New Haven (i.e., in a city setting and not on a country

road). Thus, this aspect of the gist is reconstructable. It will never totally be lost because it can be figured out. But the kind of gas that the station sells, since it is never mentioned and much more difficult to reconstruct, may well be lost forever. Similarly, the location of the wedding is not mentioned. Certainly the teller knows where he went, but we can expect that he might forget the exact details over time unless they are an important part of the story in some way. If a detail is not used and cannot be easily reconstructed, then that detail is likely to be forgotten.

The gist, then, is stored in memory and is operated upon in a variety of ways. Each of the processes described below transforms various aspects of a gist into various aspects of a story. The first process that we shall take note of is the distillation process.

Distillation

Distillation is a two-part process which reduces the events of a story to a set of simpler propositions, i.e., to its gist, and then puts those propositions into English. The first part is a memory process. A complex array of memory structures is distilled into a simpler coherent whole when a story is told for the first time. We actively try to figure out what to tell about an experience. The process of distilling a coherent story from a range of particular experiences causes a memory entity, the gist, to be constructed. After a gist is constructed, it, in effect, becomes the memory of the original set of events that comprised the story. The events themselves become lost as an easily retrievable entity, while the gist is available for use. When someone asks us about an experience, we remember what we have previously told about that experience. Rather than attempting to search all over memory to find something to say, using what we have already said is simpler. The first part of the distillation process, then, we call *gist construction*. This process searches what is known about an event and finds discrete propositions that become the gist of the story and can then be told in a given order. Once this takes place, each time a story is told, the process becomes increasingly difficult to reverse, as the new story replaces the original memories.

Let's imagine that you have just returned from a week-long vacation touring castles in England. A friend asks you how your trip was. What do you do? First, you must comb through the events of your trip to see how many of them were significant enough to mention. These choices are made in concert with consideration for the kinds of things your friend might be interested in and the amount of time he is prepared to listen to your story. When you are finished finding things that you want to tell about, you have finished the first part of the distillation process. You have constructed a memory representation of the story you are about to tell. You have constructed the gist.

The second part of the distillation process, *translation,* expresses a gist in a natural language. There are, as we have seen, many ways to express the same gist. The differences depend upon one's intentions and the story skeleton that is chosen to express those intentions. The translation process takes each of these propositions and translates them from their representation in memory into English. The translation process, then, is not a memory process but a linguistic process. Events are being translated from memory format into English format. This translation proceeds event by event and thus sentence by sentence. As each sentence appears, a new call to memory to find the next proposition occurs. These memory calls depend upon what went before. Often, how an earlier proposition was actually expressed in English can alter what propositions are composed next. So, in effect, expressing a gist in language can alter the gist somewhat by making demands upon the memory. For example, if you say that a castle you saw was beautiful, and you realize at the moment of expression that your listener might be interested in exactly what was beautiful about it, this can force you to go back to memory to find out more. Now, this information may not be in the gist and thus you might be forced to search parts of memory from which it is quite difficult to retrieve. Another alternative is to reconstruct the details from what you imagine might have been beautiful about the castle. In this way, we can see that the translation process depends, in part, upon information about the hearer, as well as upon information that may reside in memory that may not be part of the gist at all.

A gist, therefore, is an evolving kind of entity. If aspects of it are not accessed in future renditions of the story, a gist can get smaller. It also can get larger as memory reconstruction adds pieces that may not have been in the original event at all. Further, the process of translation can affect the gist. When certain words are chosen, they may express an emotional content that although not part of the original events now becomes part of the gist. A new point of view in light of subsequent events might cause the translation process actually to change the gist. We don't remember how we slanted things during a telling, by and large. But we do remember details that we may have added in translating a gist into English, and these additions can become part of a reformulated gist.

Gist construction is probably a great deal like the memory process that has the responsibility of storing away stories in the first place. We remember only the gist of the story so, in essence, what we are doing when we are initially storing away a new story is consciously trying to remember it. We are rehearsing the telling of the story, distilling it, in other words, for ourselves as part of the memory process. Telling the gist of a story for the first time may look as if we have distilled it for our listener, but we probably have already done this for ourselves.

Nevertheless, more distillation may be done during the actual telling than was done initially. The desire to keep a story short, for example, has the effect of distilling a gist so that only the essential details remain. In general, distillation leaves out descriptions of physical items unless those descriptions are critical to the story. Distillation also leaves out the particular words and ideas of the participants in a story although this distillation tends to occur at the time of storage rather than of generation. In fact, words may be put into the mouths of the participants by another story process as we shall see below. Distillation is a purist's kind of process. Distillation may never really occur in its pure form, however. That is, we like to think that we tell a subset of what we have experienced, and distillation is the process by which that subset is selected. But in actual practice, stories add details that may never have occurred at all. We shall see how this process works when we discuss other aspects of story construction. Now let's consider the next version of the first story which was told as if the teller had the intention of illustrating a previously made point about his vision problems and describing himself in the process:

STORY 1:   I was driving my Volvo once into a gas station, and what must have happened is that I was traveling forward, and I hit this big square concrete thing. It was high enough that I should have seen it, but it was over here in my right visual field. It was just another one of those cases where there is missing field here and I bashed right into it. I mean it was bright daylight, and I drove into it. Sometimes I just don't see stuff.

In this version, the teller combines the gists of two stories to make one story. The first or master story is the Volvo story; the second story is about the student's visual problems. Because the vision story has its own point, the effect of the combination process is to take everything from the Volvo story that related to the vision story and to tell it while suppressing everything else. Notice how almost nothing in the Volvo story that is unrelated to the teller's visual problems is expressed.

Two stories are also combined to illustrate the point in this version of the second story. Points may well exist independently of the stories that can be used to illustrate them. Here the point is that performance may not matter as much as emotional intent when speaking to a group. This point may, of course, be illustrated by this story, but it may also be illustrated in the mind of the teller by other stories as well. The teller combines this point with the story of the wedding, but, on the other hand, he probably could have used this story to illustrate many other points as well. Combining a point with a story means leaving out the parts of the story that don't help make the point and emphasizing those parts that do.

Combination

The combination process, therefore, causes the distillation process to suppress events unrelated to the point of the stories to be conjoined. The combination process must integrate two stories by deciding which is the master story and which is the coloration for the master. Events are interwoven to make one coherent story. The major subprocesses in combination, then, are *suppression* and *conjunction*. The suppression process examines the gist of each story to be combined to see whether it enhances the newly combined story. Aspects of the coloration story that have nothing to do with the point of the master story or with the coherence of the newly created story are thus dropped. The conjunction process must weave the two stories into one by deciding which story is dominant (dominance is often a function of affect), and which story will be used to enhance the dominant story by adding details or evidence. With the vision story dominant, the Volvo story is mined for important details which are added as evidence for the propositions of the vision story.

When a story is told in order to gain the attention of those around, the teller employs a different kind of story process. Let's consider what processes might have been active in the attention-getting versions of these two stories.

STORY 1: Let me tell you what happened to me. I was at a gas station, and I was driving this big old Volvo that I have. Let's see, I think I had gotten the gas, and I was—no, I hadn't gotten the gas yet. I was just driving in, and I was trying to get up to the pump, and there was this big planter up there. I don't know, it was this brick thing. It had dirt, and I drove the car into it and mashed the front of the car and really mashed the planter much worse than the front of the car. So I got out, and I talked to the guy at the gas station. He was really pissed off at me because he couldn't figure out how anybody could be stupid enough to drive into a planter right out there in broad daylight, and so we decided that we had to call the police, and he wanted to know the name of my insurance company. Then, the policeman got there, and I talked to him for a while. He said to me that it wasn't really a problem because I was not out on a road, so he was not going to give me a ticket, but I was still probably responsible for the damage, and the guy could still sue me if he wanted to, or he could go to my insurance company and get the money. So anyway, we exchanged insurance companies. . . .

STORY 2: Did you ever wonder what it's like when lesbians get married? Well, my sister's a lesbian, and last summer I went to her wedding, believe it or not. And it was bizarre. They—there's no legal possibility for two women to get married, so it was a civil ceremony, and it was not conducted—it was conducted by a woman who conducted rituals, women's rituals, and it was conducted as such which means that we burned incense, and we invoked goddesses, and we invoked the powers of the four directions, and we all walked in a circle, and everyone participated in the ceremony, and the bride and the groom or the bride and the bride or my sister and her fiancée or whatever the heck you want to call them wore Indian outfits—well it looked like Indian outfits. They were these strange leather outfits, matching outfits that they bought or made for the occasion. And she has two kids, my sister's intended has two kids, and they were both involved in the ceremony too, and everyone put little odd objects in the center—old photographs and old class rings, and things of significance one way or another. And it was very strange; it was a whole set of expectation violations. Everything you think's going to happen at a wedding didn't happen at this one. And vice versa, and then their house is a menagerie, so we had a dog walk through in the middle of the ceremony, and there was a bird chirping overhead. And that's what a lesbian wedding is like.

One difference between these stories and the first versions is greater length. Another difference is that the subsequent versions have more emotional content. Both of these differences are results of the elaboration process.

Elaboration

Stories can be elaborated for a variety of reasons, each of which relates to the story intentions discussed earlier. For example, a story can be elaborated in order to create an emotional impact on the hearer. Or it can be elaborated in order for the teller to hold center stage as long as possible. Each different intention causes the elaboration process to function differently.

For example, if we want to hold center stage, we might fill in as many details as possible. If we want to make a listener like us, we might elaborate the story with examples of how well we behaved, how poorly we were treated, and so on. Thus, elaboration is not the name of one story process at all. Rather, elaboration means finding additional things to say. In this story, the teller elaborated each event by adding details about how he felt to be there.

Thus, the elaboration process has three major subprocesses associated with it. *Detail addition* is a fairly straightforward process. In order to make the story take longer or seem more vivid or more realistic, details are added to the gist. Details can be added by search, by reconstruction, or by adaptation. In other words, we search memory to add details that we actually remember or that we can imagine must have been true or that we know were true in other similar situations. In the second story, the teller adds many details— strange leather outfits, walking around in a circle, invoking goddesses, etc. The intent of the teller is to hold the audience's attention. Thus, although the addition of details may have no point in terms of content, details matter a great deal in terms of storytelling. The more details added to the story, the more memorable the story becomes. Thus, the story is interesting and attention-getting.

A second elaboration process is *commentary*. In this process, we embellish by adding our own view of the situation, including comments on how well or how poorly various people behaved, what the right thing to do would have been, what others might say or think about the situation, what we would do next time, and so on. When we tell the story again, we might add different comments according to our audience and our view of the world at the time. Such comments are rarely part of the story gist in memory but are usually added at telling time.

The third elaboration subprocess is *role-playing,* another part of the telling process and not of memory. Since what people actually say is rarely part of the gist, we imagine what someone might have felt or said in that situation by accessing other stories where such feelings were experienced and stored. Thus, elaboration via role-playing tends to involve story combination. The stories that are combined are vestiges of old stories denuded of their actual points and circumstances and added to the current story in order to enhance it.

Consider, for example, the phrase "[the station owner] couldn't figure out how anyone could be stupid enough to . . ." Where does this come from? The teller probably did not recall the station owner's words. He had no real information about the owner's thoughts. Rather, the teller temporarily assumed the role of the owner by remembering his attitude, imagining where that attitude might have come from, and making up the rest. Thus, stories that start out as the relaying of factual events become fictional in a sense. Even telling true stories involves making up the events more often than not. The gist just doesn't have all you need if you want to tell a story that grabs people's attention.

The next story was told after the teller was asked to make the listener fall in love with him. The teller said that his idea of how to do this was to make himself seem vulnerable:

STORY 1: I had this old Volvo a few years ago. It was my first car, and people always have a certain special relationship to their first car, and I had one to this. I am not the type of guy that ever thought that I was really fast, the way some people do in a car, but when I was in this car I thought I was invulnerable. One day I drove the car into a gas station and drove right smack into a concrete planter, knocked it to pieces, and broke my right headlight. I wasn't injured, but I was so embarrassed. I, I felt like, I felt, I felt just completely devastated. I talked to the guy that was working at the gas station, and he told me that I was an idiot. I was going to have to pay him $10,000 to have the thing installed—it was brand-new. I realized that there was a lot more to being safe than being in a car that I wouldn't get killed in; that I was still just as vulnerable and just as potentially damaged as anybody out there. My Volvo wasn't really going to protect me at all in some way or another.

This is another example of story combination. Here the teller has decided that he needs to tell a vulnerability story to make someone fall in love with him. He uses the outline of such a story and fills in the details with an actual story. In the last story combination situation, the teller actually combined two real stories, one about his vision problems and one about his Volvo problems. Here, however, he is combining a real story with the outline of a story that he hardly knows. He may not actually have a vulnerability story. He simply assumes that one would work. This, then, is the first creation process that we have encountered.

Creation

Stories that are told via the creation process are rarely created out of whole cloth. The basic creation process combines elements of a real story or stories with a standard story the author wishes to tell. To put this another way, suppose an author wants to tell a love story. He wants two characters to meet, fall in love, have a crisis, resolve it, and live happily ever after. This outline of a story must then be fleshed out by a creation process that combines the outline with a previous story or with pieces of many previous stories. We use many different kinds of creation processes because we have many different ways to find material to flesh out a skeleton story. Here the teller uses the simplest creation process, one that fleshes out the outline by using one story to provide the details.

Such outlines are ubiquitous in both the storytelling and the story understanding process. Outlines are themselves stories, but stories of a rather neutral sort. Such stories are skeleton stories, but when skeleton stories are combined with more complex stories, more interesting stories result.

In the next version of the first story, the teller uses a skeleton story as the basis for the story addressed to his insurance agent:

STORY 1:   I was at a gas station about 11:30 this morning in Milford, and it is the one that is just before before the second Milford exit on 95 and—I can't remember the name of the gas station, but I can find out if you need to know—and I drove in. I was somewhere in the process of getting gas, I think when I was coming out of the gas station . . . no, it must have been when I was going in because I was going forward . . . I hit a concrete structure that was some kind of planter made out of loose concrete bricks that were not cemented together; knocked some of the bricks on the ground, and damaged my right front headlight. I gave the guy the name of the insurance company, and I presume that he called you, and that is why you have gotten in touch with me. He said that the thing was brand-new. I think that probably he may have been right, and it is going to cost him getting some workman out to put the cinder blocks back together. But, I don't think it is going to be much.

Here, the skeleton directs the telling of the story by outlining what information an insurance agent needs as if the teller were filling out an insurance form in his mind. Even though not very creative, the story still represents the story combination process. The creativity of that process depends to a large extent upon the creativity behind the creation of the skeleton story that is used in the first place. An insurance form skeleton story is certainly in no way creative, while a skeleton story that expresses vulnerability for making one seem lovable is somewhat more creative.

This conception of creativity in storytelling, then, is basically rather simple. After one selects a story skeleton—such as boy meets girl, boy loses girl, boy gets girl—one can then create a story around it by filling in details from real events. Thus, telling your mother about a problem that you have had is a story skeleton around which one can add the new details of a particular car accident. The more out of the ordinary one's actual experiences are, the less easy finding a relevant story skeleton is. Thus, the teller can choose the skeleton that describes going to your sister's wedding, but in the particular wedding described, that skeleton can serve only as a contrast rather than as a framework. Brand-new stories depend upon this contrast for humor. They rely upon failed expectations about what is likely to happen next by implicitly invoking a story skeleton and then abandoning it when least expected.

Captioning

The process of captioning is basically one of reducing a large amount of information to a very small amount. This happens for whole stories—*Where were you? I went to my sister's wedding*—as well as within stories. For example, let's look at one of the versions of the wedding story:

STORY 2:   Well, yeah, I was out there at my sister's wedding, and my sister is a lesbian, so she was getting married to another woman. I know that may seem very strange, and, of course, it isn't a legally binding ceremony, but it turned out to be much what you'd expect. It was two people who loved each other getting together to tell everyone else about it. And for their friends and the people that they were close to, to express their approval and hopes and best wishes for the couple. The woman that she's getting together with, that she got together with, has two kids, and so they have a family, and this new partner has a family, another family above her, and they were all there, and my family was all there, and the two families got to know each other, and that's another thing that sometimes happens at a wedding. We didn't know each other before. *And a lot of unconventional things were done there. There was some audience participation in the wedding* and *a chance for people to speak and talk about their hopes and blessings for the couple,* but it was a wedding. It was the wedding minus the religious or legal component of an ordinary one.

Now consider the sentences or phrases italicized above. We know these sentences or phrases carry more weight in other versions of the story. Here, the sentences were captioned from much larger events that the teller has decided not to relate at the moment. The particulars of the audience participation or the nature of the unconventional things are not germane to his point in this version. Therefore, he has captioned them. The captioning process is a shorthand way of telling all or parts of a story. Captioning is simply summarization of a larger story used as a means of telling that story. Woody Allen's "She's seventeen" was an example of captioning. Captioning means that there is a larger story to be told. Never telling the uncaptioned version of a story can have the effect on memory of causing the details to be forgotten, as we pointed out in Chapter 5.

Adaptation

The process of adaptation is not illustrated here. Adapting a story means taking one story and making another one out of it. If the teller of these stories decided to write a novel, he might adapt both the accident and the wedding stories to serve as chapters of that novel.

He would probably have to change various aspects of each story to make a coherent whole or to allow certain characters to reappear. Thus, new stories are created by taking old stories and altering different aspects of those stories for various purposes.

Conclusion

The central premise here is that a data base of partial stories rather than whole ones exists in memory. After a period of time, one remembers first- or secondhand experiences as a residue of partial stories. To tell a story, then, some set of events, together with a characterization of things that have been learned from those events and a characterization of the open questions in one's mind to which those events relate, are concatenated into a baseline representation, which we call the story basis or *gist* of a story. Gists are structured sets of events that function as a single unit in memory that can be transformed by a variety of processes into actual stories. Each time a story is told, its gist is accessed and manipulated for a particular purpose. A gist is a dynamic entity that can change or be replaced over time by adding or deleting details in subsequent tellings. The words we use are irrelevant, however. We don't recall the words we have added, although sometimes certain words and phrases do become an important part of a story. We do, on the other hand, recall the concepts we have added so that after retelling a gist in a certain way, with certain details left out and others emphasized, with some truths deleted and other nontruths added in, we have difficulty recognizing what actually happened. The only things we remember are the gists that we access. Accurate memories, then, are elusive entities at best.

□ 7 □

Knowing the Stories of Your Culture

□

Original Thought?

IF ALL we know is embodied in stories, and we understand everything in terms of stories we already know, then everything we say and think must be rather prescribed. When does original thinking occur? In part, much of what passes as original thinking is the coloration of neutral stories made relevant to new situations.

How to Make a Complex Decision

In the late sixties, I was introduced to an ancient decision-making process that had been revived as part of the times. When young people wanted to make a decision, they ceremoniously consulted a book of Chinese philosophy that I have previously mentioned called the *I Ching*. The consultation process had two parts. First, one of sixty-four hexagrams was chosen randomly. The selected hexagram with its accompanying commentary was then interpreted to provide advice on the correct path to take. Below are short descriptions of three hexagrams taken from the *I Ching*:

Prospering.   The inferior is going. The superior is coming. There will be good fortune and progress.

Innocence brings exceptional progress.   There is an advantage in correct persistence. If someone does not act appropriately, it would be a mistake. There is no advantage in moving toward a goal.

Learning from danger creates confidence.   Keeping a secure hold on the mind brings progress and all actions will be honorable.

Interestingly, people seem able to find relevance in *any* epigram. No matter which epigram was randomly chosen, flower children of the sixties could see fantastic relevance to their own lives and to their specific problem in it. This is not so much a comment on the "oh wow" attitude prevalent in the late sixties as it is a comment on human creative reasoning abilities. When forced to find an analogy between a general case and a specific case, if one is willing to be creative about it, it is usually possible to find a link. The creativity in this process is in the *tweaking,* by which I mean the adaptation of a general pattern to a particular case. In other words, creativity is not necessarily a process of wild innovation. The kind of mundane creativity that allows a person to invent responses like the ones that we found in the radio interviews is inherent in the process of taking what one already knows and adapting that knowledge to a new problem.

Sometimes what one already knows is what everyone knows. We don't live in a cultural vacuum. If most of what we know is stories, then most of those stories are probably not our own. We certainly can use and learn from the stories of our friends and family, but we also hear the stories of our culture and especially of various sub-cultures. We learn these stories by going to school, by watching television, by reading books, and generally by listening to those around us. These stories come in three basic flavors which are either neutral, condensed, or elaborated.

A *neutral story* contains general "wisdom" that seems intended for your particular problem but which, in fact, is applicable to almost any problem. This is the secret of the *I Ching*'s appeal.

A *condensed story* is a generalization drawn from many stories—one that predicts the outcome of events by recognizing the basic pattern inherent in certain stories. The most common form of such stories occurs as proverbs. Most cultures have proverbs that come to mind quite readily. Proverbs are condensed neutral stories that can be easily embellished with details so that they seem to apply to your particular problem.

An *elaborated story* is quite a bit like a proverb except that the case in question is filled with details and particulars. The story itself contains the names of particular players and gives particular events, but the overall intent is the same. Elaborated stories provide stories to aspire to, or to learn from, that the culture as a whole agrees are valuable. Myths, or heroic stories, are a typical form of elaborated story.

We will now consider the role of such cultural stories in more detail.

Neutral Stories

Let's return to the *I Ching* for a moment. When I give public lectures, I perform a kind of parlor trick. I ask whether anyone in the audience has a particular personal problem with which he or she would like help. Although an audience of a few hundred people is not the best place to air one's problems, I usually get a volunteer. Someone tells me a problem, and then I open a copy of the *I Ching* and read it aloud. The audience is always amazed at how relevant the answer that I have read is.

To give you an example of this, one day in Hartford, a twelve-year-old boy volunteered a problem. He said that his goldfish were dying in his fish tank, and he wondered whether I had any suggestions. Here is the advice from the *I Ching* that I randomly chose:

The great Nourisher favors righteous persistence. Good fortune results from not eating at home. It is a favorable time for crossing the great river.

The boy who asked this question was very excited. He said that he saw that the answer was very relevant to his problem. All he had to do was to change the bowl and water that the goldfish were in, give them a new place to visit, in effect, and then they would thrive. I have no idea if he actually did this or if another story from the *I Ching* would have convinced him to do something else. But he was capable of adapting this neutral story to his own problem. Most of us can do this kind of thing fairly easily if we so desire.

Condensed Stories

The more stories one has available to adapt into usefulness, the more inventive one can be. Intelligence, then, depends upon having a great many cases, often quite general cases, available for adaptation and upon the ability to find the relevance in the generalities that those cases capture to the particular problem at hand. To see this in another way, consider how you would answer the question: *Why did Swale die?*

To answer this question, you need to know that Swale was a Thoroughbred race horse who was three years old, that this is young for a horse, that he was considered the best horse of his age at the time, and that he was found dead in his stall one day before a big race. Of course, more information than this is needed to answer the question knowledgeably, but when people are pressed for an answer, they can usually make one up. Further, the answers they make up are often the same. For example, *he was killed for the insurance money* or *he was killed by the owner of a rival horse in the upcoming race* are two frequent answers to the question.

Where do answers such as these come from? Rather than attempt to create a brand-new explanation from scratch, we simply take an extant explanation, one that has worked before for some other problem, and adapt it for use in the current situation.

When I asked this question about Swale in one of my classes, one of the students said he was reminded of Jim Fixx, the man who wrote a book about the health benefits of jogging and then died while jogging at a relatively young age. He speculated that Swale, like Jim Fixx, might have died of a heart attack brought on by excessive running.

These two methods, explanation by use of standard explanations and explanation by use of reminding, are essentially not very different, and both are forms of case-based reasoning. In case-based reasoning, you find a relevant case to guide you in your task. When the task at hand is explanation, you need to find a case with a useful explanation or, alternatively, one used so often by the culture that the original case that inspired the explanation has been long forgotten. Then, you need to adapt that explanation to the current situation.

The results of this search for a relevant explanation or case and the subsequent adaptation of that case to the current situation constitute the essence of creativity. New ideas can come from this process, often in strange ways. For example, one student was reminded of the explanation pattern: *too much success too soon leads to drugs which lead to death,* a common explanation for the death of various rock stars and athletes. Swale was, after all, young, rich, very successful, and quite famous. The problem, of course, is that this reminding is silly since Swale probably didn't know all this and wasn't capable of giving himself drugs. But, and here is the key point, creativity can come from speculating about things that don't necessarily make great sense on the surface. In many ways, keeping a crazy hypothesis alive is an important part of creativity. So let's assume that the adaptation process we are using is unconcerned with these facts and attempt, instead, to establish how Swale might have gotten someone to help him use drugs. If the fact that horses can't talk doesn't matter to us, the idea that he might have asked his trainer comes to mind, and suddenly we find ourselves wondering whether his trainer gave him drugs. Since horses are drugged to speed them up, we are left with the plausible hypothesis that Swale might have died from being given too many drugs that made him fast but weakened his heart.

The point is that this hypothesis was arrived at in a fairly mechanical way. In other words, creativity, at least at this level, may not be so complex after all. Creativity needs cases to reason from and tweaking rules to apply to the cases.

Elaborated Stories

But why do all this work? We don't have to figure out the answer
to hard questions by adapting well-known stories to new situations.
Finding a story that fits exactly would be far easier. Well, actually
very little of what has gone before fits exactly in our own lives. One
remedy for this, then, is to adapt our own lives to what has gone
before. If you can't make a well-known story fit your life, make your
life fit a well-known story. Our need for heroes is powerful because
heroes are models for our own lives. Of course, heroes come in all
shapes and sizes. We can use standard heroes from our religions,
from our national history, from sports, or from our own families.
The important point is that stories of heroes' exploits are more for
copying than for adapting. We get our stories from heroes, and their
stories become our own.

Organized religion, especially the Bible-thumping religion as
practiced by modern day television evangelists, offers a wonderful
array of stories to aspire to. These preachers spend a great deal of
time telling us about problems and the solutions to these problems,
as embodied in the acts of various biblical heroes. Why are these
evangelists so appealing? One possible answer hinges upon the concept of a culturally common story. If we all share the same stories,
we feel part of a common group. Moreover, when we believe that
our most intimate stories are shared by our listener, communication
feels most intense.

For TV evangelists, the culturally common story is the basis of
their business. They tell good stories that they urge their listeners to
adopt as their own, but, more important, the stories they tell are
being heard by thousands of people. Thus, the stories automatically
build a bond among these people. They each share the same stories
to use as guidance in their lives. They can refer to them, and they
can use them for copying or adaptation.

The same possibility for establishing a bond applies to television
in general, but to a lesser extent. The fact that millions of people
watch the same show at the same time is not lost on individual
viewers. They can discuss what they saw with friends and coworkers
the next day. The difference is that the stories told on TV are usually

not stories at all in the sense that we have been discussing. They are collections of many stories, and usually the basic intention of TV stories is entertainment by humor or drama. So while TV stories may make people laugh or share the same emotions, television episodes often do not have the size of a story.

Size is actually a critical aspect to memorable stories. One cannot recall an entire TV episode by telling it in one's own words without reducing it in size. As we have seen, actually telling the story in a reasonably sized chunk is an important memory aid. Normal TV episodes are usually too long from a memory point of view, and they fail to have a point as well. But biblical stories, especially as told by TV evangelists, are just the right memory size. This quality of size and their commonality across the subculture of listeners make them quite compelling to know and talk about. They become the model for the lives of the listeners.

In addition, as we have seen with the *I Ching,* the more generic a story, the more it is of general usefulness. Bible stories have survived precisely because they are stories that typify situations in which people often find themselves. The more ubiquitous a given type of human situation, the more a biblical story relating to that situation would be told and retold, to be remembered forever by the culture.

Subcultures

One remarkable thing to notice about a subculture is that the stories that it defines itself in terms of are quite different from those of competing subcultures. Learning which stories can be told as new ones and which ones are part of the subculture is what understanding the world you live in is all about. Each subculture has its own official stories. Knowing them means gaining what one needs from the subculture. In fact, that reminds me of a story.

I was a professor at Stanford in California during the late sixties and early seventies. Those were the times of the hippies and radicals on campus—being in tune with your feelings and other non-academic ways of looking at the world were in vogue, especially in California. I received an offer to go to Switzerland to sit by a lake and think. I wanted to write a book, and the idea of taking a leave from Stanford to go do this seemed irresistible. I had to request this leave from the department chairman. He asked me why I wanted the leave, and I told him, "I need to get my head together for a while." As I heard myself say this, I was astonished. I didn't talk this way, and the real reason for the leave was that I wanted to write a book. But I knew that if I told him that, he wouldn't have found the reason compelling. This particular man had never written a book, but he had been finding plenty of time to get his head together lately. Saying this was definitely the correct way to talk to him. He understood immediately and granted the leave.

I was able to convince the chairman because I knew the stories of his subculture. Teenagers are not so lucky. How exactly does one learn the official stories of a given subculture? The answer to this question is important precisely because we need to convince others that we are or should be members of a given subculture by showing that we share the official stories. But we also need to define ourselves with respect to how we differ from the official stories. We develop stories of our own that demonstrate these differences. Thus, in some sense, growing up is the process of collecting two important classes of stories: those of the subculture(s) that one wishes to join and those that serve to define oneself as an individual who has an identity independent of the subculture.

Consider, for example, this conversation between two teenagers.

F: This guy who I don't even know, I mean he introduced himself, his name is Paul, but I've never seen him before. When he left, he gave me a kiss good-bye, and I was kind of like who the fuck are you? What egg did you hatch? Who the hell do you think you are giving me a kiss? I was kind of like OK fine. I just looked at Fred—I was like I won't ask.

R: Yeah, but drunk guys, you know.

F: I know, but it was weird though. Later on, I'm standing talking to Lee, and Scott comes over. Remember Scott Grable? His sister got married. His sister baby-sat for me for a long time. He and I dated for a while. We've been friends for a while.

R: Ick, gross, is this the one who we broke up because of?

F: No. No. No. No. No. Scott's a really wonderful guy. He goes to
     Brook.

R: Why did Scott and we break up?

F: Well, because we were never really going out.

R: OK, I get it. I remember.

F: There was never anything really physical. He comes over to me.
     He kind of said hello and gave me a hug. And then was kind of
     like—we'd been standing there for a while—and he was kind of
     like can we talk for a minute? Really seriously, and I was like, sure.
     Now Robby had been acting really weird all evening, and I kept
     saying to myself it's just that it's his house. It's his party. He has to
     mingle. It's not me. Don't be paranoid. Be calm. Right then, I like
     hit the roof, it was like oh my god. He told Scott something. He
     never wants to see me again. He's not going to tell me. Scott's
     going to tell me. Scott's really pissed about it. All that kind of stuff.

R: I can imagine.

F: Instead, we get from Scott, and I've never gotten anything like this
     from Scott. We sit down, and Scott says something like I don't
     know where to start, and I really don't know how to say this, but
     basically I want to apologize for being such an asshole to you.

R: Oh, how cute. That's nice.

F: Yeah, and he just went on about how much he really cares about
     me, and that he wanted me to know that during all that time that
     he just didn't have his shit together, and he couldn't commit to
     me and he couldn't do—

R: You should just be careful. That's such a line—I didn't have my
     shit together—that's such a line. I couldn't commit. I could name
     five guys who have said that to me. Do you know what I mean,
     like tell me, like. Josh.

F: But basically coming from Scott it was different, and we had a
     really long conversation that was really good, and we'd never had
     one of those before, and so it was really good, and so that was
     cool.

For a member of my generation, at least, this conversation is a
little difficult to understand. It uses language that I don't understand
very well, and it refers to situations that I can only understand by
guessing at them. Some of these situations are stories that are shared
only between the two participants. For example, the breakup they

refer to is a story from their shared sub-subculture, that is, from the world that only the two of them share. Other stories, however, would be understandable by members of their school only, and others would be understandable by members of their generation, and so on. To see what I mean, let's look at the continuation of this conversation with an eye toward which stories can be understood by whom:

R: Wait, I have to tell you something really funny before I forget. OK, you know I went to see Sting. So I got to see Sting. And Alison pulls, first of all I was in a bitchy mood when we left, 'cause you know how Alison is, you know Alison repeatedly lies, schemes, does things that completely irritate me, and they're always forgivable because for some reason she gets away with it. So, here we are Sunday morning. We had plans, no joke, to leave for Lake Compounce at 6 A.M. Like completely serious plans because we did want to be able to staple ourselves to Sting's leg. So we leave. I call Alison. She calls me the day before. She's like, do you mind if Sue comes? Sue is Alison's friend who I know who I don't dislike, but this was my graduation present from Alison, the tickets, and it's kind of like. Alison was supposed to go to the concert with me when I was a sophomore, and she never got to go, and so it was kind of like our rain check. It was delayed. It's hard to explain. It was kind of like a displaced thing. It was like a reenactment of what should have happened when I was a sopho-more because we bought the tickets together.

We were really pumped. I really wanted it to be just us. It's not at all that I don't like Sue; in fact, Sue and I got along better than Alison and I did this entire day. She's like do you mind if Sue comes? Fortunately, I had an excuse. I didn't want to say no because Alison did buy the tickets, whatever, even though they were a gift for me. That's fine. I go, well, I can't get her a ticket at work because our Ticketron machine is broken—which was true—I wouldn't lie about something that completely ludicrous. She's like forget it then. I call her later that night to make sure everything's OK for the next morning—she's like oh, Sue got a ticket. So, it started there. That's where it started. Because I thought that she got my hint.

So, I'm like fine. I call her in the morning. She also tells me Saturday night we can't leave at six. She doesn't want to leave until nine. I said how about eight? She said, well. So we compromised. I'm like we'll leave at 8:30. So, I finally got a hold of her at 8:30, and she's like hi. I'm like you don't seem to understand. I didn't say any of this, cause that's what I do with Alison.

I don't even bother taking it up with her especially since I wasn't going to start anything until after the show. We don't leave until 9:45. I had to go to the bank. I had to get gas. That's why I wanted to leave so early in the first place. I had to go to the Barney machine. I didn't have any money.

We leave at 9:45. Fortunately, the gates at Lake Compounce don't open until 11:00, so we were among the first people there, and we did end up waiting. We planned this six hours before they open the concert gates, and when they open the gates, it's like a mad rush to the stage. We were in the very front, just for the record, and we almost got killed. I have like two bruised ribs from being pushed into the metal bars by twenty thousand people. But I did carry on a very good conversation with Branford Marsalis, you know the saxophone, you know who he is, who I like adore. And Sting looked at us three times, and I do want to bear his children, so it was really nice, but it was painful. Physically, it was a painful concert because we had twenty thousand like thirteen-year-old Sting fans trying to get to where we were, so they were throwing us into the chrome bars.

But anyway. Alison meets a guy who was just coincidentally standing behind us and ends up the two of them like pawing each other while we're waiting for the concert to start. They let you in at six, so you still have two hours to wait before the show starts. These two meet. Sue and I are talking. We turn around and they've got their tongues in each other's mouths, and they've known each other. Fine, you can flirt with someone all you want, but there's a certain boundary that you do not cross within the first half hour of an acquaintance. I was like, Sue, we give them another half hour and we'll have a family, a house with a white picket fence, and the whole spiel. They ended up like he took her phone number or something really single-barish like that.

And we did see the concert, and the concert was great, and when we left, Alison was trying to talk about him, and Sue and I would crank the music because we didn't want to say to her we think this whole thing is really retarded, but we also didn't want to talk about it, so we figured the best way to deal with it would be to avoid the subject. So, Alison calls me the next day, and she's like Dave called, and Dave is this kid's name coincidentally. She's I think he's so nice. He's really cute, but neither of you seem to think so. I'm like, Alison, it's not that, I go, I just think the whole situation is kind of, and I couldn't finish my sentence, and she goes, sluttish, and I go, not that, I mean not, I wanted to go well basically yeah.

This is the irony of the story. We're leaving the concert. We're all really pumped. All my anger has since been channeled into passion 'cause Sting is not wearing a shirt standing above me, and he does look like Adonis, and I am drooling all over the front of my T-shirt. But he did. He looked really good. He's a beautiful, beautiful forty. I mean if I look like that when I'm forty in female version I will be one happy camper, and Branford Marsalis talked to me which did kind of make my day. So anyway, we were all really pumped in the car, and there's this beautiful—it takes like forever to get out of Lake Compounce 'cause it's like a madhouse—so there's like this guy with this red hair, like long hair, that kind of red color that no one ever has, not like bright red, and not just reddish brown, but that really pale, kind of pink, the neatest color, and it was real, completely real, and it was long, which you know how I am—long hair and guys wins hands down. Sue was like that's the guy I was trying to point out to you before. I couldn't tell if he was a girl or a guy which sounds oh great, he must be really wonderful if you couldn't tell if he was completely androgynous, but it's not that, it's that he's really pretty almost. He's got a really nice face, so he could pass for a girl with the hair from far away, but he was definitely not feminine. So we're getting in the car, and I'm looking at him, and he catches my glance, like he sees that my tongue is like on the ground, and I'm like oh, hi. And I just get back in the car. I made it my hi, the intonation, the inflection was pretty much I do want to have your children. If I had all the children I said I wanted to have, do you know how many men would have fathered children through me by now? But anyway, so coincidentally, we're following him out of the parking lot, and I'm looking in the sideview mirror, sticking my head out of the window, like oh hi, that's all I ever said, oh hi. He's looking at me, and when we're stopped for like a half hour in the backup. He puts his car in park. He has this clear rubber, you know those balls that little kids play with—they're about orange-size. With like speckles inside it 'cause it was like clear rubber. He gets out of his car, comes up to my window, and goes, a gift, hands it to me, gets back in his car, and I never saw him again.

The sheer number of culture-specific stories, ones that the teller assumes that her listener knows and need not have explained, that are contained within this story is overwhelming to attempt to detail. For example, some names of shared stories that this girl mentions are:

I went to see Sting.
I was in a bitchy mood.

You know how Alison is.

I can't hold a grudge.

I repeatedly allow her to make me completely miserable.

We did want to be able to staple ourselves to Sting's leg.

She's like, do you mind if Sue comes?

This was my graduation present from Alison.

It was kind of like our rain check.

It was like a reenactment of what should have happened when I was a sophomore.

I finally get a hold of her at 8:30, and she's like hi.

I'm like you don't seem to understand.

I had to go to the Barney machine.

When they open the gates, it's like a mad rush to the stage.

And Sting looked at us three times, and I do want to bear his children.

It was a painful concert because we had twenty thousand like thirteen-year-old Sting fans trying to get to where we were, so they were throwing us into the chrome bars.

Alison meets a guy who was just coincidentally standing behind us and ends up the two of them like pawing each other while we're waiting for the concert to start.

You can flirt with someone all you want, but there's a certain boundary that you do not cross within the first half hour of an acquaintance. I was like, Sue, we give them another half hour and we'll have a family, a house with a white picket fence, and the whole spiel.

They ended up like he took her phone number or something really single-barish like that.

Alison calls me the next day, and she's like Dave called . . . and I think he's so nice.

He's really cute, but neither of you seem to think so. I'm like, Alison, it's not that, I go, I just think the whole situation is kind of [sluttish].

Each of the sentences that I have listed above are references to culturally shared stories. The question is, to which culture? For example, "sluttish" is shared by those from many different generations, but it means different things to different cultures. Other common stories that she makes reference to are "infatuation with a new boy," "smoker's subculture," and "hero worship of a rock star." These are all culturally common stories for teenagers today and, by abstraction, can be understood by anyone who once was a teenager in similar circumstances. The understandability of this story depends upon the extent to which the understander shares the implicit and explicit culturally common stories. Many of these stories are well known to most Americans. Some can be figured out by reference to our own lives as teenagers. But many of them really require being a part of the subculture that is being discussed. Understanding, in its deepest sense, depends upon shared stories.

We live in multiple subcultures. Thus, the teller of this story uses stories that only her friends would know, but she also uses stories that only teenagers would know, or that only someone from her town would know, and so on. Some of the stories that she refers to from her own personal subculture that are the most difficult to understand, are: "You know how Alison is" and "what should have happened when I was a sophomore." Naturally, this girl can communicate with a friend on a personal level that only the two of them can understand as well as on a level that a wider and wider set of people can understand. She uses language that, to some extent, masks what she means from people not of her subculture which, one would suppose, makes what she means clearer to her compatriots.

The rock concert subculture has its stories too. Stories such as "And Sting looked at us three times, and I do want to bear his children" and "It was a painful concert because we had twenty thousand like thirteen-year-old Sting fans trying to get to where we were, so they were throwing us into the chrome bars" are easy to understand for someone who attends rock concerts and more difficult for others. You would have to be a member of the teller's generation to appreciate what is meant by "Alison meets a guy who was just coincidentally standing behind us and ends up the two of them like pawing each other while we're waiting for the concert to start" or "You can flirt with someone all you want, but there's a certain boundary that you do not cross within the first half hour of an acquaintance. I was like, Sue, we give them another half hour and we'll have a family, a house with a white picket fence, and the whole spiel." This is not to say that these stories are incomprehensible to outsiders. Certainly, others can figure out what is meant by them to some extent. And that is the key point—it is only possible to some extent. True understanding requires really knowing the story, not guessing at what it might mean.

In short, understanding someone who shares only a few of your stories is very difficult, but understanding someone whose stories are the same as yours is much easier. Self-definition means the adoption of a set of stories as one's own. Adapting to another culture means learning the stories of that culture.

Untold Stories of Foreign Cultures

People, when they operate in their native culture, rarely think about the stories that they employ in their daily lives. They know how to order a meal in a restaurant, how to mail a letter, how to transport themselves around their city, and so on. They know how to do these things because they have been doing them all their lives. Now, plop some Americans down in a Parisian café, and they are lost. They don't know whether they should tip the waiter, how long they can sit down without ordering something else, what it is possible to order, whether it is appropriate to speak to their neighbors, and so on. In short, they are so confused that they will probably do something wildly wrong and feel quite unhappy in the process. More important, they may not be able to accomplish what they wanted to accomplish, even with their high school French, because their high school French taught them to say "My pen is on the table" and not "Is the orange juice fresh-squeezed or from a can?"

Language teaching tends to concentrate on grammar and conjugations, both of which are very nice, but neither of which is something that the average speaker is consciously aware of. As speakers of English, we do know how to conjugate English verbs, and we do know the rules of English grammar. We were speaking quite fluently, however, before anyone tried to teach us these things about our own language. What we learn, as we grow up, is the stories of our culture that allow us to communicate quickly and efficiently with members of our own culture.

Obviously, then, the same should be true in learning a foreign language. You can learn, for example, the rules necessary to say "He told me" in French, but you may be unable to spit out that sentence in a real conversation if you are consciously thinking of how to place direct object pronouns, how to conjugate *avoir,* and so on. The right way to learn a language is the way people have always learned to speak, by memorizing the whole phrase as a series of sounds, without even thinking about the individual words and word placements that are involved. One must learn the phrase, *"il m'a dit,"* and say it all at once. We have a lot of evidence that language is learned phrasally, rather than word by word.

But to function effectively in France, learning French isn't all that is necessary. One must learn French stories, i.e., the stories that are only culturally common in France. Furthermore, one must also learn the shorthand way in which French people refer to their culturally common stories.

As an example of what I mean here, let's talk about cafés. The French go to cafés for four reasons: to have a drink, the way an American would go to a coffee shop (except that in France almost all the cafés sell alcoholic beverages, too); to have a place to meet with a friend to talk; or, like a kind of French happy hour, to meet with their friends from work to have an aperitif before lunch (yes, the French do drink before lunch, too) or dinner; or, on a sunny day to sit with a newspaper outside on the sidewalk and watch the world go by. The French really enjoy doing this sort of thing; almost every block in any decent-sized city has a café.

Cafés themselves have a culturally common story. You have a choice of taking a seat at a table or else standing at the bar itself. Don't expect someone to seat you—it will never happen. If you choose to sit at a table, the prices will be higher for the same drink than they would have been at the bar. Also, it costs even more to sit outside on the sidewalk than it does to sit inside. This is the story of the café. All French people know it; Americans usually have to be told. In essence, in order for Americans to operate successfully in a French café, they have to be told the story of the French café. They are missing a common story of a subculture to which they do not belong. If they are lucky, someone will tell them the story. Otherwise they will have to learn it for themselves. The problem is that most people don't realize that such common situations are expressions of a culture's stories, so no one bothers to tell these stories. Daily life is filled with the untold stories of the culture.

What follows is a typical conversation between a waiter and a two customers that might occur in a café in France:

Je vous écoute.
    Un demi.
Stella ou Kronenbourg?
    Qu'est-ce que vous avez en bouteille?
On a Heineken et Carlsberg.
    Donnez-moi une Carlsberg, très froid.
Et pour monsieur?
    Une orange pressée.
Nous ne faisons pas ça.
    Alors, je voudrais un ballon de rouge.
Ordinaire, ou Côtes du Rhône?
    Je préfère un Côtes du Rhône.
Je vous apporte ça tout de suite.

I have presented this in French with no translation because my contention is that translations aren't so simple.

Let's consider the cultural, story-based translation of this exchange:

Je vous écoute.
    Un demi.

The waiter arrives and says "I am listening to you." If an American waiter did this, we would be perplexed. What would he mean? But no Frenchman wonders what it means. It means "What'll you have, buddy?" or one of many French ways to say that a waiter is ready to take your order.

What story is being told here? The story, a rather boring one, is about preparedness. The words used, for the most part, are irrelevant. We all know what happens in a restaurant. The reality is that nothing need be said at all. The particular words actually used only indicate that the story we both know need not be told at all. We all know why waiters do what they do and why we are there, so we do nothing but indicate the start of things.

The response, *un demi,* literally means "a half." A half of what, you ask? Here then, is our second story—another dull story. Culturally common stories almost always are, especially to members of the culture. This story is about the normal size of glasses from which draft beer is served, which turn out to be half a liter. The main point is that "a half" really refers to beer. How can this be a sentence about beer? Recall that many stories don't need to be told at all. We only need to make common references to well-known stories. "A half" is a story in a café just as surely as "forty-two" is a story in jail.

Stella ou Kronenbourg?
    Qu'est-ce que vous avez en bouteille?
On a Heineken et Carlsberg.
    Donnez-moi une Carlsberg, très froid.

This next bit of conversation is about what brands of beer are available, and the last sentence asks for a very cold Carlsberg in a bottle. Herein lies another story. The French don't drink beer at the same temperature as Americans do. Our customer is telling the waiter that she is an American and that she doesn't think the French know anything about how to serve beer. The waiter can understand the request because he has probably heard this story before. Otherwise, he might respond with some question as to the customer's sanity for wanting to drink beer too cold.

Et pour monsieur?
    Une orange pressée.

The waiter asks what the male customer wants, which is the tail end of a common French story about where one sits and how one orders in a restaurant. Americans usually don't know this story: Women sit facing the main part of the restaurant, men face the wall; women order before men, older women first. The customer responds that he wants "a pressed orange," which is how one asks for fresh orange juice. Had the restaurant had it, our American customer might have been surprised to find that sugar and water were served with the juice. The French orange juice story, he would learn, is different than the American one.

> Nous ne faisons pas ça.
>   Alors, je voudrais un ballon de rouge.
> Ordinaire, ou Côtes du Rhône?
>   Je préfère un Côtes du Rhône.
> Je vous apporte ça tout de suite.

The waiter says they don't have it, so the customer asks for a glass of red. Red what, you ask? Don't be silly. This is France. You don't have to *say* wine. The waiter asks what kind of wine, giving two choices, ordinary and Côtes du Rhône. Here again he is telling a story. This is a café in France, he says, not a restaurant; we don't have lots of choices, but this isn't America either, where there are no choices. He is telling the story of his café, as it were. Next time we would know not to order orange juice if we like fresh, and we would know to order the type of wine we want because we would know the choices. In this way, we can learn the stories of the places we visit regularly. The café itself is a kind of subculture whose stories we can learn and refer to in our own conversations.

Mastering One's Own Stories

In effect, then, coping in the modern world means knowing the stories of the cultures in which you operate. Certainly, one would survive well enough in a French café even if one didn't know all the details just presented. The story of the French café isn't all that different from its American cousin. The point is that both have stories, perhaps not fascinating stories, but stories nonetheless.

Understanding a culture, then, in the sense of being able to operate easily in it, means knowing the culture's stories. And similarly, operating in the idiosyncratic world of your own subculture, you must know your own stories.

When people ask teenagers questions in their first job interview or in a college interview, for example, they often give monosyllabic answers, interspersed with frequent "I don't knows." One reason for this is that teenagers, unlike adults, haven't got their stories down. That is, they don't know what their stories are, both because they haven't thought about these things before—they haven't got answers they have used before that they can simply copy—and because their answers keep changing over time. Adults, on the other hand, needn't think at all after a while. All the stories you ever will tell have already been thought up and stored away. This process of going from not knowing what one's stories are to knowing them and telling them, ad nauseam, is what constitutes the process of self-definition. We define ourselves through the stories we tell.

But which stories do we choose to tell and which do we carefully tuck away untold or even uncomposed? The act of creating stories to tell has a great deal to do with how we see ourselves. One problem is that the stories we tell as children often are shaped for us. When the college interviewer asks a seventeen-year-old why he or she wants to go to college, there is, unfortunately, a right answer. The issue for the teenager is to learn the right answers, to learn the official stories that qualify one to be accepted into various subcultures.

Is it actually possible not to know the stories of your own culture, your subculture, or your sub-subculture? When the answer is yes, the consequences are rather interesting. Two articles that show very well what happens when one misunderstands or misuses the stories of one's culture recently appeared on the front page of *The New York Times*.

On Tuesday, September 27, 1988, an article reported the grand jury investigation of what had come to be known as the Tawana Brawley case. The article took up two full pages in the *Times,* so I will cite only some relevant parts.

EVIDENCE POINTS TO DECEIT BY BRAWLEY

A seven-month New York State grand jury inquiry has compiled overwhelming evidence that Tawana Brawley fabricated her story of abduction and sexual abuse by a gang of racist white men last year, according to investigators, witnesses, and official summaries of evidence presented to the panel. . . .

. . . She concocted, alone or with an accomplice, the degrading condition in which she was found.

. . . She tried for weeks to mislead doctors, social workers, the police, reporters . . . with a charade of medical complaints and false and fragmentary accounts of horror in the hands of racists—a tale luridly embellished by her family, lawyers, and advisers.

Miss Brawley's motives are still unclear . . . but evidence suggested that she may have feared the wrath of her mother's boyfriend for her late nights out. . . .

Thus, it appears that a case that became a national symbol of racism . . . originated as little more than the fantasy of a troubled teenager, and became grist for the racial and political agendas of her advisers.

The conclusion that Miss Brawley fabricated her story is supported by . . . evidence that she ran away and spent much of the next four days at her former apartment, evidence that she concocted the condition in which she was found, and evidence that she tried to mislead the police, doctors, and others about what had happened to her.

What does this account have to do with stories? If the grand jury is correct, Tawana Brawley ran away for four days, and she needed to tell a story. For her own reasons, she decided not to tell the true story of where she had been, but to invent one instead. When we invent a story in order to mislead people, we try to figure out the story that they want to hear, and we tell it. Children frequently tell a *he made me do it* story or an *it wasn't me that did it* story when they are caught having done something wrong. And this kind of story is what Tawana Brawley told too. Her problem was selecting a believable story. She failed to assess how many listeners would hear her story and failed to understand that what each of them wanted to hear was quite different.

Tawana told a story that is unfortunately quite standard in the general American culture: *Young girl is kidnapped and raped.* Although some details of her story were unnecessary to accomplish her goal of not getting punished by her parents, she also added a story that was appropriate for her subculture: *Young black is victim of racial attack.* While either of these standard stories is bad enough, the combination of them produced something that we can only assume Tawana had not counted on—the match of two types of stories sought by the news media and black activists. The media looks for horrifying stories involving assaults on especially innocent people. Consequently, Tawana's story matched a skeleton story that news people are always looking to report. Had she understood all this, Tawana would have been better off choosing a story, a not especially newsworthy story, that matched the *Parents forgive errant child* skeleton.

Her story also matched a skeleton story that black activists are always on the lookout for: *innocent blacks as easy victims of white officials.* She had added that her rapists were state police officers and other officials of her area. This factor, of course, had it been true, should well have caused alarm on the part of activists.

Tawana's mistake, apart from fabricating events in the first place, was to invent stories without understanding the standard nature of the stories that others look for. Thus, when doctors are handed a rape case or a case of unconsciousness from beating and deprivation, they have certain tests they perform to aid the victim. They also use skeleton stories to understand such cases, and they seek to fit the details of any new story into the familiar story. Similarly, the police know a story about rape, and in the case of Tawana Brawley, they tried to fit the details of her story into theirs. For both the doctors and the police, Tawana's story did not agree with the standard stories about rape, and this disparity caused them to question the truth of Tawana's claims.

When we move about from subculture to subculture, we attempt to interpret stories that we hear by translating them into stories we already know. When the fit is rather inexact, we wonder whether we have failed to understand something or whether the story we are being told is not what it was supposed to be. Not surprisingly, since she is young and rather unsophisticated, Tawana Brawley failed to understand how to make up a story that matched the ones that the people who were listening to her expected to hear. She did not know the stories of the other subcultures. Traveling across cultures, it seems, requires the help of a translator.

Curiously, on September 27, the *Times* also reported another case of story misunderstanding. Ben Johnson, a Canadian runner, was disqualified from the Olympics and lost his gold medal for using steroids. The story is interesting in this context because the press assumed that everyone who uses steroids also knows how to avoid getting caught.

If there were no testing, more athletes would gamble their adult lives on a gold medal, endorsements, and prize money. . . . Dr. Voy (chief medical officer of the U.S. Olympic Committee) did not show much interest in Johnson's claim that his drink had been spiked nor did he believe anything had gone wrong in the laboratory. "I'm not surprised. Steroid use is pretty rampant. My only surprise is that he got caught. My surprise is because these athletes have good information on how to mask the drugs. He must have miscalculated the dose or there is something screwy with his system, or he gambled at the end, coming close to the final event." Dr. Voy's sources among the athletes say that they are now using steroids within five to seven days of an event, assuming that the newest masking agents will take over.

This story is also interesting for our purposes because it talks about the stories of a particular culture and Ben Johnson's failure to select the right one. Dr. Voy tells the stories that a doctor knows by virtue of being a doctor who is involved with modern athletics. Doctors know the *miscalculate the dose* story, the *screwy system* story, and the *reckless gamble* story, all of which are ways for steroids to be discovered. What stories did Johnson know? Voy assumes that he knew the *masking the drug* story but might also have known the *panic to insure victory* story. After Johnson was discovered, he told the *spiked my drink with drugs* story and the *bad lab test* story. In essence, the only thinking we have here is the selection of stories.

Now, the kinds of stories that I have been referring to here are what I have previously called "explanation patterns" in my book of that name (Hillsdale, NJ: Lawrence Erlbaum Associates, 1986). The premise behind explanation patterns is that when we need to explain something to ourselves, which happens every time we fail to understand something, we choose, if we can, a standard explanation, and we try to adapt it to our current situation. Explanation patterns are cultural norms in that subcultures share them.

In other words, explanation patterns are a kind of culturally com-

mon story. We rely upon familiar explanations because we can find
them easily, and similarly, others will easily accept such explanations
because they are also familiar with them. When Tawana Brawley and
Ben Johnson chose to start telling the story of what happened to
them, they chose stories already accepted by the culture they lived
in and which they assumed would be accepted once again. When
officials analyzed those stories to see whether they were true, the
officials found other stories that sounded better and more reasonable. The major point is that no one made anything up. No story
was new but rather was standard in the subculture.

Of course, people outside a given subculture learn new stories all
the time. I learned, for example, that athletes take drugs to conceal
steroid use and that they are given information about the use of these
masking drugs in a kind of haphazard manner. This story is well-
known to Dr. Voy, but not to me. I am not a member of the
subculture of drug-taking athletes. Different cultures share different
stories; in fact, a subculture can be defined by the stories shared
within it.

The Power of a Good Story

Throughout history the most powerful demagogues have been the
best storytellers. Today we have a breed of storytellers, namely television evangelists, who manage to mesmerize people with their stories.
These storytellers share something important with their listeners,
namely a sense that the stories they are hearing are about themselves.
The television evangelists capitalize on the fact that they can tell
stories that are universally understandable by their audience—stories
their audience identifies with. Thus, evangelists tell stories about
sinners or biblical characters with problems in the hope that these
stories will speak to the audience by claiming a shared subculture.
In other words, these stories tell their listeners that they are not
alone, and as a result, the listeners behave in the way that the subculture expects by giving money or attending church or other behaviors
useful to the tellers.

One of the best of these storytellers is Jimmy Swaggart. Consider the following Jimmy Swaggart story:

1940—a long time ago—I was five years old. The night my daddy came to Jesus. He was one of the hardest men. No one thought he would come. But he stepped up that night under mighty and powerful Holy Ghost conviction. His closest friend, a businessman, wealthy—both of them in business together. Under the same kind of Holy Ghost conviction, mighty powerful conviction—so strong, the man was shaking. He wouldn't come. So my dad got up from those altars with a puddle of tears left there, and Jesus had come into his heart. The first man that he saw was his friend, his business partner. He was weeping. He threw his arms around my dad and pulled him tight—weeping and sobbing, and my dad said, "Why, why don't you come?" He said, "I can't. I can't. I can't. I can't."

It was almost like a door closed. This man that had as great a business sense as any man my dad knew. Lost it. Business after business after business after business went. He started to drink very heavily. He drank so much and stayed in a stupor of drunkenness for months at a time until his eyes—you've seen them when they're on the edge of death and their eyes are running water continually. Twenty-four hours a day running water, red, dying. His mind went.

I remember I was six years old when we went to the funeral of his little boy. The little boy was about four years old. He had black ringlet curls on his head, and it seemed that this was all the father loved anymore. The other sons had gone to hell and back. One of them was to go to the penitentiary. And that little fellow was his life. And the baby died. And I stood there with my eyes big, and it was such a striking, startling, dramatic thing that I will never forget it. I saw him as he looked into the casket—my dad trying to comfort him—but it was no use, and he was hitting the side of it with his fist and cursing God. It scared me. I was six years old, but I was scared. I was trembling. I never heard anything like that—cursing God. "You took my baby. I've got nothing left." A beautiful home gone. Business after business gone. And we were in a shack, and the casket sat in the living room. And that little fellow with his black curls lay against the pillow. And he was hitting the side—his father—and looking up and saying, "I hate you, God." Using the foulest, most horrifying language. "I hate you."

What little was left of his mind went. I would see in my dad, and if he ever prayed for a man, he prayed for this man. My dad would weep for him. He lost his cars, he lost his trucks, he lost everything he had. And you would see him stumbling along the side of the road. Cursing—constantly—this was not just one occasion. This went on for years. Cursing, cursing. Just a rolling stream of vitriolic, vituperative venom that spilled of every profanity cursing God. I would hear him sometimes when I would pass him when I was a child seven, eight, nine years old, and I would hear him cursing God for every foul thing. This went on for years. My dad would pick him up, try to talk to him. It seemed to be no hope, no use.

This story ends with the man finally finding God. Its intent is to say to its listeners that they can become part of the community—Swaggart's subculture—no matter how bad they are. This is important for a potential joiner to know. People like Jimmy Swaggart often have only one story to tell. His story is nearly always that people don't have religion at first, that they do a great many bad things, that other people try to prevent them from getting religion, but that religion can come upon them in myriad possible ways and from that point all kinds of good comes from getting religion. Telling the story in the way that I have just done is basically useless, however. The important point is to personalize it, to particularize it, to draw as many references as possible to real world events that hearers may have themselves experienced so that they can identify with the story.

What does "identify" mean in this context? Essentially, one can view Jimmy Swaggart and other demagogue storytellers as people who are looking to create indices in their stories that match those in stories their hearers already know. When such matches occur, when one's own personal stories come to mind in response to what one has heard, one feels that one has understood, in a deep sense, what the speaker has said. This means then, that storytellers who wish to convince their audience of something will find as many ways as possible to give particular details in their stories that might relate to stories their hearers know. Thus Swaggart talks about difficult fathers, drunken people, people who have had very bad luck, children confronting death, and other topics that the audience is likely to have some familiarity with; and then he ties those previously known and understood stories to the difficulty of understanding how God works and the importance of preaching. He thus adds his own conclusion to each listener's story. And his own stories become his audience's own stories. It is a powerful technique.

Now consider the following story:

God's spirit started moving through that crowd, and scores started to come to Jesus. They started—those Panamanians—coming down every aisle, weeping and crying as God's spirit flowed through that service. I guess it must have been about three or four minutes into the altar call when I saw this man step up. He was a big man, a giant of a man. You wouldn't forget a man this size because of the breadth of his shoulders, maybe six foot six inches tall. And I noticed him limping. I think it was his left leg. I'm not sure. And he came, and it was like his leg was stiff, and he came down that aisle. When he got to the front, he didn't stop. He came around to the side, walked up the steps of that old theater building on the high platform. Walked across on my side over here and walked straight toward me. Got within five feet of me, reached into the waistband of his trousers, and pulled out the longest barreled revolver I've ever seen in my life. That thing must have had a barrel on it a foot long, and it looked like it was growing. I didn't know what was going to happen. I had no idea. I stood there staring at him, him with that crippled leg. And he held that gun for a moment—it seemed like a week, a month, a year. And I thought, God—a lot of things went through my mind—Where's Frances? She always comes to my rescue. And then he laid the gun down on the old wooden pulpit, an old flattop makeshift thing, laid it on top of it and then in broken English, he starts to tell me this story.

He says, "The reason I am dragging this leg is because it's a wooden leg. A year ago tonight in the city of Panama City, Republic of Panama," he said, "I got into a fight with a man, and the man got in his car and hit me." I believe that's what he said. "And as a result of that fight and as a result of what happened, they had to take my leg off. And I am nothing but half a man." he said, "I've lived with that all year long," and he said, "I got up this morning. The reason I have this gun, I was going today to Panama City one year later, and I was going to find that man that made me half a man, and I was going to kill him." And he said, "Today was my mama's birthday." And they were both Catholic, and she said, "Son, for my birthday present, will you go to the meeting tonight with me?" Tears rolling down his cheeks, he stood there and said, "I am going tomorrow to

Panama City, but you can have the gun. And I'm going to find that man, and I'm going to not harm him or hurt him, but I'm going to tell him that he need never fear anymore. Jesus has come into my heart and changed my life." In a moment's time, in just a few moment's time, a miracle of redemption was won that night. And it's not over.

This last January, we were back in the Republic of Panama, there in the stadium. They jammed the place, and that night I closed the message by telling them what I have just told you. It happened about twenty-five years ago. And all of a sudden, the stands were filled, and there were people standing on the endfield. I saw a big man step out—dragging a leg—twenty-five years later. The man that I was talking about tonight is standing right here. He said, "I've been living for Christ for twenty years now." He said, "I don't hate that man anymore. Here is the proof of what Jesus Christ can do. Praise the Lord. Hallelujah. Hallelujah to God. Thank him for what he can do. Hallelujah to God."

He walked across that endfield with the glare of those clean lamps on him, and I threw my arms around him. That's the only power that can change society for the better. Had it not been for Jesus Christ there would have been a murder, a man living in jail the rest of his life or maybe killed himself. Untold misery for his mother and his family. An agonizing hell on earth and misery and pain and suffering for another family. But because the man of Galilee came into his heart, twenty-five years later he came across that endfield and said, "That's me. That's me. That's me. I'm the man. I'm the man. I'm the man. I'm the man. I'm the man. Glory to God."

After I finished that altar call and the service ended, I just stood there, held him like that—had to look up at him, and we talked about Jesus, the love of God, the grace of God. Tears rolled down his cheeks. I watched him a few minutes later walk away, dragging that leg, and I thought, Lord, he's not crippled, he's the most whole man you'd ever see. Hallelujah to the man.

In this story, Swaggart is telling about the value of sharing his stories, of what happens to you when you share his stories. In a sense, he is promising that these stories can be your stories if you do what he wants you to do. This is, of course, his main intention. Speakers want their hearers to believe their stories, of course. Any storyteller wants the hearers to think the story is true and interesting. Some storytellers want their hearers to learn from their stories, to change their viewpoint because of their stories. But the ultimate in storytelling is to have the stories become the stories of the listeners, to have them think that these are actually their stories.

As we said earlier, it is actually very difficult to learn from the stories of others. The tendency in understanding is to get reminded of your own story and reinforce that story slightly, knowing that others have had similar experiences. But, in general, we don't really adopt other people's stories as our own. Swaggart is trying to convince his listeners to do something that is actually very difficult to do. He wants his listeners to buy his stories, not only to believe them, but in a sense to reenact them. He probably knows, at least implicitly, that, to the extent that he gets his listeners to tell his stories and to live his stories, he can manipulate people to do what he wants them to do. Story adoption, the taking of other's stories as your own, is a very important principle of any organized religion.

The last of the Swaggart stories is the one that he surely wants his audience to make into a story of their own, to relive the story for themselves, so to speak.

A lady walked up to me just this week. She introduced herself, a very lovely lady. She said, "Jimmy Swaggart, you would never look at me and tell it, but just a few months ago, I was a drunk, an alcoholic, and you were number one on my hit list. I hated you. The day I really hated you was when you told me that alcoholism was not a disease. It is a sin." She said, "I had hidden behind my *disease* for years. I was dying and going to hell, and my home was gone, and everything was shot to hell." She said, "I walked over to that TV set, and I turned it off so loud till I almost broke the knob. Bam." And she said, "When I walked back, and the screen was black, and you were gone, but what you preached was still here. Hallelujah."

Tears rolling down her cheeks, she said, "You preached the truth. I know you caught flak. I know half the churches got on your back, but keep preaching it. I'm free tonight. I'm free today because of the word today of almighty God." I said, "God, where are the preachers?" If everybody in town loves your pastor—oh, he's a member of the catch 'em all club and the whodunit club and the civic con betterment growing tulips, lilies, and roses club, and they wrote him up in the paper how he's joining the ecumenical council, and he is so loved—find somebody who doesn't care what the Better Business Bureau thinks of his council for civic improvement, but find someone fresh from the prayer closet full of the Holy Ghost, full of the power of almighty God, and listen to him preach the word without fear or without favor. My God, help us. My word, clap your hands. Stand up and shout. Say, "Jesus is alive." We have something to shout about. We have something to proclaim. We have something to sing about. We have something to lift us up. It is Jesus the King of Kings and the Lord of Lords. On the face of the entire earth, Jesus saves, Jesus saves, Jesus heals. Jesus fills with the Holy Ghost. Jesus is coming again. Hallelujah. Hallelujah. Hallelujah. I said, "God, where are the preachers?" And I was sobbing, and he said, "I'm going to raise up the preachers. I'm going to fill them with my spirit. They are going to go in the spirit and power of Elijah. They are going to sound like John the Baptist. I am going to raise them up. I will bring them and fill them with my power and all of hell will not be able to stand against them."

When we hear the stories of others, the issue becomes whether we choose to adopt these stories for ourselves. We define ourselves through our own stories, but through teaching (and preaching), we also define ourselves through the stories of others. Many people who are good storytellers know how to take advantage of this basic human need to define oneself through the stories other people live.

The stories of our culture are those stories that we hear so often that they cease to seem like stories to us. They are the stories that we take for granted. They are the stories we live by. The more independent we are, the more the stories we tell that are uniquely our own. The more connected with others that we wish to be, the more the stories we tell are those that are already well understood by our listeners. Outsiders tell more interesting stories because they tell stories that are not known to their audience. Insiders tell stories that everyone accepts and that everyone has heard before. It takes a great storyteller to make such insider stories interesting.

□ 8 □

Stories and Intelligence

□

PEOPLE THINK in terms of stories. They understand the world in terms of stories that they have already understood. New events or problems are understood by reference to old previously understood stories and explained to others by the use of stories. We understand personal problems and relationships between people through stories that typify those situations. We also understand just about everything else this way as well. Scientists have prototypical scientific success and failure stories that they use to help them with new problems. Historians have their favorite stories in terms of which they understand and explain the world. Stories are very basic to the human thinking process. But people also use stories to avoid thinking.

Are these two statements contradictory? It is all too easy to get caught in the trap of assuming that the mechanisms that underlie human intelligence are so complex that it would be a mammoth feat to replicate them. One implication of the view of story-based understanding expressed here is that people's minds are inherently simpler than AI researchers have wanted to admit. There are a great many underwhelming intellects out there. Maybe AI people should stop using their perceptions of themselves at their most innovative as models. This doesn't mean that creating a storytelling story-referring machine will be an easy process—far from it. But it does mean that a machine that stores and retrieves stories would display a fair amount of intelligence and would be possible to build.

Intelligence is more likely to be a continuum than a *now you have it, now you don't* affair. People differ in intelligence for reasons other than that one person has a property that another is lacking. Similarly, a machine is unlikely to be missing some quality or other that would keep it from being as intelligent as a person. Rather, an intelligent machine probably needs to have certain basic capabilities. The extent of its intelligence would reflect how well it exploited those capabilities. What might those capabilities be?

The abilities that characterize very intelligent people are really a set of processes that these people execute, and they are the very same processes that average people execute. It simply isn't the case that smart people have some property that dull people are missing. Nor is it the case that smart people have more of something that dull people have less of. In some sense, it isn't even true that humans have something that animals don't have. It isn't the presence or absence of a feature, but how that feature is used. The features of intelligence are what they are, and everybody has all of them. What differentiates smart from stupid is the way in which the processes that employ features are run.

Below, I have characterized some dimensions of intelligence along which these processes operate. Each of us has these processes. We don't, however, all use these processes in the same way. For each of them, there is a normal way in which they are employed. In order to operate in the world, we must have some ability to process information in the normal way. To be considered to be really intelligent, however, we must do more than proceed in the normal way. We must extend each dimension of intelligence in a particular way. It is the ability to make this extension of the normal dimensions of intelligence that is the aspect of intelligence that is variable and differentiates us from each other according to intelligence.

The first dimension of intelligence is *data finding*.
As a matter of course we are *reminded*.
Some people can find data of which they have not been
    naturally reminded. They have learned how to *search* for
    data.

Intelligence is characterized by the *ability to get reminded*. Why is reminding so important? Quite obviously, if you don't get reminded of stories, you can't tell them, nor can you recognize new problems as instances of old, previously solved problems. Reminding has a purpose. It is the means by which our memories present us with data for our consideration. It follows, then, that one aspect of the intelligence of a system is how well it labels its experiences. No one experience should be labeled only one way. We might want to recall an experience because of who was involved in it, where it took place, an unusual feature related to it, or one of many points that were derived from it. But in order to do this, we must either consider all the aspects of that experience at the time of processing and storage of that experience, or else we must be able to retrieve that experience again in order to reconsider it.

Obviously, labeling is not a conscious process. But thinking about an experience is. We are not aware, in mulling over an event in which we have participated, of exactly why we are mulling it or what it means to be mulling it. The claim here is that mulling is a process critical to intelligence, one that creates labels for events in myriad ways so that they can be seen again in memory.

It also follows, therefore, that the process of searching memory for those events is an intelligent process, dependent upon a knowledge of the labels that have previously been used and also dependent upon an ability to look at an experience in a novel enough way so as to be able to create new labels to consider.

We cannot say for sure if higher-level animals get reminded, but there is reason enough to assume that they do. They do not rediscover each day where the best sources of food are, for example. They remember them at just the right time. And it is safe to say that all people get reminded of past experiences from time to time. Thus, the intelligence in this process is not in the reminding itself. That is a natural phenomenon. And retrieving experiences from memory does not seem like such a remarkably intelligent process.

But finding those experiences when they are not obviously connected to what you are now processing is a special kind of reminding. When search requires thinking it is a more conscious type of search than the search that the normal reminding process entails. What makes one person's memory better than another's? The answer has to be two things: labeling and search techniques.

Let's consider labeling first. Imagine two people undergoing the same experience. Let's say they both attend a baseball game and somebody next to them gets hit by a batted ball, is taken to a first aid room, and returns to watch the game an inning later. Now, let's imagine that it is two years later. What might our hypothetical experiencers of this day have remembered of it? Obviously, the possibilities are myriad. Would they remember the score of the game? Who won? Where they were sitting? What the person who was hurt looked like? What the attendants who took the person away were wearing? What inning this occurred in? What they thought about it all?

In some sense, it is the last question that is most important here. What they remember depends heavily on what they thought about the incident. One could, after all, see this incident in a variety of ways: as an annoying interruption of the game, for example, or as an indication of the potential violence of sport, or as an example of how badly fans want to see a game (even if they are injured they come back to watch), or as an example of God's will in keeping the ball from hitting them, or all of the above.

An incident is remembered in terms of how it is seen in the first place. That is, labeling is in many aspects an arbitrary process. Of course, both viewers would label this as something that happened at a baseball game. But one might see it as having relevance with respect to any sporting event, while the other might see it as being worthy of calling up any time that one is seated next to someone who looks like the victim in this incident. And, of course, even that last categorization is arbitrary since one person might characterize the victim as being blond, while the other might characterize him as being fat.

Is it possible that one of the viewers might easily recall this incident while the other might forget it? Of course. Would one then have a good memory while the other was seen as forgetful? Naturally, those characterizations are easy to make. What is actually happening, however, has nothing to do with how many brain cells are allocated for this particular experience with more going to the person with the better memory. The difference between the two viewers is a function of how they labeled the event. If the first viewer was very taken by this incident, seeing it as relevant to his views of sports, religion, health, and whatever, he would of course recall it often and reinforce the memory with each recall. To do this, he would have had to have labeled the event extensively at the time. Or, to put this another way, he would have had to have mulled over the event, relating it to other things he thought about life shortly after the event took place. For him, this event would be easily recalled later, because he had thought about it at the time.

But for a viewer for whom this event had little significance in a day otherwise occupied with an exciting and significant baseball game, it is likely that the game would be remembered and the hitting of the patron would be almost forgotten. In other words, if you don't think about something you aren't likely to remember much.

There is a variable that changes all this, however, namely, the number of baseball games attended prior to and after this event. If this game were the only game a viewer had attended it is likely that this incident would be easily recalled anytime that baseball were brought up, because the incident would have become part of the baseball-attending script itself. It is almost as if, were this person to attend another game, he would *expect* a patron near him to be hit by a ball. Similarly, if numerous incidents of this kind had occurred in the life of the viewer, this particular incident would be easily forgotten, especially if nothing were especially different about this one.

A good memory, then, means an attentive labeling facility during processing or, to put this another way, you aren't going to remember what you don't find interesting, so the more that interests you the better memory you are likely to have. Search, obviously, depends upon labeling. You can't find what you have failed to label or have mislabeled in the first place.

Obviously all higher animals, and certainly all humans, label experiences and store them away in memory. Intelligence in this arena manifests itself before the retrieval process even starts. You can remember better what you have understood more completely, that is, what you have seen from many different vantage points. This mulling process occurs prior to storage. In other words, what you haven't thought about sufficiently is less likely to be available to you in situations later in life where it might be relevant.

In sum, then, we can say that it is a normal part of intelligence to be able to find, without looking for it, a story that will help you know what to do in a new situation. It is an exceptional aspect of intelligence to be able to find stories that are superficially not so obviously connected to the current situation. If you have labeled a story in a complex fashion prior to storage, it will be available in a large variety of ways in the future. Higher intelligence depends upon complex perception and labeling.

But how do you know what events to store away as stories worth remembering? It seems obvious that we can't make a story out of everything. Simply walking down a busy street for an hour could supply you with enough different things to think about to occupy you for the rest of your mental life. Intelligence requires you to forget many things and to ignore most things. Learning to ignore and forget effectively can enhance remembering and effective retrieval of information. If you are not concerned with the trivial you can focus on the significant. This means, in effect, that one must establish a set of standard cases into which the vast majority of experiences can be remembered in the short term and forgotten in the long term.

Case recognition is a very important process in memory, but, here again, it is also an ability that everybody can be assumed to have. We can all recognize particular cases—the faces of our friends and relatives, for example. Generic situations, such as a restaurant, are easy to spot, even if we have never seen that particular restaurant before.

And, similarly, if we encounter a situation that is new to us, a broken leg, for example, we can relate it to other similar types of cases—someone else's broken leg, our own broken arm, another illness or injury we may have had—and invoke the appropriate script. The ability to recognize an event as an instance of a previously processed case is very important because we use prior cases to help us process new events. Thus, case recognition is a critical and quite common aspect of human intelligence.

Here again, what is a part of normal everyday intelligence is also in its extended form an important aspect of what we consider to be highly intelligent behavior. It is one thing to recognize a restaurant as a restaurant when one has never been there before, but it seems qualitatively different to recognize a new piece of music as being by Beethoven, a newly encountered painting as being by Picasso, a new legal case as being like another, or a new situation in business as being like a superficially dissimilar case. Of course, these are all aspects of the same process of case recognition.

Knowing that you have seen an analogous case before means no more than knowing what you know, which of course means knowing what indices you have employed before. Thus, one must have a consistency to one's indexing algorithm in the long term. This consistency is very relevant for being able to make comparisons and generalizations. Intelligence depends upon finding what you have previously labeled, which in turn depends on labeling things the same way each time. This is actually not so easy to do and is one reason why some people are smarter than others. Smarter people index less randomly as well as more complexly.

The second dimension of intelligence is *data manipulation*.
As a matter of course we can do *partial matching*.
Some people can find matches that do not directly fit and,
    instead of rejecting them, use them. They have learned
    how to *adapt* old data for use in new situations.

It is a part of everyday intelligence to do partial matching. This means that you will not fail to recognize somebody who has shaved off his mustache although you may realize that there is something different about him without knowing exactly what. A total match between your memory of that person and what he looks like just now may not occur, but this does not cause you to fail to recognize the person. A partial match suffices.

The same phenomenon occurs in matching stories. Here the problem of matching is different, however. We match new events to stories we already know that are not exactly like those stories. We might, for example, recall an earlier attempt to get a teacher to change a grade while thinking about getting our boss to change his or her salary decision. We might recognize that a certain food we like isn't fit for eating when it displays certain properties, and we would want to know not to eat it when we saw the same type of food again.

To do all this, we must be capable of thinking about stories we have acquired in the past to see if one of them matches closely enough to what we need to know now. Thus, partial matching of one story to another is a critical aspect of human intelligence.

The extension of this capability shows itself in the extent to which very partial matches can be made useful in a new situation. It is all too easy to reject a partial match when the match is very superficial or improbable. More difficult is to keep a very unlikely match alive, to think about it enough to find a way in which it could be helpful.

Then, the tricky part comes when one has to adapt an old story that one has found in such a way as to make it useful for processing a new story. The more successfully you adapt old stories, the more creative you are. Adaptation of old theorems helps mathematicians prove new ones; adaptation of old programs helps programmers write new programs; adaptation of old cases helps lawyers argue new cases and helps doctors prescribe treatment. The better you can adapt an old case to a new situation, the more able you are to cope with the unforeseen. Much of what we assume is creativity is better seen as the adaptation of old stories to new purposes, purposes to which they have never been applied before. Insight is often the recognition (note the word "recognition" means, literally, "cognizing again") that an old story could have a new use.

When you decide to purchase a stock, you want to recall other stock purchases and how they turned out. The other purchases that you recall will not match on very many features. The name, the date, the price, the state of the economy, just to name a few, are likely to be different. But what if the business the company engages in, its price-earnings ratio, its selling price relative to its historical low, its position in its industry, and such are different as well? Which of these criteria are normally different and which, if they are different, make the comparison absurd?

In fact, individual decision-makers have theories about which features are criterial and which are irrelevant. Partial matching is an art. We must guess what we can ignore because no match is ever really a complete match. The intelligence problem is one of finding effective theories of partial matches. We must know when stories are relevant enough to tell, when cases are paradigmatic enough to base future actions upon. There are no hard-and-fast rules for doing this correctly. The making and testing of new theories of usefulness of a partial match is thus another hallmark of intelligence.

Any intelligent being can recognize that a partial match is good enough and can learn to treat such matches as if they were complete matches. The high end of this aspect of intelligence requires that one can find a match where there may not obviously be one and utilize that possibly errant match to help one cope with brand-new situations.

The third dimension of intelligence is *comprehension.*
As a matter of course we can *connect new stories to old stories.*
Some people can figure out what a new story might mean
    even when there is no obvious candidate old story to
    which to relate it. They have learned how to *invent*
    coherency for otherwise incomprehensible data.

Part of being intelligent is figuring out where the actions of others fit. Dumb animals perceive everything unknown as a potential threat. Perhaps not so brilliant, but as the guy said who dropped popcorn around him to keep the elephants away, "See? It works."

TOKYO, SEPT 23, 1985—A Japan Air Lines official who had been negotiating with relatives of the 520 people killed in last month's Boeing 747 crash has killed himself to apologize for the disaster, the police said.

They said Saturday that Hiro Tominaga, 59, a manager of JAL's Haneda Airport maintenance shop near Tokyo, stabbed himself in the neck and chest.

He left a note saying, "I offer my apology with my life," the police said.

Do this man's actions make sense? In some cultures they do, in some they don't. Interpreting what you see and hear involves referring to established norms. Being intelligent, therefore, requires knowing wide ranges of different norms, so that unusual actions can be interpreted in a context that makes them sensible. Intelligence involves ascertaining what plan the action of another might be part of, what goal that plan was intended to satisfy, and what belief the actor held would explain why that goal was a goal at all.

People whom we would characterize as less intelligent than others often also display the property of seeing the behavior of people outside their own social world as being crazy. People from other cultures are crazy because they eat funny foods or wear funny clothes. We characterize the ambitions of others in other social worlds according to the extent to which we have attempted to invent coherence for them. It sometimes takes a great deal of work to consider the rationale behind others' actions. It is much easier to dismiss their seemingly unusual behavior as incoherent and let it go at that.

This aspect of intelligence is, in a sense, just hard work. You have got to know what goes on in the world and be able to figure out where what you just saw fits. As is often the case with human intelligence, what appears to be a very difficult process can be short-circuited in actual practice by learning some tricks. One of the most common of these tricks is the *script,* which I have discussed at length elsewhere.

The real value of scripts is that they allow us not to think. We either know the *Japanese official takes responsibility* script or we do not. If we don't, then his action appears crazy. If we know the script, his action seems obvious and straightforward. Either way we didn't have to think too much.

That, then, is a key point. Part of human intelligence is the ability to find a context for actions that we observe that make them comprehensible to us or allow us to dismiss them as irrelevant. What makes for really intelligent behavior here is again a difference in degree rather than in kind. Intelligent people don't easily accept either the answer that a given action fits into a script or the answer that if it does not then the action in question is crazy.

Intelligence in this arena means having no story to match a new input to but being able to comprehend it nevertheless. In other words, when intelligent people see an action they try to see it as different from what they know rather than similar to what they know (if they are interested in that action, of course, otherwise they can ignore it like everybody else). And when they see actions that are obviously different and out of the bounds of what they know, they try to find similarities with what they have experiences of in order to render crazy actions comprehensible. To put this another way, intelligence here means being interested in explaining as much as possible rather than explaining away as much as possible. The more you find of interest, that is, the more actions you find to be in need of explanation, the more you have to think about. And, quite simply, the more there is to think about, the more you think.

In a sense, then, finding where some action fits is a matter of invention. This is, then, the intelligent aspect to this otherwise mundane process. We can see easily enough why the waitress has brought the food we asked for, but why she has flung it down angrily on the table may be more difficult to understand. We must invent a coherent reason for her actions or else we must see her as being crazy in some way. This ability to see the disconnected behaviors of others as part of a coherent plan of action is an important aspect of intelligence.

Intelligence means finding coherence where it isn't obvious that it exists. Humans, in the normal course of processing experiences, must find out why people do what they do. But intelligence in this arena means doing the extra processing to find coherence where it may not be obvious, or to invent coherence where it actually cannot be found.

The fourth dimension of intelligence is *explanation*.
As a matter of course we can *explain our expectation failures*.

Some people can recover from their expectation failures and
     will not make the same mistake twice. They have learned
     how to *discover predictive rules* on the basis of past failures.

Intelligence involves failure and therefore explanations about circumstances where failure has occurred. But every aspect of life, every
little failure, is not worth dwelling on. Intelligence thus involves the
ability to know where to spend one's intellectual time.

Often people explain problems in such a way as to make them
disappear. It is important not to feel that every noise is a possible
bomb. We hear threatening noises and try to figure out why they are
not problems. We observe people doing something odd and we
attempt to figure a good reason why we need not be concerned with
that odd action. "They're just crazy, don't worry about them" is a
good thing to believe after all. In a sense, we must see the world as
being a normal, well-ordered place, even if it actually isn't true. We
can't go around wondering about everything after all. Or can we?

My daughter, when she was three years old, used to ask me every
time we passed a man on the street why he was doing what he was
doing. Now sometimes those questions were easy to answer, and
sometimes they were completely impossible to answer. But naturally
my daughter expected me to know and kept on asking. In fact, as
I write this, she is a teenager, and still asks such questions. These days
the questions are a kind of joke between us, but the key point is she
still is wondering why people do what they do. Children have to
learn to stop asking such questions. They learn this in several ways,
but mostly by their not getting answered. Often those questions are
not answered because they are answered by the technique of explaining away. Whatever curiosity the child has an adult can and often will
stifle by explaining that the interesting phenomenon is not interesting at all.

It seems fairly obvious that speculating about what may be going
on in an anomalous situation is an important form of thinking.
Moreover, children who naturally seek explanations, and who learn
easily enough to explain away, can also learn to explain things themselves. There are really three parts to this process then. Children ask
for explanations and two things can happen. Either they can have the

phenomena explained away for them—"It's nothing to worry about, dear. Elephants do that all the time"—or they can have explanations given to them—"The sky is blue because of the way molecules in the atmosphere disperse sunlight." Either way, children fail to advance to the next aspect of this dimension of intelligence.

To learn to explain failure (and here I mean the failure to predict correctly what would happen next, not the failure to achieve some goal), one must practice. There really is only one right answer for a child then—"Why do *you* think that man is doing that?"—although it often isn't so simple to answer a child in that fashion. In any case the point is that the more curiosity there is about the world in general and the actors in it, the more one finds anomalous. And the more anomalies the more explanations needed, and the more explanations needed the more explanations invented.

Learning to explain phenomena such that one continues to be fascinated by the failure of one's explanations creates a continuing cycle of thinking that is the crux of intelligence. It isn't that one person knows more than another, then. In a sense, it is important to know *less* than the next person, or at least to be certain of less, thus enabling more curiosity and less explaining away because one has again encountered a well-known phenomenon. The less you know the more you can find out about, and finding out for oneself is what intelligence is all about.

From what I said above, it follows that intelligence is intimately connected with failure. "Well, then I must be very intelligent because I fail all the time," I hear you saying. Actually that statement is not so very far from the truth. A characteristic of dumb systems is that they never fail. Every day is like every other for them. They know a limited amount, never venture outside their limits, and thus never need to grow or change. Change comes about because of failure. Why change anything if it is working well? *If it ain't broke don't fix it.*

Learning depends upon a system venturing beyond known borders into places where the rules may not be so clear-cut and where failure may occur. But this venturing out will never take place unless some failure has occurred that would motivate it.

Failure is valuable because it encourages explanation. One must wonder why one has failed and invent a strategy that will eliminate the failure next time. The more intelligent you are the more you will fail. Ultimately the value of failure and the explanation of failure is to come up with new rules that predict how events will turn out. Of course, these too will fail. This is one of the reasons that one must keep one's stories available. If all you recall is the rule, it will be hard to figure out what to do when the rule fails. But if the story that generated the rule is still available, you can look at the data again and create a new rule. No story worthy of the name has only one possible rule that can be derived from it. We can all see a given story, if it has sufficient complexity, in a variety of ways. Thus, the task for an intelligent system is to be looking for failures that it can use its stories to explain in order to create new rules to be tried and considered again.

The fifth dimension of intelligence is *planning*.
As a matter of course we can *execute plans* that we have copied from others.
Some people can execute plans of their own invention. They have learned how to *create plans*.

Everybody plans. Cats plan. Dogs plan. Babies plan. Planning would seem to be a very complex mental activity. In fact, efforts to simulate human planning behavior by computer in Artificial Intelligence labs have indicated that planning is overwhelmingly complex. How is it then that planning is possible by beings who are not overwhelmingly intelligent? The answer is that most beings don't create plans, they copy plans. If animals had to figure out how to get fed by reasoning it out from general principles, there would be a great many starving animals. Fortunately, animals have other animals to copy. Even so, from time to time a pet has to have food shoved under its face for it to realize that the food is there and that the animal might consider eating it.

Leaving aside the possibility that some planning is done entirely by instinct, that is nonconsciously, we should ask ourselves if there is ever a time that animals have to create plans for themselves. Or, to put this question differently, can all human planning behavior be accounted for by the concept of copying? I ask this question because this is the issue that differentiates intelligence along the dimension of planning. Can a sentient being create its own plans?

This is really not a frivolous question. Think of how many times you have done something just because you did it that way before or because that is how your parents did it or because that is how a friend told you to do it. Reasoning out a plan from first principles can be quite difficult. One thing that is easier is modifying old plans. So when a new plan is needed, a standard human trick is to find a plan that is a lot like the needed plan, that satisfies a goal a lot like the new goal, and to try to modify the old plan in such a way as to make it work in the new situation. Cooks do this when they are missing an ingredient for a recipe, drivers do this when they are trying to get to a new destination, and chess players and generals do this when they are trying to find a new strategy for winning. They look for an old strategy that has worked before and see if it will fit somehow in the new situation.

Certainly there are times when even this adaptive planning won't work and genuinely new plans must be created from scratch. The argument is that this kind of planning behavior occurs quite rarely, not because it wouldn't be a good idea, but because it is quite difficult to do.

So, along the dimension of planning, we all use the plans of others, we all can adapt some of these plans to fit new situations. But the extent of our abilities to find plans to adapt is just like the extent of our ability to be reminded that was discussed before. It depends upon clever indexing strategies and the accumulation of a great deal of experience.

The ability to create brand-new plans is one of the real hallmarks of intelligence. These plans need not be new to society in general, of course, but just to the individual who created them. In general, then, the more intelligent you are, the more you can create new plans.

The sixth dimension of intelligence is *communication*.
As a matter of course we can *tell stories*.
Some people can tell stories that are not simply direct
     descriptions of what has happened to them. They have

learned how to *generalize, crystallize,* and *elaborate* so that
they tell stories that express insights not obvious in the
original story.

Intelligent beings communicate. It is an interesting property of
human beings that the process of communication itself can alter
what is being communicated. When an animal communicates something, such as the fact that it is hungry or frightened, the act of
communication itself does not lead it to new insights about the
situation. But people can have a dialogue with themselves in effect.
They can notice things about what they say that can cause them to
change their view of what they are saying in midstream. This is the
process of communication/discovery.

Normally, the communication process for humans is very case-
dependent. People tell about their experiences and these experiences
can be considered as cases in point, intended to illustrate some point
that a speaker wants to make. The ability to illustrate a point with
one's own experience is thus an important aspect of intelligence.

The relevant extension here is in being able either to come to new
generalizations as a result of the communication process, or the
ability to crystallize a complex experience in a simple way. To put
this bluntly, dull people tell you what happened to them, leaving no
detail out, and often without point. Intelligent people quickly find
the essence of the experience they are conveying and try to relate it
to the topic at hand in a way that sheds light on the generalizations
between them.

The crystallization-generalization aspect of intelligence in the
communication/discovery process can tend to exemplify intelligence
in many ways. In some sense, this is a learned skill, but it depends
upon having something to say in the first place, which depends upon
initially having interpreted an experience in an interesting way. In
other words, while the ability is learned the precedent abilities that
this skill depends upon may not be learnable.

We all have a desire to communicate. When something happens
to us, we want to tell about it. Why this is so is an open question.
But it seems that for most people the telling of an experience makes
that experience live again. And perhaps more importantly, telling

about an experience forces us to crystallize that experience in terms of its essence. We cannot relay the entirety of what has occurred of course. Describing a two-week trip would take about two weeks, maybe more. So we eliminate the unessential.

Now recall that a human's memory cannot be bothered by all the details either. We cannot afford to devote mental resources, storage facilities in the brain so to speak, to every single detail of our two-week trip. Some of the details we cannot reconstruct if necessary. We need not remember the details of the airplane ride unless something unusual occurred. One airplane trip is like another and, if we have traveled often, such things are good candidates for aspects of the trip to forget.

On the other hand, there are some things we would especially like to remember. They were important in some way to us. Further, there are some aspects of the trip that we would like to keep thinking about. We may not be sure what we think about certain events, what we felt at the time or why, how we behaved in critical events and how we feel we should have behaved.

This is one reason why telling about an experience is important to us. It helps us to understand that experience ourselves. And, here again, one can see the difference in intelligence along this dimension. We all know how to present a case, to tell about what happened to us. But knowing how to get the event into a few short sentences that convey the most important aspects of that event, or the aspects of that event that would be of most interest to the person who we are talking to, is more difficult.

And, here again, the differences along that dimension are not necessarily one of innate abilities. Rather, it may be possible that the more one does the communication/discovery process well, the more one has to communicate and discover. New insights are, in essence, generalizations that one discovers oneself while talking about (or thinking about) an experience. Further, the more one communicates well, the more one's listeners may be able to respond with relevant experiences of their own that may aid the generalization process.

The idea here is that the more ideas are discussed, the more insights one will come to. This seems fairly obvious, but how this appears in actual practice may be less obvious. The analysis of an experience is critical to understanding. Unexamined experiences may contain many possible lessons for future use, but they remain there dormant unless discussed with others or discussed with oneself. In other words, the more one examines one's experiences and the more one tries to crystallize the essence of an experience for the consumption of another, the more one can be reminded of or remind others of similar experiences that can then be compared and contrasted, yielding new generalizations. Good crystallizations enhance discovery, and discovery is at the heart of intelligence.

It is a property of intelligence to be able to tell what has happened to us and to be able to know the extent to which that experience might be relevant to others and to know when to tell it. We have a sense of what people want to hear when—of what constitutes communication. The idea of a dialogue, two people taking part in a kind of mutual storytelling, is an interesting aspect of intelligence. Other animals don't really do anything like this, yet all human cultures do.

The extension of this ability is seen in the creation of new stories and in the elaboration of old ones. To talk about things that didn't happen is, ironically, an important aspect of intelligence. In a sense, intelligence here depends upon the concept of entertainment. Knowing that it is possible to entertain people in various ways, storytellers learn to hone the skills necessary to be entertaining. Thus, the ability to create new entertaining stories is an important aspect of intelligence.

Another side of intelligence relates to what we discussed above. Knowing what to leave out can be as important as knowing what to add. Dull people have the facility to bore their listeners by telling every detail of a story. People who are intelligent along this dimension say just what needs to be said. Further, they present things in the right order and in the right way for maximum impact.

Certainly, the ability to tell stories is there from the time one learns to speak. Children are asked to relate their experiences of the day and in so doing become storytellers. The extra step along this dimension requires an ability to see yourself as your audience is seeing you and to care about improving. People are not born as fascinating storytellers; they grow into it if they choose to by paying attention to their listeners. In the process of doing this they, in this sense, become more intelligent because they learn from the process of talking.

The seventh dimension of intelligence is *integration*.
As a matter of course we *understand stories that we have been told*.
Some people seek to find out more than simply what they have been told. They have become (or have not forgotten how to be) *curious*.

At the Yale AI lab in the late 1970s, the problem of getting a computer program to understand stories was investigated. What would it mean for a program to understand a story? Below is the input and output of one of those programs, called Fast Reading and Understanding Memory Program (FRUMP).

FRUMP

INPUT

Washington, March 15—The State Department announced today the suspension of diplomatic relations with Equatorial Guinea. The announcement came five days after the department received a message from the foreign minister of the West African country saying that his government had declared two United States diplomats persona non grata.

The two are Ambassador Herbert J. Spiro and Consul William C. Mithoefer, Jr., both stationed in neighboring Cameroon but also accredited to Equatorial Guinea.

Robert L. Funseth, State Department spokesman, said Mr. Spiro and Mr. Mithoefer spent five days in Equatorial Guinea earlier this month and were given "a warm reception."

But at the conclusion of their visit, Mr. Funseth said, Equatorial Guinea's acting chief of protocol handed them a five-page letter that cast "unwarranted and insulting slurs" on both diplomats.

Selected sketchy script $BREAK-RELATIONS CPU TIME FOR UNDERSTANDING - 2515 MILLISECONDS

ENGLISH SUMMARY

The US State Department and Guinea have broken diplomatic relations.

FRENCH SUMMARY

Le departement d'état des états-unis et la guinée ont coupe leurs relations diplomatiques.

CHINESE SUMMARY

Meeigwo gwowuhyuann gen jiinahyah duannjyuele way jiau guanshih.

SPANISH SUMMARY

El departamento de relaciones exteriores de los ee uu y Guinea cortaron sus relaciones diplomaticas.

It became clear to us from working on such programs that, while understanding stories might entail being able to summarize them, some deeper concept of understanding was also implied when we talked about understanding. Below is the input and output of some Yale graduate students who were asked to ask questions after having read a newspaper story.

THE STORY

JERUSALEM, April 13—A sixteen-year-old Lebanese was captured by Israeli troops hours before he was supposed to get into an explosive-laden car and go on a suicide bombing mission to blow up the Israeli Army headquarters in Lebanon, according to Israeli officials and an account from the youth himself.

The teenager, Mohammed Mohmoud Burro, was captured by Israeli soldiers in a raid on a southern Lebanese village on February 23.

It is believed to be the first time that a trained suicide car bomber has been seized alive.

THE STUDENTS' QUESTIONS

Why would someone commit suicide if they are not depressed?
Why does the news tell us only about Lebanese truck bombers?

Aren't there any Israeli truck bombers?

These kids remind one of kamikaze pilots in World War II. Are they
    motivated in the same way?

Why is it that every Arab seems to be named Mohammed?

How do the Israelis know where to make their raids?

How do Lebanese teenagers compare with US teenagers?

Why hadn't they been caught alive before?

What do the parents of suicide bombers think of their children's
    training for this job?

Is there a political group organizing the kids?

This story reminds one of Oliver Twist. Is there a Lebanese Fagin
    around who organizes homeless kids into suicide bombers?

What property did these students exhibit that our program did
not? The simple answer is curiosity. FRUMP wasn't a very intelligent program. It seems safe to say that, but why? The answer is that
FRUMP didn't learn anything from what it read. Every story was
grist for the mill that chewed up stories and summarized them.
FRUMP seemed intelligent because it could summarize stories and
thus seemed to understand them, and computers that understand
stories were not then, nor are they now, everyday phenomena.

FRUMP didn't learn. Of course it wasn't intended to learn, so that
is not a terrible criticism. But people who read stories do learn from
them. At least some people learn some things from them sometimes.
The variable in all this is curiosity. If you care about a subject enough
to speculate about it some, then you are likely to become more
interested in what you read. The way that happens is that anomalies
that you don't readily have a context for present themselves to be
explained. If you cannot explain them by yourself you generate a
question for later. Later may be years later, but fortunately curiosity
is often quite patient.

To get back to our discussion of intelligence then, intelligence
along the dimension of integration means trying to get everything
you see and hear to fit into your internal model of how the world
works. The problem of course is what to do when things don't fit.
If you fall apart every time that happens you will be incapable of

reading anything, for example, because everything you read would have to have the feature of never containing anything new, and that seems quite unlikely. So integration of new material requires one to decide to what extent each unusual thing is worth updating one's memory about. In other words, you can read about an earthquake in Iran or of the breaking of diplomatic relations between two countries, but how much of what you read should you remember?

It might seem that the answer to this question is obvious: all of it. But, in fact, if you really did remember every article you read in one Sunday's *New York Times,* you might never have room in your head for anything else ever again. The trick in reading is knowing what to forget, and, of course, that is the trick in the integration of new information into memory as well.

Not everything is worthy of remembering. Go back and look at the news stories that I presented above. How many of the details did you remember? A smart reader would not have paid much attention to any of it since the content was neither germane nor up-to-date. Smart readers learn to ignore a great deal of what they read, partially by never reading it in the first place in any serious sense and also by quickly forgetting what they find irrelevant to their own needs. This kind of forgetting is not really a loss of information in memory, of course; the information was never integrated into memory in the first place. This is why integration is so important.

And, here again, the basics of integration are done by every human being. We all must decide what to retain and what to discard, because we all process tremendous amounts of information every day. And, here again, the smartest of us becomes curious about certain aspects of what we encounter, and it is precisely those aspects that are worth focusing on.

Now what constitutes a payoff is a question of values and not of fact. There is no law that mandates where mental processing time is best spent. Of course, if what you are curious about and spend time integrating into memory is what has happened on the daily soap operas or what is for sale and in fashion, it is fairly likely that the intelligence that will be developed by this particular domain of curiosity will not earn kudos among those people who evaluate intelligence.

Intelligence in the area of integration, then, is a very subjective thing. We spend integration time becoming expert, and in a sense almost everyone is an expert on something. Being an expert on certain things, or having curiosity about certain things with the memory store to make that curiosity quite particular, which is how I would prefer to put it, implies intelligence in the eyes of the world if those arenas are in vogue among the intelligentsia. Or to put this another way, children who know a great deal about computers, who are very curious about computers, who spend mental processing time integrating new information about computers into their memories are not necessarily more intelligent than those who spend the same effort on motorcycles, but they are more in fashion and are likely to be more employable.

So the issue with respect to stories is this: We know them, find them, reconsider them, manipulate them, use them to understand the world and to operate in the world, adapt them to new purposes, tell them in new ways, and we invent them. We live in a world of stories. Our ability to utilize these stories in novel ways is a hallmark of what we consider to be intelligence.

Artificial Intelligence

We started this book with a brief discussion of artificial intelligence and some of its problems. Since then, we have virtually ignored the issue. One reason for this is that you cannot really make progress on artificial intelligence until you have a handle on real intelligence. Given what we have said about intelligence, then, what are the implications for the computer modeling of intelligence?

Intelligent machines would be good storytellers. Sometimes they might relay culturally common stories as answers to questions that were asked of them, and other times they might tell careful and pertinent stories as a way of making a point in response to requests for advice. But in the end machines, like people, will have to be the repository of an extraordinarily large number of stories in order to have something useful to say. Intelligence, for machines as well as for humans, is the telling of the right story at the right time in the right way. Thus, the key problem in artificial intelligence is the indexing problem. Stories must be labeled well enough, and new information must be understood well enough, so that the indices that are extracted from new information that is input to an intelligent system can be matched with the indices that have been used to label previously processed information.

Of course there is a great deal more to intelligence than just finding the right thing to say back. We want to learn from the comparison of the new information and the old information, for example. We want to know what to store away from a new experience and what to ignore. We need to know what to say to whom and under what circumstances. But at the core of all these issues is the basic problem of extracting indices and finding memories that have been labeled by those indices. In many ways, it seems that indexing is the basis of intelligence.

It may well be that it will take many years to create truly intelligent machines. The problems in getting reminded of a good story are myriad, and they will not easily be solved soon. However, there are useful intermediate steps along the way. A program that only knew a few thousand stories, even a program that simply contained a few thousand stories without even knowing what they were about in a serious sense, would be quite useful. A librarian who can point out a good book to read, in response to what you have indicated as your need or interests, need not have read the book in order to be a useful librarian. Just enabling the right story to be told at the right time is something that can be of great use if the stories themselves are of use.

And what of this storytelling machine? Would it be intelligent? We don't ask that question of human storytellers. We don't need to know if they fully understand the stories that they are telling if the stories they are telling are of use to us. We will grant intelligence to a storyteller if we like the story we were told.

In the future, machines that we interact with will have to be good storytellers. We will forgive them if they fail to understand us, but we will simply not use them if they fail to be entertaining. People today are used to being entertained by good storytellers. The most common media of these storytellers are movies and television. But these are passive forms of storytelling. We are used to such passive story listening. Books are passive too, after all. We have been content to lie back and be entertained for centuries.

The day of interactive storytelling is coming, however. Computers could tell different stories to different people in ways that those people could best understand. With the advent of video data bases, such computer-interactive storytelling could be done according to the visual standards of today's television. But the passivity would be gone. And the aim of the storyteller at the lowest common denominator of viewer would be gone. The more stories the computer knew how to tell, the more different ways that those stories could be told, the more likely that the idea of the interactive video storytelling machine would become a reality.

The impact of such a machine would be tremendous, especially in education. If we can learn from a machine that is trying to respond to our needs and can do so in an entertaining way, then storytelling and learning may become what they were in the past—an interaction with an entity that knew something you wanted to know and was willing to tell it to you in the most interesting possible way. Private tutors have done this for centuries, and wandering storytellers had done this for centuries as both sources of entertainment and news.

The French have an expression I rather like: *La plus ça change, la plus la même chose*, which means "The more things change, the more they stay the same." One thing that has stayed the same is the basic human ability to hear and understand stories and to tell stories. As we have become part of a larger and larger society, some of the individuality of that storytelling and receiving process has been lost. We all get fed the same stories (on television), must learn the same stories (in school), and wind up believing the same stories. Computers, oddly enough, offer the prospect of increased individuality. A computer with millions of stories to tell, the entire collection of the stories that people can put into them, will allow listeners to learn a larger variety of stories, thus enabling them to compare, contrast, generalize, crystallize, and in general become more intelligent.

Human beings are naturally predisposed to hear, remember, and to tell stories. The problem—for teachers, parents, government leaders, friends, and computers—is to have more interesting stories to tell.

Index

◻